Living Together as Equals

Living Together as Equals

The Demands of Citizenship

Andrew Mason

OXFORD
UNIVERSITY PRESS

OXFORD
UNIVERSITY PRESS

Great Clarendon Street, Oxford, OX2 6DP
United Kingdom

Oxford University Press is a department of the University of Oxford.
It furthers the University's objective of excellence in research, scholarship,
and education by publishing worldwide. Oxford is a registered trade mark of
Oxford University Press in the UK and in certain other countries

First Edition published in 2012

British Library Cataloguing in Publication Data
Data available

Library of Congress Cataloging in Publication Data
Data available

ISBN 978-0-19-960624-5

Printed on acid-free paper

For Lynn, once again

Preface

Many of those who think that citizenship matters, not only in terms of the obvious benefits it provides but also the demands it makes on us, can't help feeling that they don't do enough. Balancing the demands of citizenship against those of parenthood, family, and friendship, and against the pressures that our jobs and leisure activities exert, is a tremendous challenge and it is hard to feel that one has got that balance right. This book is intended as a partial corrective to these feelings of failure. It tries to show that we can be decent enough citizens without devoting our lives to serving the political communities to which we belong. By acting in more mundane ways in the private sphere and in civil society we can be reasonably good citizens, though greater public-spiritedness would no doubt help to make us better ones.

I couldn't have written this book without various forms of support. The Leverhulme Trust made it possible by awarding me one of their Major Research Fellowships and I owe them my warmest thanks. Although I've resisted the idea—encouraged by the practice of so-called 'Full Economic Costing'—that my period of Leverhulme-funded research leave has been subsidized by my institution, there's no doubt that my colleagues have taken on more burdens as a result of it and I'm grateful to them for not complaining.

I also have a number of particular debts of gratitude. Chris Armstrong, Roger Crisp, John Horton, David Miller, David Owen, and Shlomi Segall kindly read an earlier draft of the manuscript, as did three anonymous referees for Oxford University Press. Though no doubt there is still much wrong with it, the book has been improved a lot by their comments. I am very grateful for the help they have given me and the time and energy they devoted to doing so.

I would also like to thank Ludvig Beckman, Richard Bellamy, Clare Chambers, Iseult Honohan, Brad Hooker, Cécile Laborde, Derek McGhee, Bhikhu Parekh, Jonathan Quong, Jonathan Seglow, Graham Smith, Varun Uberoi, Corinne Wales, and Albert Weale, who read either drafts of chapters or papers which those chapters drew upon, or gave me advice when I asked for it. I am also grateful to Dominic Byatt, my editor at OUP, for his encouragement and efficiency.

Several parts of the book benefited from being presented at conferences, workshops, and research seminars. In particular I would like to thank participants in: the conference on 'Virtue and Social Diversity' held at Florida State University in March 2007; the conference on 'The Politics of Social Cohesion' held at the University of Copenhagen in September 2009; the Association for Legal and Social Philosophy annual conference on 'The Future(s) of Democratic Citizenship' held at the University of Southampton in April 2010; the conference on 'The Dynamics of Citizenship' held at the University of Stockholm in May 2010; the conference on 'Inclusive Futures' held at Macquarie University in February 2011; the Philosophy Department research seminar at the University of Hull in February 2007; the Political Theory research seminar at the Department of Government, London School of Economics and Political Science in January 2007, and the Political Theory seminar at the Manchester Centre for Political Theory, University of Manchester, April 2007.

And, finally, I am grateful to my family—Lynn, Sam, and Matthew—who have provided a welcome distraction from it all—well, most of the time the distraction has been welcome.

Contents

Introduction

Traditional understandings of citizenship are facing a number of challenges. Ideas of cosmopolitan and environmental citizenship have emerged in the light of concerns about global inequality and climate change, whilst new models of multicultural citizenship have been developed in response to the issues raised by immigration and the presence of national minorities. At the same time, more particular debates take place about the demands that citizenship places upon us in our everyday lives. Do we have a duty as citizens to take steps to reduce the risk of having to rely upon state benefits, including health care? Does good citizenship require that we send our children to the local school even when it performs poorly? Does a parent fail in his duty as a citizen—not just as a father, say—when he is less involved in the raising of his children than their mother? Should citizens refrain from appealing to religious reasons in public debate? Do we have duties of citizenship to minimize the size of our ecological footprints? What we need is a normative theory of citizenship that brings these issues together under a common framework rather than treating them in isolation in the way that often happens. In this book, I develop such a framework, made up of a minimal core concept of citizenship together with two accounts that provide different ways of elaborating this core concept. I then employ these accounts to cast light on a range of different demands that citizenship might be thought to make upon us in our everyday lives.

1 Concept and conceptions

The minimal core concept of citizenship that I shall rely upon can be characterized in a straightforward and indeed familiar way: citizenship is a relationship in which the parties enjoy rights or entitlements within a common framework of enforcement and provision, and incur special obligations, duties, or responsibilities to each other. This characterization picks out elements of the idea of citizenship that are central to our ordinary understanding of it, but it does not provide a sufficient condition of citizenship, nor a definition of it, since there are other relationships that also possess these features, for example, family relationships. Particular conceptions of citizenship add further elements to those contained in this characterization by giving a more precise account of what type of relationship is to count as one of citizenship, by specifying the rights, entitlements, duties, and responsibilities that are to be attributed to citizens, and by explaining how these are grounded.[1]

I am primarily concerned with conceptions of citizenship which construe it as a moral ideal, in effect as specifying a set of moral rights or entitlements that individuals must enjoy if they are to count as full and equal citizens, together with a set of moral obligations, duties, or responsibilities that they incur in this relationship. These conceptions allow us to stand in judgement on the packages of rights and entitlements that are enshrined in the laws and constitutions of particular states, and also provide us with a basis for evaluating the behaviour of citizens: we might conclude that a person is not really a citizen in a state, or not really a full citizen, because she lacks the complete range of rights which, morally speaking, are required for full citizenship, and we might conclude that an individual is a bad citizen on the grounds that she does not fulfil her obligations as a citizen. (This is not to deny that what we classify as relationships of citizenship from a purely legal standpoint, but which fall short when judged from the perspective of a moral conception, may nevertheless have significant value, even if some or all citizens in this legal sense lack the full moral rights or entitlements that they ought to enjoy.)

In Chapter 1, I distinguish some different families to which conceptions of citizenship belong that treat it as a moral ideal. The two most important of these families I refer to as the justice account and the equal membership account. Very roughly, the justice account regards citizenship as a vehicle for delivering justice, whereas the equal membership account supposes that citizenship consists in full and equal membership of a social and political community. More precisely, according to the justice account, the rights, duties, and virtues of citizenship derive solely from the rights, duties, and virtues of justice—or at least, are related in some direct or indirect way to such considerations, typically being understood as the best means of fulfilling principles of justice. In other words, the concept of justice is regarded as logically prior to that of citizenship, with the rights, duties, and virtues of citizenship being parasitic on that concept. According to the equal membership account, in contrast, the rights, duties, and virtues of citizenship are grounded in an important good which I shall refer to as the good of equal membership: namely, the good realized by a social and political community the members of which have equal standing. In effect, the good of equal membership consists in the value of living together as equals in an inclusive community. The justice account and the equal membership account represent different families of views because they can be elaborated in different ways. Different versions of the justice account are generated by different theories of justice, whereas different versions of the equal membership account are generated by different ways of understanding the good of equal membership.

It might be argued, however, that when it is properly thought through, the equal membership account collapses into the justice account (or at least that it represents a narrow version of the justice account) because the good of equal membership is simply the good of political equality, which consists in a just distribution of political rights and opportunities. In Chapter 2, I resist this argument by various means, for example, by maintaining that if the good of equal membership involves not only political equality but also social equality, that is, treating one's fellow citizens as equals in social interactions with them in civil society and beyond, then it goes further than what justice requires; by arguing that even if versions of the justice account and of the equal membership account converge in terms of the rights, duties, and virtues they underpin, they nevertheless give these rights distinctively different groundings; and by suggesting that the good of equal membership may be an organic whole with a non-instrumental value that is more than the sum of the value of its component parts.

Properly understood, however, the justice account and the equal membership account are not in competition and may complement each other. Not only are they grounded in different considerations, they also focus on partially different relationships. The standard framing assumptions of the justice account mean that it does not focus exclusively on *citizens* but instead is concerned more broadly with those living together in the same state, subject to the same set of legal, political, and economic institutions. This will include resident aliens, who possess a legal right of residence but lack the status of citizenship, as well as resident citizens. In effect the justice account and the equal membership account are concerned with overlapping but partly distinct relationships, and this provides a further reason for thinking that we do not have to choose between them. They may not always provide us with complementary perspectives on different issues, however. Sometimes the perspectives they provide come into conflict with each other, in a way that raises questions about the idea that justice always has primacy. Whatever their precise relationship in particular cases, my claim is that they each provide some illumination, and that our mapping of the terrain suffers when we neglect the perspective that is provided by the equal membership account.

But do we really need the distinction between justice and equal membership accounts that I have drawn? Could we not make do with the distinction that is commonly drawn between liberal and republican conceptions of citizenship, or the distinction between Greek and Roman models of citizenship upon which that between liberal and republican conceptions is to some extent founded?[2] Indeed, is not my distinction just another way of classifying liberal and republican conceptions? Although there are ways of making the contrast between liberal and republican views of citizenship that may seem to come close to the one I am proposing, it nevertheless has a different basis, and indeed I argue in Chapter 1 that the distinction between the justice account and the equal membership account *cuts across* that between liberal and republican views of citizenship and equips us better in understanding the demands made by citizenship.

Of course, there are several other distinctions that might be drawn between ways of thinking about citizenship. James Tully, for example, distinguishes between modern and diverse traditions, which find expression not only at the level of the state but also at the transnational or global level.[3] In relation to the nation state, the modern tradition conceives of citizenship in terms of the possession of a particular set of rights and duties and their corresponding institutional preconditions. These rights are regarded as providing universal standards which can be used to assess the imperfect institutional forms that citizenship takes in practice. In contrast, the diverse tradition recognizes a multiplicity of different practices rather than a single set of standards. It conceives of citizenship as a cooperative relationship that does not require any particular institutional setting, and which may cross territorial boundaries, but which takes place in the context of relations of governance. It obtains either between the governed and their governors, or between equals exercising power together, and is oriented towards securing the enjoyment of public or civic goods, whether through (creative) use of the options available to them, or by employing strategies of negotiation or confrontation in order to expand that range of options. Although there are some similarities between the distinction I am drawing and Tully's, there are clearly differences as well, and his purposes are rather different from mine. I make no claim that my distinction is the only one that is important; how we chart the terrain of citizenship will of course depend upon the questions we are addressing. My claim is merely that the distinction between justice and equal membership accounts illuminates the demands made by citizenship. (I shall return to Tully's conception of diverse citizenship in Chapter 8, in the context of discussing the issue of whether there is a duty to act as a global or transnational citizen.)

2 The duties of citizenship

My purpose is to develop the two different accounts of citizenship I have sketched and then use them to illuminate a number of issues concerning the duties and responsibilities of citizenship. It has been a common complaint over the past several decades that citizens have focused too much on their rights and entitlements and not enough on their duties and responsibilities. No doubt there is some truth in this accusation, as there is likewise in the claim that political theorists have concentrated on what the state owes its citizens at the expense of what citizens owe the state or indeed each other. But at the level of political theory, at least, the idea that the responsibilities and duties of citizenship have been entirely neglected cannot be sustained A consideration of whether we have a duty to obey the law, and if so, how it is to be justified and what are its limits, has been at the heart of much theorizing about citizenship, and even when the notion of distributive justice took centre stage, it did so in the context of Rawls's theory which postulated a natural duty to support just institutions. The real debate has not been about whether citizens have any duties or responsibilities, but about their precise content, how demanding they are, and whether duties of citizenship grounded in principles of justice need to be supplemented by other duties of citizenship grounded in some other way. This book focuses on the duties and responsibilities of citizenship, not because they have been ignored but because their content and basis is still less well understood.

What sort of duties are the duties of citizenship? They are moral duties but they need not be legal duties. Indeed there are often strong reasons—sometimes principled, sometimes pragmatic—for not enforcing them. Kant believed that moral duties may be either perfect or imperfect, that is, they may be duties that require one to behave in some way on any occasion when they apply—for example, he believed that we have a perfect duty not to lie that requires us never to lie—or they may be duties to behave in some way on some occasions and/or to some extent when they apply—for example, he thought that we have an imperfect duty of charity that requires us to look after the welfare of others on some occasions and to some extent, thus allowing us some leeway to decide when and to what degree.[4] Since imperfect duties allow the agent some choice in determining how best to fulfil them, it is hard to encode them in laws, even if we were to think that their fulfilment is sufficiently important to justify enforcing them. Many citizenship duties look as if they are imperfect duties, for example, if there is a duty to serve the political community, it would seem to be a duty to do so on some occasions and to some extent. (Civic virtue could play a crucial role in understanding how imperfect duties of this sort are fulfilled, for it can be conceived as a disposition which involves a capacity to discern what these imperfect duties require in the context of series of decisions that extends over time.)

There is room for scepticism, however, about the very existence of imperfect duties.[5] It might be thought that all duties are perfect, and that duties which appear to be imperfect can be spelt out in a way that reveals them to be perfect, for example, we could spell out the Kantian duty of charity by specifying the circumstances in which we are morally required to come to the aid of those in need. This would have the benefit of being more precise and it would enable us to distinguish more readily between dutiful acts and supererogatory acts (roughly speaking, acts which it is good to perform but not wrong not to perform), which is hard to do so long as the notion of imperfect duty is in play. But even if a duty to come to the aid of others when they are in need could be translated into a perfect duty, it would be difficult to do the same for at least some of the duties of citizenship. Given the diversity of forms that even reasonably just states may take, including federal arrangements with multilevel governance as well as unitary states, it is hard to specify in anything other than highly general terms what a duty to participate politically or serve the political community would require of us, and specified in these terms it is likely that it will still have the shape of an imperfect duty.

In the light of these difficulties, a two-tier model may seem attractive: we might suppose that, at the fundamental level, the duties of citizenship are all perfect duties, but at the level of practical decision-making, they have the form of imperfect duties, and the agent has some choice in deciding how to fulfil them. For example, it might be thought that the duty to participate politically and the duty to serve one's political community are imperfect but that both are derived from the perfect duty to shoulder one's fair share of the burdens of a practice when one enjoys its benefits: in practice, the best way for each citizen to satisfy this perfect duty is for her to recognize, and conscientiously fulfil, imperfect duties to participate politically and serve her political community—and in that way 'do her bit'. But although a two-tier model of this kind seems well-equipped to explain how imperfect duties might be grounded in a perfect duty of fair play, I am not so convinced that it can be applied in the same way to duties derived from the more fundamental one to support and promote just institutions since that duty looks as if it may be irreducibly imperfect.[6]

My aim is to demonstrate that the justice account and the equal membership account each provide a valuable perspective on the duties of citizenship, whether perfect or imperfect, and that we miss something of importance if we look at this issue through only one lens. I focus in particular on the following questions: whether citizens have a duty not to become dependent on the state in so far as they can avoid doing so (Chapter 3); whether they have a duty to take a share of domestic burdens, including a duty to be equally involved in raising their children (Chapter 4); whether they have a duty not to seek or gain unfair advantages (Chapter 5); whether they have a duty to offer only public reasons in public debate (Chapter 6); whether they have a duty to integrate with other cultural, religious, or ethnic groups (Chapter 7); whether they have a duty as 'ecological citizens' to ensure that their environmental footprints are sustainable, and more generally whether they have a duty to act as global citizens (Chapter 8).

Some of these duties have received less attention in the literature on citizenship than others that I do not discuss in the same depth, such as the duty to obey the law, the duty to participate politically, and the duty to serve the political community. Although I make some remarks about these other duties, particularly in Chapter 1 where I use them to illustrate various points, I do not devote whole chapters to their exploration. I do not deny their importance, but the way in which the justice account and the equal membership account bear upon them is more obvious and they are already better understood.[7] With the exception of Chapter 6 (which discusses the issue of whether we have a duty to give only public reasons in public debate), I have also chosen to focus on what might be called 'everyday citizenship'. By 'everyday citizenship', I mean the low-level decisions that we make in the course of our everyday lives that, on reflection, our duties of citizenship might be thought to bear upon—such as the decisions people take about where to live, where to send their children to school, whether to lead healthy lifestyles, whether to use their personal connections in seeking advantages for their children, what share of domestic burdens to shoulder—and which in practice in liberal-democratic societies have often been treated as of merely private significance, at least when they do not involve any law-breaking.

The duty to avoid state dependency

The question of whether citizens have an unconditional entitlement to welfare benefits and health care is the main context in which the debate about rights and responsibilities has taken place. One way in which it might seem that we can steer a path through this debate, neither denying such an entitlement nor the responsibility of the citizen, is to argue that citizens have a duty to avoid becoming dependent upon state aid, including perhaps a duty to lead a healthy life so that they reduce the demands that they place upon the state, including its health-care provision. Whether such a position is available to us, however, is complex, and the justice and equal membership accounts provide us with different perspectives on the issue. From the perspective of the justice account this issue is inextricably bound up with the question of whether justice requires people to bear the costs of their choices. If it does, then it may seem a short distance from here to the conclusion that citizens have a duty to avoid becoming dependent upon state aid. But I shall argue that things are not that simple. If the entitlement to state benefits is conditional upon not being responsible for one's inability to meet one's own needs, then there is little, if any space, for a citizen's duty to avoid becoming dependent upon the state: either one cannot avoid doing so, in which case such a duty would be irrelevant, or one becomes dependent in a way that is a foreseeable and avoidable consequence of one's own choices, in which case one has no entitlement to state aid. This dilemma does not exhaust the range of possible positions, however. Even though it is hard to deny that responsibility for an outcome makes a difference to a person's entitlements, there are a number of different possible positions on the precise effect that responsibility for one's predicament makes to one's entitlement to state aid, some of which can make space for the idea that citizens are under a duty to avoid becoming dependent upon it.

The issues here look rather different from the perspective of the equal membership account, for it seems to involve an unconditional commitment to meeting each citizen's needs in so far as this is required in order to provide them with equal opportunity to participate on equal terms in social and political life. Indeed, the justice account and the equal membership account potentially conflict in this context, raising the question of whether the good of equal membership may sometimes legitimately take priority over consid- erations of justice. If it may legitimately take priority, then there is room for a justification of a duty to avoid state dependency even if we were to suppose that there is no reason of justice to help a person who is responsible for his or her own needs—and indeed even if we were to suppose that it would be unjust to force others to do so through taxation.

The duty to share domestic burdens

Feminists have sought to re-chart the terrain of citizenship. One of the crucial issues in this context is the place of unpaid care work, especially that which is involved in the raising of children, in our understanding of citizenship. If we endorse a principle of reciprocity which holds that citizens are justified in receiving state benefits only if they have made a contribution to society when they had the opportunity to do so, then we can allow that the performance of unpaid care work enables a citizen to satisfy this requirement.[8] Reflecting upon these issues from the perspective of the justice account, we might also think that each parent has a duty of citizenship to take a fair share of the work associated with raising their children, grounded in principles of justice which govern the distribution of domestic burdens. This is more problematic than it might appear, however, and there are a number of sources of resistance to the idea that principles of distributive justice apply to domestic burdens. For example, it might be thought that if we are truly to respect moral and religious pluralism, we have to allow different family units to organize their domestic lives in accordance with their own moral and religious doctrines, which may involve particular views about the proper role of men and women and the distribution of domestic burdens between them. I shall consider a variety of different reasons for resisting the application of principles of distributive justice to domestic burdens, but I argue that none of them are persuasive.

It is not clear, however, that the principles of justice appropriate in this context entail that mothers and fathers have a duty to share the burdens of childcare *equally*. These principles may, for example, permit burdens that are experienced as a result of performing paid work for others to offset burdens shouldered whilst performing unpaid domestic work. Formulating precise principles to govern the division of domestic burdens is challenging and it may be that the best we can hope for is a requirement that each parent does their bit, seen as an imperfect duty. (This imperfect duty might perhaps be understood as derived from a perfect duty that requires us to take on our fair share of these burdens.) I argue that, on various assumptions at least, it can properly be conceived as a duty of *citizenship* as opposed to merely a duty owed to one's co-parent.

Many versions of the justice account will require parents to bear the lion's share of the burdens of raising their child, on the grounds that parents choose to have their children (or, at least, that their children are a foreseeable consequence of their sexual activity) so should bear the costs of doing so. One of these costs, however, may be that while their children are young they do not have the same opportunities as non-parents (or parents of older children) to participate fully in the social and political life of the polity. But if honouring the good of equal membership involves an unconditional commitment to providing each citizen with an equal opportunity to participate on equal terms in the political sphere and in civil society, an equal membership account may not be so sanguine about the effects of the burdens of caring for young children. The tension between the justice account and the equal membership account in this context may be partially resolved, however, by supposing that each parent has a *pro tanto* duty of citizenship to take an equal share of the burdens of raising their children should the other desire to reduce their greater share, and that employers have a duty to provide flexible work arrangements for their employees so that they are able to engage in equal parenting, in so far as employers can do so in a way that is relatively costless. Even if having the opportunity for equal parenting does not mean that parents of young children will have an opportunity equal to others in their society to participate in social and political life, it does involve a movement in the direction of greater equality of opportunity in this respect.

The duty not to seek or gain unfair advantages

The justice account maintains that citizens are under a duty to support and to further reasonably just laws and institutions. But even in a society whose basic institutions and laws were perfectly just, there would be scope for individuals to act unjustly, to seek an unfair share of benefits or advantages for themselves, or for their friends or relations. This is not merely a practical problem with devising institutions, laws and policies so that they deter such behaviour or punish it when it occurs. It is a deeper problem because there are many instances where we think it desirable to allow people the liberty to act unjustly. For example, we may think it is important to permit private education because it allows parents to choose schools for their children with a particular educational philosophy or distinctive curriculum, even though we know that some of these schools will undermine equality of opportunity by giving their pupils unfair advantages in the competition for jobs or elite higher education. We also know that some parents will choose these schools for their child to give him competitive advantages rather than because of their conception of what constitutes an intrinsically valuable education, yet arguably such behaviour violates a duty not to seek or gain unfair advantage for oneself or others.

The idea that there is a duty not to seek unfair advantages for oneself or for others is most at home within a justice account of citizenship; there is no interestingly different 'equal membership' account perspective on it. If there is such a duty, what it implies will depend upon what constitutes an unfair advantage, and this will be determined by our best theory of justice. I shall assume that justice requires us to counteract the effects of differences in people's 'unchosen' circumstances, but I shall not presuppose any particular view of what that involves. Instead I shall draw out the implications of two broadly different approaches, which I call the neutralization approach and the mitigation approach.

The duty to give only public reasons

Many liberal theorists have argued that citizens have a duty to exercise self-restraint in public debate by offering only public reasons for the laws and policies they favour, at least when these involve matters of basic justice. Often they defend this position from within a justice account by appealing to a notion of legitimacy. I argue that this approach is unpromising, however. Even if political principles can be legitimate only if they are acceptable to all, this does not rule out the possibility that principles may be legitimate if they are endorsed by different citizens for different 'private' reasons. If they can be legitimate even when they are endorsed for different private reasons, why limit public debate to the giving of only public reasons? Other ways of tying the giving of public reasons to the legitimate exercise of political power run into related difficulties.

The idea that citizens have a duty to give only public reasons in public debate is also sometimes defended by an appeal to the importance of respect for one's fellow citizens, or by appeal to what it is to be reasonable. The first of these arguments is most at home within an equal membership account. Both face a number of problems, however. For it would seem that we can respect our fellow citizens whilst, for example, giving a religious reason that they do not share, so long as we are not dismissive of them and do not ridicule their arguments. We may also be reasonable whilst offering such reasons so long as we give due weight to the burdens of judgements and do not seek to justify laws and policies which would require others to conform to religious doctrines that they can reasonably reject.

The duty to integrate

A number of governments in Europe and elsewhere have declared that immigrants have a duty to integrate. They have grounded this duty in the importance of social (or community) cohesion for the stability of social institutions. From the perspective of justice accounts, this duty is best understood as deriving from a duty to support just institutions. If the achievement and stability of reasonably just institutions depends upon social cohesion, and social cohesion depends upon integration, then there would be a basis for the idea that citizens are under a duty to integrate. An argument of this sort relies upon empirical evidence. But before we can even determine whether the evidence supports it, we need some clarity concerning the concepts of social cohesion and integration, and what empirical hypotheses are being entertained in relation to them. When we probe further, it seems that the idea of integration is often associated with two rather different ideas that bear very little relation to each other. First, the idea of members of different groups leading more of their lives together in what we might call 'meaningful interaction', and second, the idea of sharing a national identity. Weaker and stronger claims are then possible about the connection between each of these phenomena and the cultivation and maintenance of reasonably just institutions. Is it being claimed that a shared national identity is a necessary condition for the achievement and stability of reasonably just institutions, or more weakly, that a shared national identity tends to make these institutions easier to achieve, and more stable and enduring? And if it is being claimed that meaningful interaction is a necessary condition for the creation and maintenance of these institutions, then we need to know what level or intensity of interaction is required. I argue that when levels of trust are sufficiently low to threaten the viability of reasonably just institutions, the connection between meaningful interaction and mutual trust may be able to underpin a duty to integrate that binds the majority as well as minorities, and that requires both to make different choices about where they live or where they send their children to school. Under these circumstances, there may also be scope to defend some specific duties, for example, a duty that requires immigrants to learn the language of the society they have joined, and a duty that requires parents to send their children to schools that are diverse in terms of religion, culture, and ethnicity when they have the choice.

The equal membership account has a potentially different perspective on these issues. It may suppose that lack of integration, or different cultural groups leading 'parallel lives' within the same society, is a product of a failure of social equality, that is, a failure of citizens to treat each other as equals, often as a result of racial prejudice which lies behind behaviour which, even if it is not unjust, leads to a separation between different groups. For example, as a result of such prejudice a couple might decide not to buy a house in a neighbourhood that has a high proportion of members of an ethnic minority living there, or decide not to send their son to the local school because it has a high proportion of children from that minority, or decide not to allow him to play with children in the neighbourhood from it. If these patterns of behaviour are reproduced across a society, then different groups will lead different lives within the same society. Even if the prejudiced forms of behaviour that generate a lack of integration are not unjust, it may be possible to justify a duty to integrate that bears primarily on those behaving in this way, especially when lack of integration causes minorities to suffer from various forms of disadvantage.

The duty to act as a global or ecological citizen

The idea that a person may be in a relationship of citizenship to others who live beyond the borders of the state to which she belongs, even when they are not all subject to any common political authority, has gained momentum over the past decade or so. It is implicit in the contention that each of us owes a duty of ecological citizenship, to those in the developing world who bear the brunt of climate change, to reduce our environmental footprints to a sustainable size by making different choices in our everyday lives, and it is implicit in the contention that we owe duties of global citizenship to those who live in grinding poverty to help them raise their standards of living. But even if these duties are properly regarded as duties of justice, it is not clear that a justice account can legitimately characterize them as duties of ecological or global *citizenship*. This is not simply because citizenship is about the enjoyment of rights as well as the incurring of duties, though that might make one worry about extending the relationship of citizenship into contexts where there is no common political authority to protect rights. It is also because it is part of the core concept of citizenship that the duties of citizenship are special duties which fellow citizens owe to each other as part of that relationship. In their standard form, these duties emerge from the fact that one is subject to the same social, political, and economic institutions, or part of a cooperative scheme for mutual advantage, or part of a scheme that is in place to facilitate mutual aid. In the absence of some background such as this, it is hard to see how any duties that are owed as part of justice can be construed as special duties that fellow citizens owe to each other. This is not to say that notions of global or transnational citizenship are unintelligible in the absence of global or transnational political institutions. They can gain a foothold where agents act together across state borders in a way that creates associative obligations between them: in these cases even if they do not enjoy rights through the protection of transnational institutions, the fact that they incur duties to one another to promote various civic and public goods at least gives the language of citizenship a foothold.

3 Essentialism

The core concept of citizenship to which I appeal is flexible and accommodating, perhaps more so than it may initially appear. According to it, citizenship is a relationship in which the parties enjoy rights or entitlements within a common framework of enforcement and provision, and incur special obligations, duties, or responsibilities to each other. This allows the possibility that the obligations of citizenship extend to what is conventionally regarded as the private sphere and include obligations to perform one's fair share of domestic labour, such as the work involved in caring for children and other dependants. It also allows the possibility that equal citizenship for all may require group differentiated rights that give different packages of rights to different groups of citizens, perhaps distinguished in terms of culture or ethnicity.[9] As I have already suggested, however, it does run counter to conceptions of citizenship which maintain that people can lie in a relationship of global or transnational citizenship *simply* through sharing obligations of justice to those in poverty beyond the borders of the states in which they live, in the absence of anything else that connects them, and even in the absence of any common framework of rights protection. Indeed I appeal to the core concept of citizenship to cast doubt on these new usages of the term. But an approach which adheres to the idea that there is such a core concept, no matter how minimal, will strike many as fundamentally misguided, especially when it is applied as a brake on new ways of thinking about citizenship.

Those influenced by Wittgenstein's later work may resist the idea that there is a core concept of citizenship by arguing that there is a variety of different uses of the term with nothing that unifies them, and will be inclined to think that the approach I favour involves an objectionable form of essentialism.[10] In a well-known passage in the *Philosophical Investigations*, Wittgenstein points out that there is no set of properties or characteristics which serve to define what makes an activity a game. He encourages us to look and see whether there is anything in common between what we quite properly call games and concludes that 'the result of this examination is: we see a complicated network of similarities over-lapping and criss-crossing: sometimes overall similarities, sometimes similarities of detail'[11] but not a set of properties which all and only games possess. It is important to situate Wittgenstein's remarks in context, however. He is seeking to displace a particular idea of what it is to grasp a concept or understand the meaning of a term, according to which grasping a concept or understanding a term consists in knowing the rules for its proper application and where those rules are thought to determine how it should be used on each and every occasion. He insists that there are no such rules, and that we do not need to suppose otherwise in order to make sense of the idea that a term may be meaningful and used correctly or incorrectly. But the notion that there is a core concept of citizenship need not involve denying any of these insights. The specification of a core concept of this kind need not provide a set of rules for applying the concept that determine its proper use on each and every occasion: indeed the account I have given is incomplete and open-ended in various ways, thus allowing for differing interpretations.

These remarks are unlikely to satisfy those opposed to the idea that there is a core concept of citizenship. They will think that any attempt to recover such a concept must fail to appreciate that the use of the term 'citizenship' has evolved in response to changing social and political circumstances in such a way that it would simply be miraculous if some abstract formula, whether partial or complete, could account for, or explain the limits of, its diverse legitimate uses. Even if such a miracle were to occur, we have no reason to think that future uses will conform to that abstract formula. Indeed the search for abstract formulae of this kind, and adherence to them, is likely to mean that we will be slow to come to understand and appreciate conceptual innovations: theorists will complain that some new usage represents a conceptual confusion because it does not conform to the abstract formula they have identified, failing to appreciate that this new usage constitutes an imaginative rethinking of a concept, perhaps in the light of changing circumstances. Moreover, the very idea of a core concept seems to be on shaky ground in so far as it assumes that we can identify an uncontested, and indeed uncontestable, set of conceptual truths which serve to constrain the different conceptions or interpretations of citizenship that are possible. From this perspective, it can seem that postulating a core concept is to stipulate a set of conditions that different conceptions of citizenship must meet in a way that lacks any authority to constrain the way in which the concept may evolve in the face of changing social, political, and economic circumstances and the intellectual developments that may occur in the light of these changes.[12]

This is a powerful challenge that should trouble anyone who thinks there is value in seeking to identify core concepts that reflect the use of the key terms of political discourse. It would be futile for theorists to think that they can police the boundaries for the proper use of these terms, or indeed to believe that, even if they could, this would be desirable. Put more philosophically, it might seem that the difficulty with the approach I am proposing (or that part of it which involves adherence to the idea that there is a core concept of citizenship) is that it assumes a too rigid division of statements into analytic or synthetic, that is, into statements which are true solely in virtue of the meaning of the terms that are used to express them, and statements which, if true, are true not only in virtue of those meanings but also because of the way the world is or ought to be.[13] Those who reject the analytic/synthetic distinction, so understood, can nevertheless suppose that there are statements that we are reluctant to give up in the face of changing circumstances because of the intellectual costs this would impose on us, without maintaining that to do so would *simply* be to change the meaning of the terms we are using. From this perspective, insisting on my analysis of the concept of citizenship in the face of challenges to it which have arisen in the light of changes in our social, political or economic circumstances would be to refuse to engage in an important debate about the costs and benefits involved in changing our ways of thinking about citizenship.

But whilst reflection on Wittgenstein's remarks about family resemblances gives us reason to be suspicious of attempts to capture the use of complex concepts by definitions that pick out common properties, even he emphasizes that terms can be misused. Indeed, he supposed that many philosophical problems arise from language 'going on holiday', when philosophers prise terms away from their ordinary contexts, perhaps as a result of being misled by their superficial grammar, and raise questions which misunderstand the role of these terms in our lives. We at least need to leave open the possibility that some radically different usages of terms such as 'citizenship' do violence to the concept it expresses, in effect emptying it of content, and collapsing distinctions that are worth preserving between citizenship and other ideals. The core concept I have described is not intended to constrain new ways of thinking about citizenship, but rather to give us a better sense of what features of our ordinary thought and practice are deeply rooted and which are relatively superficial. When a new way of thinking is proposed that runs counter to these deeply rooted features, we are in a better position to assess its costs and benefits. That assessment may then guide us in reaching a conclusion about whether it represents a worthwhile form of conceptual innovation, or is better seen as a conceptual confusion. So the notion of a core concept should not be regarded as drawing a line between what can be contested and what is beyond contest, and it need not presuppose a rigid distinction between analytic and synthetic statements. The analysis I give can be interpreted as identifying deeply rooted assumptions about the nature of citizenship that are presupposed in a range of central uses of the term, though they might in principle come to be rejected without us having to conclude that the term was being given an entirely new meaning (in a way that might preclude the need to choose one usage rather than another). When new models of citizenship are proposed which abandon one or more of these assumptions, the question then becomes: what are the costs and benefits of doing so? So in Chapter 8 when I examine an ecological notion of citizenship which abandons elements that I regard as partly constitutive of our core concept, including the idea that the duties of citizenship are owed by fellow citizens *to each other*, I argue that this notion is flawed not merely because it runs counter to our core concept of citizenship, but because the costs of rejecting this idea are not worth bearing.

4 Citizenship duties as associative obligations

According to the minimal core concept of citizenship with which I am working, citizenship duties are special duties since they are duties that fellow citizens owe to each other. (It is this notion which creates difficulties for some versions of the idea that we are fellow global or ecological citizens.) Citizenship duties seem to be associative obligations that arise from the particular relationship of which they are part. But the very existence of associative obligations has been called into question. Samuel Scheffler argues that such duties face two potential objections, which he calls the voluntarist objection and the distributive objection. According to the voluntarist objection, mere membership of a group or participation in a relationship cannot by itself give rise to any duties, whereas according to the distributive objection, the beneficiaries of the fulfilment of special duties obtain unfair advantages.[14]

The voluntarist objection arises from the thought that special duties cannot be justified unless they are in some sense voluntarily incurred.[15] This creates a pressure to construe citizenship obligations as the product of some act of will. In particular it encourages us to think of them as either contractually grounded or as deriving from a principle of fair play that requires a person to shoulder his fair share of the burdens of a practice when he has enjoyed (a fair share of) the benefits of it. Both of these approaches to justifying duties of citizenship face well-known difficulties, however. Most citizens have not entered into any explicit contract with each other, and the idea that they have done so tacitly is fraught with problems, especially in a world where people are not free to move from one state to another. That citizens have received various benefits from a practice, such as the enjoyment of rights, seems insufficient on its own to generate any duty to shoulder a share of the burdens of it, yet the idea that they have willingly accepted these benefits is hard to establish when they cannot refuse them. When they have *claimed* benefits, such as welfare payments, the case may be stronger, but it will apply only to a subset of citizens. One way round the voluntarist objection might be to suppose that each of us has a natural duty to support and further just institutions from which various more particular duties of citizenship can be derived, such as a duty to obey the law, a duty to pay one's taxes, a duty to participate politically, and a duty to serve in the military when needed. But it is hard to see why this should be regarded as a duty that applies to the citizens of a particular country in relation to *their* institutions, rather than as a duty to which everyone is subject regardless of their citizenship and which binds a person whenever she is in a position to undermine or promote a just institution.[16] If that is so, then it is not a duty of citizenship as such.

Each of the approaches to meeting the voluntarist objection that I have described can be developed in creative ways in the face of the difficulties raised with them. Indeed, in Chapter 1, I shall defend the idea that a duty to support and promote just institutions can be interpreted as a special duty that fellow citizens owe to each other. But even if none of these strategies were successful, the voluntarist objection might simply be met head-on by denying that all special duties must be voluntarily incurred. As Scheffler himself points out, ordinary moral opinion endorses a wide range of associative obligations that are incurred from being born into a particular family or state and does not suppose that they must be a product in some way of voluntary choice.[17] In a way that resonates with ordinary moral opinion, I shall argue in Chapter 1, in the context of the equal membership account, that at least some citizenship duties are non-voluntary associative obligations that are grounded in a non-instrumentally valuable relationship of which they are part.

The distributive objection to associative duties that Scheffler also identifies poses a further challenge for duties of citizenship. In relation to these duties it is an objection that arises from the perspective of outsiders: it maintains that fellow citizens (especially those who belong to an affluent state) enjoy unfair advantages as a result of the fulfilment of special duties to one another. The distributive objection might also be met head-on, by arguing that relationships such as citizenship are an independent source of obligations that, in some circumstances at least, can outweigh general duties when they come into conflict, including general duties that are grounded in principles of justice. Even though I have some sympathy with this line of argument (and will end up endorsing a restricted version of it), it seems to imply that the special concern warranted by relationships such as citizenship justifies some unfairness towards those who are not part of these relationships. For many that would be hard to swallow. This line of argument has to be made easier to accommodate, preferably by showing that compliance with special duties need not involve any unfairness. Let me consider how this might be done, beginning with various ways in which conflict between general duties and special duties could be avoided.

First, some special duties of citizenship might be derived from general duties of justice owed to persons as such. Assigning these special duties might be regarded as the best means in practice of fulfilling general duties, in which case those who benefit from them would not be enjoying unfair advantages. For example, Robert Goodin maintains that we have a general obligation to protect the vulnerable, and argues that our special obligations derive largely from this general obligation: 'special obligations are ... merely devices whereby the moral community's general duties get assigned to particular agents'.[18] The idea considered in Chapter 4, that citizens have a special obligation to each other to take their fair share of domestic burdens, and the idea considered in Chapter 5, that citizens have a special obligation to each other not to seek or gain unfair advantages, might also be defended by appealing to the way in which these obligations can be derived from general principles of justice. Indeed this is the characteristic form that the defence of special obligations takes within the justice account of citizenship. (Of course, some argument would be required to show that the preference that *actual* states give to the interests of their own citizens in our imperfect world promotes rather than undermines impartial principles of justice, and there will be scope for the plausible view that these principles would be much better fulfilled by dispersing the sovereignty that is currently concentrated in states by creating a variety of different political units above and below.[19] But a transformed system of global governance of this kind might then underpin special obligations amongst the members of these new political units.)

Second, even when the special duties that citizens owe to each other are not derived in some way from general duties that are owed to persons as such, they might be *additional* duties that do not compete with the general duties.[20] If they are additional duties and do not compete with general duties, this would undermine the idea that those who are the beneficiaries of the fulfilment of the special duties are receiving *unfair* advantages. This response is particularly effective when the general duties are regarded as lexically prior to the special duties. Consider two different types of case where this might apply. First, when the special duties are *less* demanding than the general duties in terms of the distributive shares they require fellow citizens to receive, but the general duties cannot in practice be met in full; second, when the general duties are less demanding than the special duties. An example of the first type of case would be when the general duty requires us to bring about a state of affairs in which everyone is equal in terms of the distributive shares they receive, or as equal as possible when complete equality is unachievable, whereas the special duty merely requires us to make sure that as many citizens as possible have enough to be able to lead a decent life. The special duty kicks in when equal shares are impossible to achieve and we are selecting between distributions that involve the same degree of equality or inequality. An example of the second type of case would be when the general duties governing the distribution of resources are less demanding than the special duties and are non-egalitarian in character, for example, when they merely require us to do our bit to ensure that each person, regardless of his or her nationality or citizenship, is in a position to lead a decent life. In that case, the special duties kick in after this general duty has been satisfied.[21]

The idea that the special duties of citizenship are additional duties that do not compete with general duties also has force when these special duties do not directly govern the distribution of resources. Several of the proposed duties that I shall consider in Part II would govern the behaviour of citizens without being directly involved in distributing resources between them: for example, the duty to give only public reasons in public debate, and the duty to integrate. Of course, even when duties of citizenship do not directly govern the distribution of resources, their fulfilment may nevertheless involve the use of resources, for they may have implications for where citizens should direct their efforts: if citizens are under a special duty to participate in public life or to serve their political community, then the fulfilment of these duties would require citizens to devote time and energy to these activities at the expense of other projects, including some which may have global or transnational reach and which are concerned with promoting the well-being of those in other countries.[22] Here there is the potential for conflict between the fulfilment of special duties and general duties but there is no compelling reason for supposing that the general duties must always take priority, or that any unfairness would be involved in giving the special duties priority. Whether the general duties should take priority will depend on the specific ones involved and the circumstances in which they come into conflict.[23]

Even when the general duties and special duties directly govern the distribution of resources and the former are not given lexical priority, it may still be possible to justify the advantages received by the beneficiaries of the fulfilment of these special duties. For it might be argued that there need be nothing objectionable about the way in which fellow citizens receive additional benefits from the fulfilment of special obligations, provided that there is a fair opportunity for outsiders to become part of that relationship—though, of course, there would need to be further elaboration of what is to count as a fair opportunity in this context.[24] Any plausible egalitarian view will have to allow that some inequalities may be permissible, and in principle at least, those which emerge from relationships which everyone has the fair opportunity to join are plausible candidates.

Notes

1. The distinction between concept and conception is usually credited to John Rawls. J. Rawls, *A Theory of Justice* (Cambridge, MA: Harvard University Press, 1971), pp. 5–6; J. Rawls, *A Theory of Justice*, revised edition (Oxford: Oxford University Press, 1999), p. 5. (In the citations that follow, references will be given in the form 'p. x/y', where 'x' denotes the page number in the 1971 edition and 'y' denotes the page number in the 1999 edition.) The distinction I am drawing is somewhat different because my characterization of the core concept does not serve to distinguish citizenship from all other relationships since it does not provide sufficient conditions of it.
2. See J. Pocock, 'The Ideal of Citizenship since Classical Times', in R. Beiner (ed.), *Theorizing Citizenship* (Albany, NY: State University of New York Press, 1995), pp. 29–52.
3. See J. Tully, *Public Philosophy in a New Key, Vol. II, Imperialism and Civic Freedom* (Cambridge: Cambridge University Press, 2008), pp. 246ff.
4. The idea that imperfect duties, unlike perfect duties, allow the agent some choice in determining how to satisfy them doesn't quite capture the distinction, however. For even perfect duties allow the agent some leeway in deciding how to satisfy them. For example, even if there is a perfect duty not to lie, an agent may satisfy this by being silent when asked a question or by giving an evasive answer. The point is rather that if A is under a perfect duty to do X or not to do X (under circumstances Y), then if A is to comply with that duty she has to do X or not do X (under circumstances Y), whereas if A is under an imperfect duty to do X, then she may decide when to do X.
5. See D. Statman, 'Who Needs Imperfect Duties?', *American Philosophical Quarterly*, Vol. 33, 1996, pp. 211–24.
6. See Chapter 1, section 1 for further discussion.
7. I do not mean to imply that there cannot be new and surprising defences of the duty to participate politically, or the duty to serve one's political community, from within either a justice account or an equal membership account. For a recent novel defence of the idea that there is an enforceable duty to serve that is congruent with a justice account, see C. Fabre, *Whose Body Is it Anyway? Justice and the Integrity of the Person* (Oxford: Oxford University Press, 2006), Ch. 3.
8. See S. White, *The Civic Minimum: On the Rights and Obligations of Economic Citizenship* (Oxford: Oxford University Press, 2003), pp. 108–13.
9. Some have argued that equal citizenship requires special representation rights for women, whilst others have argued that it requires cultural minorities to have group differentiated rights in order to redress the disadvantages they experience through being marginalized in a society where the dominant culture and first language is different from their own. See, for example, I. Young, 'Polity and Group Difference: A Critique of the Ideal of Universal Citizenship', *Ethics*, Vol. 99, pp. 250–74; W. Kymlicka, *Multicultural Citizenship: A Liberal Theory of Minority Rights* (Oxford: Oxford University Press, 1995).

10. See Tully, *Public Philosophy in a New Key, Vol. II*, pp. 244–6.

11. L. Wittgenstein, *Philosophical Investigations*, third edition, trans. G. E. M. Anscombe (Oxford: Blackwell, 1967), para. 66.

12. Tully, for example, argues that we can extend the use of 'citizenship' in a legitimate way simply by enacting that use, provided it bears some resemblance to its use in the past. See Tully, *Public Philosophy in a New Key, Vol. II*, pp. 298, 245. See also L. Bosniak, *The Citizen and the Alien: Dilemmas of Contemporary Membership* (Princeton, NJ: Princeton University Press, 2006), pp. 12, 26–7.

13. The paradigmatic example of an analytic statement is 'All bachelors are unmarried men'; 'all bachelors are lonely' would be an example of a synthetic statement. The distinction between analytic and synthetic statements was first drawn by Kant, although other philosophers had made similar distinctions: see I. Kant, *Critique of Pure Reason*, trans. N. Kemp Smith (London: Macmillan, 1929), A6/B7ff. The most influential challenge to it comes from W. Quine, 'Two Dogmas of Empiricism' in his *From a Logical Point of View*, second edition (Cambridge, MA: Harvard University Press, 1961). The philosophical literature on the distinction is extensive. William Connolly argues that the distinction is unhelpful in relation to political concepts on the grounds that these are cluster concepts and statements applying these concepts are generally neither purely analytic or purely synthetic: see W. Connolly, *The Terms of Political Discourse*, second edition (Oxford: Martin Robertson, 1983), pp. 17–20.

14. See S. Scheffler, 'Families, Nations, and Strangers', section III, in his *Boundaries and Allegiances: Problems of Justice and Responsibility in Liberal Thought* (Oxford: Oxford University Press, 2001).

15. Sometimes the word 'obligation' is reserved for moral requirements that are voluntarily incurred, whereas the word 'duty' is used to refer to moral requirements that are incurred non-voluntarily. (See, for example, Rawls, *A Theory of Justice*, Ch. VI.) Framed in these terms, the voluntarist objection in effect challenges the very existence of special duties. But in this book I shall use the terms 'duty' and 'obligation' interchangeably.

16. See A. J. Simmons, *Moral Principles and Political Obligations* (Princeton: Princeton University Press, 1979), Ch. 2; J. Waldron, 'Special Ties and Natural Duties', *Philosophy and Public Affairs*, Vol. 22, 1993, pp. 5–7.

17. Scheffler, 'Families, Nations, and Strangers', p. 64.

18. R. Goodin, 'What Is So Special about Our Fellow Countrymen?', *Ethics*, Vol. 98, 1988, p. 678.

19. See, for example, T. Pogge, *World Poverty and Human Rights* (Cambridge: Polity, 2002), Ch. 7.

20. See D. Jeske, 'Associative Obligations, Voluntarism and Equality', *Pacific Philosophical Quarterly*, Vol. 77, 1996, p. 300; D. Jeske, 'Special Obligations', *Stanford Encyclopedia of Philosophy*, section 5, at <http://plato.stanford.edu/entries/special-obligations/>, accessed 30 July 2010.

21. See J. Seglow, 'Associative Duties and Global Justice', *Journal of Moral Philosophy*, Vol. 7, 2010, pp. 65–7.

22. Seglow, 'Associative Duties and Global Justice', p. 69.
23. For relevant discussion, see D. Miller, 'Reasonable Partiality Towards Compatriots', *Ethical Theory and Moral Practice*, Vol. 8, 2005, pp. 63–81, especially pp. 71–80.
24. See Chapter 2, section 3, for some reflection on this issue of what it is for long-term residents to have a fair opportunity to become citizens.

Part I
The Normative Foundations of Citizenship

1

Conceptions of Citizenship

Citizenship is (in part) a relationship in which those involved enjoy rights or entitlements within a common framework of protection and provision, and incur special obligations, duties, or responsibilities to each other. Or so I claim. In this chapter, I distinguish three different conceptions which put flesh on the bones of this core concept of citizenship: the justice account, the common good account, and the equal membership account.[1] But I then go on to reject the common good account because it has counterintuitive implications concerning what it is to act as a citizen. The equal membership account avoids these problems, and indeed it can be regarded as the common good account better conceived. That in effect leaves me with two conceptions of citizenship. At this point it may look as if I am in danger of reinventing the wheel. But the distinction between the justice account and the equal membership account is not simply a refashioning of the distinction between liberal and republican conceptions, nor indeed is it a reinterpretation of the so-called Roman and ancient Greek models of citizenship. There are points of contact here, but my contrast cuts across these traditional ways of thinking about citizenship. Indeed the distinctions I draw are sufficiently different from the way in which the terrain of citizenship is normally mapped that it can be hard to locate particular thinkers within them.

1 The justice account

The justice account maintains that all the rights, duties, and virtues of citizenship are ultimately derived in some way from considerations of justice. The rights of citizenship are understood as requirements of justice and the duties of citizenship are understood as either the means through which a citizen sustains or promotes justice in her society or discharges the duties of justice that she owes to her fellow citizens. As a result, a normative theory of citizenship is parasitic upon a logically prior theory of justice.[2]

The justice account is really a family of views because different theories of justice generate different versions of it. (Questions may be raised about what constitutes a theory of justice rather than some other value, and answers to these questions may serve to place limits on what can constitute a justice account of citizenship, but in this chapter I shall bracket these issues.) Some versions take the view that all fundamental principles of justice apply independently of how individuals are related to each other, and assign moral rights and entitlements with no regard to citizenship, but argue that the institutions of particular states should be designed with a view to protecting the moral rights of their own citizens, and to forcing or enabling fellow citizens to discharge their duties of justice specifically in relation to each other, on the grounds that this constitutes the best way of realizing these fundamental principles.[3] These versions can still allow that the legal rights and entitlements granted to citizens may vary from one state to another without compromising the fundamental principles of justice because cultural and other particularities may affect what counts as the best means of realizing these principles. Other versions maintain that fellow citizens are related to each other in a way which means that some fundamental principles of justice apply to them that do not necessarily apply to others (for example, fellow citizens might be regarded as part of a cooperative scheme for mutual advantage, and this might be thought to license the application of egalitarian principles to them but not to outsiders), whilst allowing that there are other such principles (for example, those that concern human rights) that apply equally to everyone.[4]

According to the justice account, to act as a citizen is to act out of a concern for what justice requires in relation to one's fellow citizens. Citizens are conceived as being under special duties towards one another to sustain and promote the institutions that secure their rights and entitlements.[5] When citizens live under just, or reasonably just, institutions, they are regarded as being under a duty to their fellow citizens to support these institutions. In a society where institutions and policies are significantly unjust, the justice account holds that citizens owe a duty to each other to work to reform them. This general duty to support and further just institutions might be deployed in defence of a range of more specific duties, both perfect and imperfect: for example, a perfect duty to obey just laws and even some unjust ones;[6] a perfect duty to serve in the military when one is physically able to do so and the institutions of one's country are reasonably just but under grave threat from outside; an imperfect duty to participate politically in both formal and informal ways, at least in so far as the moral health of those institutions depends to some degree on the presence of an active citizenry; an imperfect duty to serve one's political community in so far as its institutions are reasonably just and a contribution from citizens is required for (or at least is conducive to) the flourishing of these institutions.[7]

The general duty to support and further just institutions can be understood in more or less demanding ways. It might be understood in a radically consequentialist manner, as a duty to promote the justice of society's laws and institutions over time, with any specific duties that are derived from it, such as a duty to obey reasonably just laws, governed by this overarching aim, thus allowing or even requiring citizens to break such laws when this would better promote just laws and institutions on balance over time.[8] This way of understanding the general duty would make it potentially very demanding, however, for in unjust societies it would require us to devote our energies to reform even when the costs to ourselves were extremely high. Other approaches might suppose that although the general duty to support and further just institutions justifies a perfect duty to comply with reasonably just laws and institutions, it underwrites only an imperfect duty to work to reform unjust institutions, or a perfect duty to do so only when this does not impose excessive costs on us. Rawls, for example, maintains that there is a natural duty of justice 'to support and to comply with just institutions that exist and apply to us' and which 'constrains us to further just arrangements not yet established, at least when this can be done without too much cost to ourselves'. He adds that 'if the basic structure of society is just, or as just as it is reasonable to expect in the circumstances, everyone has a natural duty to do his part in the existing scheme'.[9]

Rawls's position does, however, raise the question of why we should suppose that citizens are exempted from a duty to work to reform unjust institutions when this would impose excessive costs on them, whilst no similar concession is made in relation to their duty to comply with reasonably just laws and institutions.[10] Even if the difficulty in justifying this apparent asymmetry does not steer us towards a radically consequentialist understanding of the duty to support and further just institutions, it at least suggests that this duty should accommodate the idea that citizens have moral permission to break reasonably just laws in circumstances where these laws impose excessive costs on them. For example, it should allow that we might be morally permitted to refuse to comply with a legal injunction that required us to give evidence against a defendant in court when that would put us at grave risk of reprisal and where the only way of reducing that risk to an acceptable level would involve re-locating and being given a new identity. The duty to support and further just institutions is best thought of as a combination of two different general duties—a general duty to support and comply with reasonably just institutions and a general duty to work towards establishing just institutions or reforming unjust ones—both of which are *pro tanto* duties that allow exceptions when complying with them would impose excessive costs. The second of these duties seems to be an imperfect duty even when it incorporates an exceptions clause of this kind, for the duty to work towards establishing just institutions or reforming unjust ones would seem to allow citizens some discretion in relation to when and how they devote their energies to these tasks.[11]

Irrespective of how the duty to support and further just institutions is fleshed out, it is hard to show that it is owed *specifically* to fellow citizens, casting doubt on whether it can therefore count as an obligation of citizenship. For much the same reasons that it is hard to explain why citizens are under a special duty to support their own institutions in particular—rather than a duty to support and further just institutions in general, irrespective of whether they are subject to them—it is also hard to explain why the duty to support just institutions is owed to fellow citizens rather than to humanity in general.[12] (Those who defend the idea that there is a duty to support just institutions might of course deny that it is specifically a duty of citizenship, or indeed that citizens have any special reason to support and further their own just institutions rather than the just institutions of other states, but to some extent this is counterintuitive.) It is not enough here to say that we are under a special obligation to each other to support these institutions because they 'apply to us', for it would seem that a just institution may apply to a group of people without that placing them under a special obligation to each other to comply with its demands and do their share in it. John Simmons gives the example of an 'Institute for the Advancement of Philosophers' that is designed to promote the interests of philosophers and does so in a just way.[13] Even if this Institute looks after the philosophy-related interests of all philosophers in a particular network of universities, and in that sense applies to all those philosophers who work in them, it is hard to see why any of them should be under a special duty to join it or support it in other ways.

However, this is not an insuperable problem for the idea that the duty to support and further just institutions is a duty of citizenship. As Jeremy Waldron argues, a citizen may be an insider in relation to the institutions which apply to her in the sense that it is part of their point to do justice to her claims and those of her fellows.[14] When such institutions are successful, there is a difference between 'being one of the parties in respect of whose interests a just institution is just, and being a person who is merely capable of interfering with a just institution in some way'.[15] Those who are insiders in relation to a set of reasonably just institutions have a duty to support those institutions that is owed to each other in particular,[16] in addition to the duty they have to support any just institutions they relate to as outsiders that is owed to persons in general.[17] In this context we also need to distinguish between institutions the very point of which is to do justice to the claims of the individuals to whom it applies, and an institution which has some other point, for example, to promote the interests of those to whom it applies (even though it may be committed to doing so in a way that is just both in relation to insiders and outsiders). The main reason why we do not think that the philosophers are under an obligation to support the Institute that Simmons describes is that it is not a just institution in the relevant sense. It is not part of the basic structure of society since that is made up of institutions that have a profound and pervasive effect on the lives of those who live under them. Nor is it the case that its very point is to do justice to the claims of those to whom it applies; indeed it does not play any significant role in delivering justice for them. It is a just institution merely in the sense that its aims are not unjust and it pursues them in a just manner.[18] (It is better characterized as a good institution and it is implausible to suppose that we have a duty to support and further *good* institutions that is analogous to our duty to support and further just institutions.)

A justice account can also incorporate the idea that citizens are under a duty of justice to bear a fair share of the burdens of a practice when they enjoy a fair share of its benefits, which may be able to underwrite various specific obligations, such as an imperfect duty to participate politically and an imperfect duty to serve the political community, by appealing to the idea that when citizens enjoy the benefits of just institutions, then they have a duty to bear their fair share of the burdens of sustaining them. The scope of a principle of fair play of this sort, and the conditions under which it applies, have been a matter of considerable dispute, however. For good reason, there is a consensus that mere receipt of benefits is insufficient to place a person under a duty to bear a fair share of the burdens of the practice that was responsible for creating those benefits.[19] Some argue that the principle applies only when benefits are accepted rather than merely received,[20] where acceptance of these benefits requires a meaningful possibility that they might be refused and some consciousness of that fact. Others argue that what matters is that the benefits received should be essential for leading a decent life, so we are entitled to assume that everyone wants them.[21] If a principle of fair play applies when a weaker condition of this latter sort is satisfied, it may be able to underpin the idea that citizens have a duty to each other to participate politically on the grounds that the secure enjoyment of various basic liberties which are in practice indispensable to leading a decent life relies on the presence of a reasonably active citizenry. It might also allow us to justify the idea that citizens have a duty to serve the political community, on the grounds that the various formal and informal institutions which make up such a community, and which play a key role in enabling them to lead decent lives, cannot be sustained in the absence of a willingness to contribute to them in various ways.[22]

A principle of fair play might also ground a duty to make a productive contribution to society. Stuart White, for example, argues that

> where the institutions that govern economic life are sufficiently fair in terms of the opportunities they afford for productive contribution, and the awards they apportion to it, those citizens who claim the high share of the social product available to them under these institutions have an obligation to make a decent productive contribution, proportionate to their abilities, to the community in return.[23]

This principle of 'fair reciprocity' could be highly inclusive in terms of what it counts as a productive contribution, for example, it might include not only paid work, but also unpaid voluntary work and the caring work (generally done by women) performed in looking after dependants, whether young, elderly, or disabled, in domestic contexts.[24]

Different versions of the justice account will hold different views concerning what further demands citizenship places upon us.[25] Some versions suppose that principles of justice apply primarily to the basic structure of society in such a way that the duties of citizens are very limited. (For example, these versions may suppose that the only duty of citizenship is a duty to support and promote just institutions, including any specific duties this entails, and that citizens have no other or further duties.) This position is hard to sustain, however. Consider the principle of non-discrimination, a principle of justice that is generally thought to apply to the institutions which make up the basic structure of society. This principle should surely govern not only the selection decisions made by officials in public institutions but also those taken within private firms and corporations.[26] But how much further does the principle extend? For example, does it also apply to the membership rules of associations in civil society, and the rules governing who can hold offices within them? Some will resist this conclusion, but there is a general argument for applying principles of justice widely, including to such matters. For if the reason for applying principles of justice to the basic structure of society is that this structure has profound effects on the life chances of individuals, then this provides grounds for applying principles of justice to any practices or patterns of behaviour that also have such effects, including those that are part of civil society. On the basis of a nuanced version of this argument, G. A. Cohen has argued that Rawls cannot consistently deny that the difference principle should apply to personal economic choices, such as an individual's decisions about what career to pursue, what wages to negotiate, and how hard to work, as well as to the basic structure of society.[27] If this argument can be sustained, acting on duties of justice and corresponding duties of citizenship may require considerable self-sacrifice, even if (as Cohen allows) there are personal prerogatives which permit citizens to depart from these duties when compliance with them would be particularly burdensome. I shall return to these issues in section 1 of the next chapter.

It might be thought that the dominant liberal political theories give a justice account of the duties of citizenship.[28] As we have seen, Rawls maintains that citizens have a duty to support and to further just institutions. He also allows that there are duties of citizenship that do not derive from the duty to support just institutions but which have their place within the virtues of citizenship (such as the virtue of civility), with these virtues justified at least in part by the role they play in sustaining and promoting just institutions. It would be too quick, however, to conclude that Rawls endorses the justice account of citizenship. In his later writings he is not committed to it when it is understood as providing an *exhaustive* account of how the rights, duties, and virtues of citizenship are to be justified. Indeed, given that Rawls is seeking to avoid appeal to controversial doctrines, he should refrain from endorsing any account of this sort, since he need not deny the possibility of duties of citizenship which are grounded independently of considerations of justice, for example, in some aspect of the common good.[29] The question of whether there are such duties goes beyond the remit of his theory of justice.

2 The common good account

According to the common good account, the rights, duties, and virtues of citizenship are grounded in the common good: standardly, rights protect the conditions required to secure the common good, whilst duties and virtues promote the common good. To act as a citizen is to act in the light of the common good, a wider concern than that of justice;[30] whenever one does so, one acts as a citizen. The common good account can in principle underwrite different kinds of duties. For example, it might maintain that we have a perfect duty to promote the common good in whatever ways we are able to do. Or, more plausibly perhaps, it can maintain that we have an imperfect duty to do so, that is, a duty sometimes and to some extent to act so as to promote the common good (combined, perhaps, with a perfect duty not to *undermine* that good). The latter view, though vague, will be less demanding that the former view, unless the former permits a person not to promote the common good when that would impose excessive costs on her. The latter view can give a key role to the idea of civic virtue, conceived as the dispositions required for citizens to be able to judge what their imperfect duties require of them in particular circumstances and act accordingly.

The relationship between citizenship, so understood, and considerations of justice depends upon how we understand the common good.[31] Some of the rights needed to protect the common good might turn out also to be rights of justice, and some of the duties which promote the common good might also be duties of justice, even if they are not justified in these terms. How then should the common good be conceived? First, it might be conceived as an aggregate of individual goods, so that promoting the common good is equivalent to promoting utility within the confines of the state.[32] Second, it might be conceived as the set of conditions that in general need to be met before each individual can achieve his or her own good. (This would include some of what are technically public goods because they are non-excludable, such as security or unpolluted air, but not all of the relevant conditions will be public goods in this sense.) Third, it might be conceived as involving, in addition to those conditions that in general need to be met before each person can achieve his or her own good, various goods that are partially constitutive of the good of each and every individual.[33] Amongst such goods, those which are *irreducibly social* might be given special significance. Irreducibly social goods are those goods which can only be enjoyed with others, out of necessity rather than mere contingent fact,[34] either because their realization depends upon the existence of various social forms[35] or because they essentially involve interaction with others, for example, friendship.[36] Irreducibly social goods are part of the common good in the relevant sense only if they are part of each person's good.

If the common good is understood in either the second or the third way, then some of the rights and duties of citizenship that are grounded in the need to protect or promote conditions or components of each individual's good will also be rights and duties of justice, for in at least some cases securing these conditions and components will also be a requirement of justice.[37] This would nevertheless constitute a common good account rather than a justice account because the rights, duties, and virtues of citizenship are grounded in the common good rather than in considerations of justice. Suppose, however, that the rights of citizenship are conceived as the conditions for the realization of the common good, and these conditions are in turn simply conceived as rights of justice, so that in effect, principles of justice are derived from the common good. This theory of citizenship would be both a justice account *and* a common good account, which shows that these categories are not necessarily mutually exclusive.

Does the common good in the third sense distinguished include the good of political participation as a component or ingredient? Political participation might plausibly be regarded as an irreducibly social good, but in order to defend the idea that it is a component of the common good, we would need to show that it was also partially constitutive of each person's good. This claim is harder to justify, though there is a weak and a strong version of it. The weak version claims that political participation is an ingredient of each person's good—other things being equal, a person's life goes better when she is politically active compared to when she is not—without being essential to her flourishing, whereas the strong version maintains that it is such an important ingredient of each person's good that a person cannot flourish in its absence. But even the weak version of the claim that political participation is part of each person's good is open to question. It needs to be distinguished from two other, more mundane, claims which are much more plausible. First, that unless there is active political participation, a society will be vulnerable to domination and corruption, so that some degree of political participation, on the part of some citizens, is an empirically necessary condition for each citizen to flourish—in other words, it is a common good in only the second sense distinguished above. Second, that political participation is an ingredient of some people's flourishing (and indeed always contributes to a person's flourishing when it is a part of her life that she values) but, given the diversity of people's tastes and what they find fulfilling, is not an ingredient of the good life for everyone—any more than is playing a musical instrument or engaging in philosophical contemplation.

Common good accounts, whatever view they hold on the issue of whether political participation is an ingredient of each person's good, seem unacceptably broad because they suppose we can demonstrate that someone has acted as a citizen simply by showing that she has acted in the light of the common good. There are ways of acting in the light of the common good, in each of the three senses I have distinguished, that do not seem to have much to do with citizenship. Voluntary work generally involves acting in this way in at least two of these senses (it promotes the aggregate of individual goods, and may also help to secure some of the conditions required for each individual to be able to achieve his or her own good), but it does not necessarily have a strong connection with citizenship. Helping out in a charity shop which supports cancer research may be virtuous, a good act, but is it really an act of good citizenship, even if the benefits would mainly be felt by fellow citizens? The same question might be asked of various forms of paid employment which contribute to the common good, for example, school crossing attendant, doctor, nurse, teacher, firefighter, or civil servant. These are all forms of *public service* but the mere fact that they promote the common good does not seem sufficient to justify the idea that they are acts of (good) citizenship.

In response it might be said that in order for paid employment to count as an act of good citizenship, the primary motivation for engaging in it must be to contribute to the common good, rather than, say, to earn a higher salary, in the sense that the reason why one chooses this form of employment rather than another must be that it involves this contribution rather than that it pays more money or provides greater job security or other benefits. We might even require that one's choice of employment must involve some sacrifice, financial or otherwise, if it is to count as a form of good citizenship, so, for example, giving up one's job as a barrister in order to work as a High Court judge could count, but not giving up a poorly paid administrative job in the private sector in order to join the civil service. This still seems counterintuitive, however, for it seems inappropriate to regard someone as engaged in an act of good citizenship simply in virtue of being motivated primarily to contribute to the common good. We surely need to distinguish between merely being a good public servant and being a good citizen—just as we need to distinguish between merely acting in an altruistic fashion and being a good citizen even when the beneficiaries of one's altruism are fellow citizens.

I do not mean to imply that public service can never be an act of good citizenship. Even justice accounts can regard public service in this way. As I pointed out in the previous section of this chapter, a justice account may claim that citizens have an imperfect duty to serve their political community that is grounded in a duty to support and further just institutions, or in a principle of fair play. But from this perspective, when public service is an act of good citizenship, it is not merely the fact that it is motivated by a concern for the common good that constitutes it as such, but rather that it can properly be regarded as discharging one's duty to support and further just institutions (since public service is often conducive to the flourishing of these institutions—consider again in this context the barrister who takes a cut in salary to become a High Court judge), or as a way of complying with the principle of fair play (since public service can be a way of bearing one's fair share of the burdens of a set of institutions). This is one point at which common good accounts diverge from justice accounts, and in a way that suggests the former are too broad and undiscriminating. If they are too broad and undiscriminating, then they cannot provide a plausible account of the source of the rights, duties, and virtues of citizenship in particular. In the next section I shall consider an account which seems to preserve what is important in the common good account yet avoids the problems that beset it. Indeed, what I call the equal membership account can be regarded as the common good account better conceived. It can also underwrite the idea that there is a duty to serve one's political community, though it does not regard this as grounded in a duty to promote the common good.

3 The equal membership account

In attempting to draw the distinction between mere public service and acts of citizenship, we might suppose that acting as a citizen involves being oriented to a particular part or aspect of the common good, very roughly, the good of a community whose members have equal standing, which I shall refer to as the good of equal membership, and that to be a good citizen is, at least in part, to act in ways that express or promote this good. The good of equal membership might be regarded as part of the common good in the second sense distinguished above, on the grounds that it is a condition for the realization of each person's good; it might also be regarded as part of the common good in the third sense distinguished, on the grounds that the good of equal membership is an ingredient of each person's good. I shall call this *the equal membership account*. Again, it is really a family of different accounts which vary depending on how the good of equal membership is understood, which will also affect its precise relationship to the common good in its various senses.

How, then, should the good of equal membership be understood? This good consists in the value of a collective body that makes decisions that importantly affect its members' conditions of existence, and in which they have equal standing because they have equal opportunity to participate on equal terms and treat each others as equals.[38] Different versions of the equal membership account will divide on the issue of whether the value of a collective body of this kind derives solely from its contribution to the good of individuals. But any plausible version will acknowledge that at least some of its value consists in its contribution to the good of its members. Being an equal member of such a body might be regarded not just as a condition of each person's good, but also as an irreducibly social good that is partially constitutive of each person's good, namely, the good of being recognized and treated as an equal member of a collective body that makes important decisions that concern one's conditions of existence.[39] This claim is not, by itself, incompatible with welfarism, that is, the doctrine that individual well-being is the *only* good or value that has basic moral significance.[40] However, when it is combined with the idea that equal standing in a collective body that makes decisions that importantly affect its members conditions of existence has some non-instrumental value, then it becomes so—and, indeed, someone who takes this view is committed to the notion that in at least one respect a collective body of this kind is better than one in which there is inequality of status but everyone is better off.

According to the equal membership account, the rights and entitlements of citizenship are grounded in the conditions required to secure the good of equal membership. (The legal rights and entitlements accorded to citizens may vary from one state to another without necessarily compromising the ability of these rights and entitlements to secure the good of equal membership since what counts as treating others as equals may depend to some extent at least on cultural and other particularities.) To act as a citizen is to act in a way that is oriented towards this good. This includes acting in order to express or promote it, including acting from various duties that are grounded in it, and acting to secure the conditions necessary for its realization. Acting in ways that express the good of equal membership can take many different forms, ranging from, for example, voting in an election to sitting at the front of a bus in order to make some wider point about one's equal status. (According to the equal membership account, one of the ways in which people can be good citizens in non-ideal societies is by striving to bring the good of equal membership fully into existence.)

More generally, acting as a citizen requires treating others as equals in one's political dealings, which involves giving at least some weight—generally equal weight—to their interests when deliberating about what policies should be implemented or what laws should be enacted. The equal membership account therefore implies that citizens should, to at least some extent, pursue the common good in their political actions, even though it does not maintain that this concern with the common good must govern their behaviour outside of the political process, in the way that the common good account supposes. The equal membership account can also endorse the idea that there is a duty of citizenship to serve one's political community. Indeed various forms of voluntary work which take place in civil society and which serve the common good may also be conceived as acts of good citizenship in so far as they promote the conditions necessary for realizing the good of equal membership. The equal membership account can, like the other two accounts, give a central role to civic virtues: in the equal membership account they are understood mainly as the dispositions that citizens need in order to discern what behaviour is required in order to treat their fellows as equals, and to motivate them to act accordingly.

What precisely is the relationship between the equal membership account and the justice account? Do they really provide us with different normative theories of citizenship? Our ability to keep these accounts apart seems to rely on at least one of the following conditions being met:

(i) there being some rights or entitlements of citizenship grounded in considerations of justice that cannot simply be regarded as conditions for the realization of the good of equal membership;

(ii) there being some duties of citizenship grounded in considerations of justice that cannot simply be regarded as expressing or promoting the good of equal membership;

(iii) there being some rights or entitlements of citizenship grounded in the conditions required to secure the good of equal membership that cannot simply be regarded as rights of justice;

(iv) there being some duties of citizenship that are grounded in the good of equal membership that cannot simply be regarded as duties of justice.

Even if conditions (i) and (ii) can be met, unless at least one of (iii) and (iv) is met it might seem that the equal membership account is *redundant*. Indeed it might be thought that the equal membership account is dispensable on the grounds that the good of equal membership is equivalent to an equal, and therefore just, distribution of political rights and opportunities. From this perspective, the value of a collective body which makes key decisions and in which each member has equal standing is simply the value of a society that is just in terms of its distribution of political rights and opportunities.

Equating the good of equal membership with an equal (and therefore just) distribution of political rights and opportunities is open to contest since it is not clear that securing this good in full is *necessary* for such a distribution. The good of equal membership involves the members of a political community not only possessing equal opportunity to participate on equal terms in decisions that importantly affect their lives, but also treating each other as equals in the process of making those decisions, including the public debates surrounding them. I shall refer to this wider notion as 'political equality'. Since the good of equal membership requires political equality, it seems to go beyond a just distribution of political rights and opportunities, thus suggesting that condition (iv) above can be met. It might be thought that a justice account can embrace the full ideal of political equality by endorsing a further duty of civility or mutual respect in the political process. This is not as straightforward as it might seem, however, for if a duty of civility or mutual respect is to be regarded as a duty of citizenship and made compatible with the justice account, then it would have to be grounded in considerations of justice.[41]

Nor is it clear that a just distribution of political rights and opportunities entails that citizens must have equal opportunity to participate on equal terms in the political process. Many contemporary theories of justice, including Rawls's, suppose that it is *equal political liberties* that are fundamental for the just distribution of political rights and opportunities. Whether equal political liberties require or entail each citizen having an equal opportunity to participate on equal terms in the political process, will depend in part on how political liberty is understood; if political liberty is understood in such a way that a person may possess it without having the means required to exercise it, such as the time or resources needed to do so, then equal political liberty may fall short of this. In *A Theory of Justice*, Rawls notoriously distinguishes between liberty and its value, claiming that:

> The inability to take advantage of one's rights and opportunities as a result of poverty and ignorance, and a lack of means generally, is sometimes counted among the constraints definitive of liberty. I shall not, however, say this, but rather I shall think of these things as affecting the worth of liberty.[42]

In *Political Liberalism*, however, Rawls insists that this distinction is not intended to settle any substantive issues, and argues that it is important to ensure that each person's political liberties have a fair value.[43] That brings his theory closer to a commitment to each citizen having an equal opportunity to participate on equal terms in the political process, but there is still a potential gap here. That gap may be even greater on those theories of justice which allow that an individual's ability to exercise his political liberties may be justly limited by his own choices, including the decision he may make to have children.[44] So the equal membership account may diverge from the justice account because the former but not the latter involves an unconditional commitment to each citizen possessing equal opportunity to participate on equal terms in the political process. An unconditional commitment to full political equality may generate some rights of citizenship that cannot simply be regarded as rights of justice, thereby satisfying condition (iii) above.

Even if it were true that the good of equal membership is equivalent to an equal distribution of political rights and opportunities, the equal membership account and the justice account generally diverge in terms of the ways in which they *justify* the value of an equal distribution of this kind, which allows us to keep them apart. Equal membership accounts suppose that there is something non-instrumentally valuable about what I have called political equality, of which the equal distribution of political rights and opportunities is a component. Although justice accounts regard an equal distribution of this kind as a fair way of distributing political power, they have to acknowledge that it is not unique in this respect. If a single individual was vested with the power to make political decisions but required to do so by giving equal weight to each citizen's interests, then that would seem to be equally fair. In order to explain why they nevertheless favour an equal distribution of political rights and opportunities, justice accounts generally appeal to the way in which such a distribution promotes just outcomes, such as the role it plays in securing various basic rights. Even though Rawls, for example, regards political liberty as a basic liberty, within his theory the basic liberties count as such because of the role they play in the development and exercise of two fundamental moral powers (namely, the capacity for a sense of justice, and the capacity for a conception of the good) and in enabling and protecting the pursuit of a wide range of specific conceptions of the good.[45] He also suggests that the political liberties in particular may be justified mainly in terms of the part they play in securing other basic liberties.[46] So Rawls's central defence of equal political liberty has a doubly instrumental character.

Whatever the precise relationship between political equality and the just distribution of political rights and opportunities, and whatever differences arise in the justification of each, there are independent reasons for thinking that the equal membership account is non-redundant and can be kept apart from the justice account. Like the justice account, the equal membership account is really a family of conceptions. Particular conceptions of it can understand the good of equal membership in a way that takes it beyond political equality, even in the full sense I have distinguished, to embrace *social* equality: that is, each person enjoying equal standing not only in the political process but also in their social lives within and beyond civil society, because each has equal opportunity to participate on equal terms in that sphere and is treated as an equal in it. Social equality might be regarded as an irreducibly social good that is partly constitutive of each citizen's good but at least partially independent of justice.[47] (David Miller, for example, maintains that a society in which people regard and treat each other as equals, and where there are no status divisions that allow us to rank people in different cate gories, has value in its own right independent of justice.[48]) Those versions of the equal membership account which regard the good of equal membership as embracing social equality are particularly appealing; in section 1 of Chapter 2, I shall defend further the idea that social equality has a value that is partially independent of justice by showing that there are duties to treat one's fellow citizens as equals that are not straightforwardly reducible to duties of justice, thereby satisfying (iv) above.

The good of equal membership may also have a distinctive kind of value. There is a tendency to think about value in an atomist way. If we understand the good of equal membership as consisting in both political equality and social equality (with political equality including components of justice), the value of that good might then be regarded as simply the sum of the value of its component parts. But there is another, more holistic way of thinking about the value of the good of equal membership: namely, that part of its non-instrumental value emerges from the interaction of these components, and indeed that this aspect of its value is conditional upon the presence of all of them. The value of the good of equal membership might properly be regarded as arising at least in part as a result of the fact that both social and political equality are enjoyed in the context of a collective the members of which have equal standing and which exercises significant control over their conditions of existence. This is in effect to treat the value of the good of equal membership as an organic whole, in G. E. Moore's sense:

> It is certain that a good thing may exist in such a relation to another good thing that the value of the whole thus formed is immensely greater than the sum of the values of the two good things. It is certain that a whole formed of a good thing and an indifferent thing may have immensely greater value than that good thing itself possesses ... The value of a whole must not be assumed to be the same as the sum of the value of its parts.[49]

The organic whole formed by political equality and social equality in the context of a collective the members of which have equal standing and that exercises control over their conditions of existence might be held to possess value that is more than simply the sum of the value of those parts.

Moore insists that the intrinsic value of the constituent parts that make up an organic whole does not vary; the value of the whole is explained by the way in which these parts are related to each other in the whole:

> The part of a valuable whole retains exactly the same value when it is, as when it is not, a part of that whole. If it had value under other circumstances, its value is not any greater, when it is part of a far more valuable whole; and if it had no value by itself, it has none still, however great be that of the whole of which it now forms a part.[50]

This idea that the intrinsic value of a component remains constant is largely a product of Moore's view that the intrinsic value of a thing can be understood as the value it would possess if it were absolutely by itself.[51] But intrinsic value does not have to be understood in these terms; the intrinsic value of a thing can be understood instead as any value it possesses that is grounded entirely in its intrinsic properties. This conception of intrinsic value allows that the value of the component of an organic whole may in fact be greater *as a result* of its role within that whole; its value would nevertheless be intrinsic so long as that value was grounded solely in its intrinsic properties, despite being (in part) a result of its place within the whole.[52] The intrinsic value of political equality, for example, might be greater as a result of being realized in a collective which exercises significant control over its members' conditions of existence whilst at the same time achieving social equality.

The equal membership account may regard the duty to treat fellow citizens as one's social and political equals as partially constitutive of the complex good of equal membership, rather than simply a means to its promotion. Indeed, doing so helps to explain why it is an obligation that is owed to fellow citizens in particular. For if the obligation to treat one's fellow citizens as equals were grounded simply in the idea that this best promotes the good of equal membership, then it is unclear why it should be owed to one's fellow citizens rather than to humanity in general. (There may be a general obligation to promote the good of equal membership that is relevant whenever a person is in a position to promote that good, irrespective of whether it pertains to her membership in her own polity, but this is not specifically an obligation of citizenship in the relevant sense.) I have suggested elsewhere that we can understand how, without circularity, such a special duty owed to one's fellow citizens might be *grounded* in the good of equal membership, by analogy with a different good, that of friendship, and the way in which it can ground special duties of friendship.[53] I draw upon Joseph Raz's brief but suggestive discussion of this issue.

Raz makes three central claims about the nature of friendship: first, friendship is a non-instrumentally valuable relationship; second, part of what it is for two people to be friends is for each to be under certain duties to the other,[54] and these duties are justified by the good of friendship; third, these special duties are internally related to the good of friendship, i.e. they are part of that good. We might expand on these claims. Friendship is valuable for its own sake because it involves the expression of mutual concern; it allots a central role to altruistic emotions such as sympathy and compassion, and a willingness to give oneself to another. Part of what it is for two people to be friends is to be under a moral duty (other things being equal) not to betray each other's confidences or to use those confidences manipulatively, and to have responsibilities towards each other to provide comfort and support when needed. (A good friend is one who, amongst other things, complies with the various duties he has to his friends.) On Raz's view, the duties of friendship are internally related to the good which justifies them: they are partially constitutive of the good of friendship since this relationship is specified in part by these duties. As a result, the duties cannot be adequately conceived as the means of realizing the good of friendship, for that good includes the fulfilment of the duties. Raz resists the objection that this justification of the special duties is viciously circular: the justification consists in placing them in a wider context (that is, the relationship as a whole, and perhaps also its contribution to the well-being of the parties involved in it) to which these duties contribute and which is non-instrumentally valuable. That wider context gives reasons for accepting the duties. Raz's view has the virtue of preserving the intuition shared by many defenders of special duties that duties of friendship are not contingent upon any role they might play in maximizing general well-being, but are grounded in the nature of friendship itself.

It seems to me that a comparable defence of the special duties of citizenship can be mounted from within the equal membership account. Consider the following proposal. The good of equal membership has non-instrumental value in virtue of its realization of both political equality and social equality.[55] (Some but not all of that non-instrumental value consists in the fact that political equality constitutes a fair way of distributing political rights and opportunities.) Part of what it is to be a citizen is to incur special duties: these duties give content to, or express, what it is to treat others as equals, both socially and politically, and are justified by the good of the wider relationship to which they contribute, that is, the good of equal membership.[56] Fellow citizens have a duty to behave respectfully towards each other in public debate, and indeed in their multiplicity of interactions in civil society. A good citizen is, in part, someone who complies with these various duties and responsibilities, and in doing so realizes the good of equal membership.

This account can also make space for the idea that citizens have special duties to give additional weight to each others' needs so that their fellow citizens are in a position to participate fully in the life of the collective, and can truly be said to possess equal standing. In effect the duties of citizenship might include a duty to promote and sustain social and political equality between them (rather than simply a duty to treat each other as equals in their social and political interactions). This duty might be understood as either perfect or imperfect: it might be a duty to promote social and political equality (and its conditions) between them whenever one is able to do so, or it might be a duty sometimes and to some extent to promote social and political equality of this sort (and its conditions). In order to avoid Scheffler's distributive objection to associative obligations,[57] we would need to acknowledge the way in which this obligation might compete with general obligations to outsiders which at least sometimes, perhaps always, take priority. (Even if these general obligations always take priority, the special obligations might have force in circumstances when it was impossible to fulfil the general obligations completely. For example, even if these general obligations require us to ensure that everyone's needs are met, in circumstances where this was impossible our special obligations might direct us to meet the needs of our fellow citizens first.)

4 Liberal versus republican conceptions of citizenship

Conceiving of the good of equal membership in terms of the combination of social and political equality makes the equal membership account distinguishable from both the common good account (it is narrower in one respect, since the good of equal membership consists of only some aspects of the common good) and the justice account (it is broader in one respect since it embraces social equality, and it can appeal to the idea that the good of equal membership is an organic whole).[58] The equal membership account seems to preserve the strengths of the common good account whilst avoiding the potential problems with its scope, which gives us sufficient reason to put aside the common good account. But is the distinction that remains, between the justice account and the equal membership account, simply a disguised version of the one which is commonly drawn between liberal and republican conceptions of citizenship? (Or indeed, is it a version of the distinction between Roman and Greek models of citizenship on which the one between liberal and republican conceptions is often thought to be founded?[59]) One might think that there is a close correspondence between the liberal view and the justice account on the one hand, and the republican view and the equal membership account on the other, on the grounds that the justice account, like the liberal view, offers an undemanding conception of what it is to be a good citizen, whereas the equal membership account, like the republican view, offers a much more demanding conception. This is mistaken, however: some justice accounts are very demanding because they suppose that principles of justice apply to personal behaviour and generate a range of duties of citizenship, whilst some equal membership accounts are undemanding because they have a limited conception of social and political equality and the duties that are constitutive of it. Moreover, it seems to me that the distinction between justice and equal membership accounts has more resources to explain how different views can emerge about the scope and nature of the duties of citizenship.

The distinction between liberalism and republicanism is drawn in different ways and for different purposes. Some regard republicanism as a particular form of liberalism, whilst others see them as mutually exclusive. One might attempt to characterize the difference between them either in terms of the rights, duties, and virtues to which they are committed, or in terms of their different theoretical foundations, in effect how these rights, duties, and virtues are grounded. As an example of the first approach, consider the commonly expressed view that the liberal conception treats citizenship as a status that is exhausted by the enjoyment of rights whilst the republican conception treats it as a matter of discharging responsibilities, so (unlike the liberal conception) gives a central place to a range of civic virtues. David Miller, for example, argues that according to the republican view, citizenship is active rather than passive because it amounts to more than the possession of rights and duties. Being a citizen involves 'being willing to take active steps to defend the rights of other members of the political community, and more generally to promote its common interests. The citizen is someone who goes to the aid of a fellow-citizen who collapses in the street, or who intervenes when he is able to prevent a criminal act being committed.' Being a citizen also involves playing 'an active role in both the formal and informal arenas of politics'.[60]

Miller's way of drawing the distinction runs the risk of confusing what it is to be a citizen with what it is to be a *good* or virtuous citizen. Being under an obligation to participate politically or to contribute to one's political community is different from fulfilling that obligation: being a citizen may involve being under such obligations but it does not necessarily involve *acting* on them. A person does not cease to be a citizen because she fails to fulfil the obligations she incurs as a citizen; we do not ordinarily suppose that someone who fails to come to the aid of a fellow citizen who collapses in the street is not a citizen. There is some historical basis for the idea that a person who shuns political participation is not really a citizen even if he has political rights and an unconditional right of permanent abode, for this idea resonates with the Aristotelian notion that part of what it is to be a citizen is to take turns at ruling and being ruled. This Aristotelian notion has some point in the context of participatory or direct forms of government, but extending it to embrace the idea that in representative democracy the politically inactive fail to be citizens surely stretches things too far: those with political rights who are politically inactive in modern liberal democracies may be bad citizens, but they are surely citizens nonetheless. It might therefore seem that a better way of capturing the distinction at this level is simply in terms of the *range* of responsibilities these perspectives acknowledge. Republican theorists hold the view that citizens have a responsibility or duty to take active steps to defend the rights of other members of the political community, and to come to the aid of fellow citizens when needed, and for that reason endorse a wider range of civic virtues, whereas liberal theorists suppose that citizens merely have a duty to obey the law and support and promote just institutions, and therefore endorse a much narrower range of civic virtues. But this has no power to *explain* why these two traditions embody different views of the scope and responsibilities of citizenship; it is simply a description of the different views they hold on these matters.

In order to explain how different views of the scope of these duties and responsibilities arise, we need to look at how they are justified, that is, at their deeper theoretical foundations. Here the republican tradition tends to divide. Some republican theorists see their position as grounded in the idea that political participation is the highest good, and that even if it is not an essential ingredient of human flourishing for everyone, it is at least a very important aspect of that flourishing for all. But this part of the republican tradition founders in the face of the argument that human flourishing is diverse: that individuals may lead fulfilling lives in a variety of different ways, and that political activity, like playing a musical instrument, or studying the history of one's society, is just one such (non-instrumentally valuable) way of doing so. To retreat to the more plausible claim that some degree of political participation, on the part of some or most citizens, is essential for sustaining a free society would deprive republicanism of any distinctiveness, for this is a claim that many liberals would happily accept.

This is not the only direction in which the republican tradition has been developed, however. Much of the best recent work within this tradition has taken the view that what at root distinguishes it from (other forms of) liberalism is a particular conception of liberty: republicans understand liberty as non-domination, whereas liberals conceive of it simply as non-interference.[61] It might then seem that republicanism is bound to generate more demanding duties of citizenship because it will require an active citizenry to support the structures and participate in the practices which secure them against the arbitrary exercise of power.

I doubt that liberalism as it is commonly understood is committed to understanding liberty as non-interference; indeed, there are many strands of liberalism which recognize that intervention is required in order to *enhance* individual freedom. But there is still a potential contrast to be made here: we might say that liberalism has generally conceived of liberty as the absence of constraints on action, or as the non-restriction of options, though there has been considerable dispute amongst liberals on the issue of what is to count as a constraint on action in the relevant sense[62]—for example, liberals have disagreed about whether a lack of resources may do so. Within such accounts, threats or the probability that one will be subject to the exercise of power, can restrict one's freedom by acting as a constraint without there needing to be any actual intervention. If a person knows that if she tries to perform some action, an agent with power over her will prevent her, or is likely to prevent her—and perhaps even punish her for attempting to do so—then this constrains her actions.[63] But a theory of liberty as non-domination appears to go further, for it allows that one's liberty may be restricted even in the absence of any constraints on one's actions, for example, when a slave is allowed by his master to do everything that a free person may do and the slave knows that there is no significant probability that his master will change her mind.[64]

Even if liberals do have a different conception of liberty from republicans in this way, their judgements concerning what counts as loss of freedom will converge in most ordinary cases. Liberals have reason to be concerned about what republicans call 'domination', for they have reason to value the secure enjoyment of various basic liberties, understood as the absence of certain sorts of constraint, and to be vigilant against both potential and actual threats to these liberties. And they will care about the stability of institutions that protect individuals against constraints or restrictions and be concerned to promote liberty (as they conceive it) in both the short term and the long term. So even if republicans have raised an important challenge to understanding liberty (purely) in terms of the absence of constraints on action or the non-restriction of options, it is unclear that the alternative conception they propose will in practice justify a different set of duties or virtues of citizenship, or indeed a different set of institutions or political procedures.[65] This is not to deny that those who think of themselves as republicans have devoted more energy to these issues, and thought more profoundly about the best way of securing individuals against the ills of domination—nor is it to deny that this is a distinctive feature of the republican tradition both now and historically; it is merely to suggest that there is no reason internal to their own theoretical commitments why this *must* be so.

If we see liberalism and republicanism as grounded in different understandings of liberty, we might be inclined to think of them as expressing different theories of justice, in effect as providing competing versions of the justice account of citizenship. But it is questionable whether the ideal of non-domination is best understood as an interpretation of justice rather than as a (partial) interpretation of the good of equal membership, and the idea that liberty is best conceived as non-domination can figure in either a justice or an equal membership account. Domination is a serious evil, and its counterpart non-domination is an important value, but does it provide us with an interpretation of justice? Non-domination is surely an aspect of justice, but arguably justice has a non-instrumental concern with inequalities in the distribution of wealth and income that goes beyond a commitment to non-domination.[66] Furthermore, it seems to me that the notion of non-domination can be regarded as a way of giving partial content to the good of equal membership, for when one person dominates another there is a violation of social or political equality (or both).

So rather than thinking of liberalism and republicanism as different versions of the justice account, we would do better to see the distinction between them as cutting across both the justice account and the equal membership account, with there being liberal and republican variants of each. If republicanism is distinguished from liberalism by being founded upon an ideal of liberty as non-domination, then it may express a justice account which sees justice itself as wholly or partially constituted by liberty understood in these terms, or it may express a equal membership account which sees that good as wholly or partially constituted by liberty so understood. For reasons I have given, however, if republican variants are founded on an ideal of liberty as non-domination, regardless of whether this ideal provides the basis for a justice account or an equal membership account, it is not clear that these variants must hold a different view of the virtues or duties of citizenship from those liberal variants which are founded on an ideal of liberty as the absence of constraints or the non-restriction of options.

If, on the other hand, what distinguishes republicanism from liberalism is *simply* a belief in the importance of an active citizenry rather than a different view of liberty, then republicanism can be grounded in a justice account that takes a demanding view of what citizens need to do in order to sustain just institutions or it can be grounded in a equal membership account that takes a demanding view of what citizens need to do in order to sustain social and political equality. Liberalism on this view could be grounded in either a 'narrow' justice account that has a restricted view of what is required of citizens in order to secure just institutions, or in a version of the equal membership account which supposes that social and political equality can be sustained even when much of the citizenry simply go about their own business. But in that case the distinction between liberalism and republicanism may be useful for other reasons, but it possesses no power to *explain* divergences between different views of the demandingness of citizenship; what is doing the work in explaining these differences is the contrast between the two justificatory bases and variations within them.

5 Concluding remarks

The justice and good of citizenship accounts provide us with two different ways of thinking about citizenship. The justice account is perhaps the dominant approach to normative theorizing about the rights, duties, and virtues of citizenship, but the equal membership account emerges from a set of concerns that can be understood as only partially overlapping with considerations of justice, namely, the value of being an equal member of a collective which makes decisions that importantly affect one's conditions of existence, being recognized and treated as an equal not only in the political process but also in social interactions within and beyond civil society. It is tempting to think that we have to choose between these two accounts, but in the next chapter I shall explore some reasons for thinking that it is a mistake to treat them as competitors. If the justice account and the equal membership account are not even competitors, then it would be a misconception to suppose that it is the need to choose between them that explains why divergent views of the demandingness of citizenship emerge. It would only be variations within each account that could create well-founded or reasonable disagreements on this issue.

Notes

1. This chapter draws upon my 'Citizenship and Justice', *Politics, Philosophy, and Economics*, Vol. 10, 2011, pp. 263–81.
2. For this reason John Tomasi refers to the justice account as the derivative interpretation of citizenship: see his *Liberalism Beyond Justice: Citizens, Society, and the Boundaries of Political Theory* (Princeton, NJ: Princeton University Press, 2001), pp. 57–61.
3. According to this view, there may be duties of justice that extend beyond state borders, and not all duties of justice will be duties of citizenship. Some justice views are radically critical of the existing state system on the grounds that in practice the preference that states give to the interests of their own citizens undermines rather than realizes impartial principles of justice. Some of these critics of the state system favour dispersing the sovereignty that is currently concentrated in states in order to create a variety of different political units, above and below. See, for example, Pogge, *World Poverty and Human Rights*, Ch. 7. These new units would protect the rights of their members and provide the basis for special obligations between them, but in a way that (it is supposed) is better able to serve fundamental principles of justice.
4. See, for example, T. Nagel, 'The Problem of Global Justice,' *Philosophy and Public Affairs*, Vol. 33, 2005, pp. 113–47; A. Sangiovanni, 'Global Justice, Reciprocity, and the State', *Philosophy and Public Affairs*, Vol. 35, 2007, pp. 3–39. For relevant discussion, see also M. Blake, 'Distributive Justice, Coercion, and Autonomy', *Philosophy and Public Affairs*, Vol. 30, 2001, pp. 257–96; M. Risse, 'What to Say About the State', *Social Theory and Practice*, Vol. 32, 2006, pp. 671–98; C. Armstrong, 'Coercion, Reciprocity, and Equality Beyond the State', *Journal of Social Philosophy*, Vol. 40, 2009, pp. 297–316.

5. To the extent that duties of justice are universal in scope, a citizen will continue to have duties to outsiders, and indeed may have duties to support the development and maintenance of transnational institutions, owed to persons as such, when these institutions would facilitate the fulfilment of his or her duties to outsiders and enable them to receive their just entitlements.

6. See Rawls, *A Theory of Justice*, section 53.

7. The duty to support and further just institutions may also underwrite perfect duties to serve one's political community in particular ways, for example, to serve conscientiously on a jury when selected.

8. See A. J. Simmons, 'The Duty to Obey and Our Natural Moral Duties', in C. H. Wellman and A. J. Simmons, *Is There a Duty to Obey the Law?* (Cambridge: Cambridge University Press, 2005), pp. 124–6.

9. Rawls, *A Theory of Justice*, p. 115/99.

10. See Simmons, 'The Duty to Obey and Our Natural Moral Duties', pp. 157, 160–1.

11. As I noted in section 2 of the Introduction, some are sceptical about the very existence of imperfect duties, at least at a fundamental level. It is unclear, however, that a duty to work towards establishing just institutions or reforming unjust ones can be properly regarded as a perfect duty, even if it is formulated to allow exceptions when complying with it would impose excessive costs. If it were a perfect duty, then in principle at least we would have to be able to specify what it required of citizens in particular cases when they were in a position to contribute towards establishing just institutions (or reforming unjust ones) in a way that did not allow the discretion characteristic of imperfect duties.

12. The duty to support and further just institutions seems to fall foul of what Simmons calls 'the particularity requirement': see Simmons, *Moral Principles and Political Obligations*, p. 31. Rawls regards it as a natural duty and maintains that these 'hold between persons irrespective of their institutional relationships; they obtain between all as equal moral persons' and 'are owed not only to definite individuals . . . but to persons generally' (Rawls, *A Theory of Justice*, p. 115/99).

13. See Simmons, *Moral Principles and Political Obligations*, p. 148.

14. Waldron, 'Special Ties and Natural Duties', p. 16. See also J. Quong, *Liberalism Without Perfection* (Oxford: Oxford University Press, 2011), pp. 129–30. Quong in effect argues that we have a special duty to support and further just institutions in the state in which we live because just institutions more generally are best promoted by citizens across the globe recognizing that they are under a special duty of this kind to their fellows.

15. Waldron, 'Special Ties and Natural Duties', p. 19.

16. Resident aliens may also be insiders in relation to an institution, so there is still an issue about whether obligations justified in this way would be owed to fellow citizens as opposed to some wider group, e.g. all residents. I raise this issue again in section 2 of the next chapter.

17. This does of course raise the question of how the obligation they owe to their fellow citizens is to be weighed against the obligation they owe to outsiders when the two come into conflict. But the fact such conflicts may occur does not undermine this kind of response to the particularity objection.

18. See Waldron, 'Special Ties and Natural Duties', pp. 29–30.

19. See R. Nozick, *Anarchy, State and Utopia* (Oxford: Blackwell, 1974), pp. 90–5.

20. See Simmons, *Moral Principles and Political Obligations*, p. 129.

21. See G. Klosko, *The Principle of Fairness and Political Obligation* (Lanham, MD: Rowman and Littlefield, 1992), p. 39. See also R. Dagger, *Civic Virtues: Rights, Citizenship, and Republican Liberalism* (Oxford: Oxford University Press, 1997), pp. 68–78. For criticism, see A. J. Simmons, *Justification and Legitimacy: Essays on Rights and Obligations* (Cambridge: Cambridge University Press, 2001), pp. 34–6.

22. Whether the *enforcement* of such a duty in particular contexts could be defended is open to question, however. It might be argued that it has the character of an imperfect duty, which would make it impossible to enforce in a justifiable way (see A. J. Simmons, *Justification and Legitimacy: Essays on Rights and Obligations* (Cambridge: Cambridge University Press, 2001), p. 60). The principle of fair play might, however, be applied to specific institutions and practices in order to justify a range of enforceable perfect duties to serve one's political community, for example, when applied to legal institutions it might justify the idea that there is a perfect duty to perform jury service when selected.

23. White, *The Civic Minimum*, p. 49.

24. See D. Bubeck, 'A Feminist Approach to Citizenship', EUI Working Paper, 1995, EUF No. 95/1.

25. The justice account can also give a role to a range of virtues. Some of these virtues are conceived as dispositions which enable citizens to discern what their duties of justice to their fellow citizens require of them in particular circumstances and motivate them to act accordingly. Other virtues might be conceived more broadly as dispositions which support or promote just institutions or a just society. The defences that William Galston and Stephen Macedo offer for a range of 'liberal virtues' are consistent with the justice account, since they appeal to the role that the exercise of these virtues plays in sustaining just institutions: see W. Galston, *Liberal Purposes: Goods, Virtues, and Diversity in the Liberal State* (Cambridge: Cambridge University Press, 1991); S. Macedo, *Liberal Virtues: Citizenship, Virtue, and Community in Liberal Constitutionalism* (Oxford: Oxford University Press, 1990).

26. Some libertarians would, however, resist this extension, on the grounds that private employers are entitled to hire who they want, for whatever reason they want, as a result of their property rights.

27. See G. A. Cohen, *Rescuing Justice and Equality* (Cambridge, MA: Harvard University Press, 2008), Part I. For relevant discussion, see also L. Murphy, 'Institutions and the Demands of Justice', *Philosophy and Public Affairs*, Vol. 27, 1998, 251–91; T. Pogge, 'On the Site of Distributive Justice: Reflections on Cohen and Murphy', *Philosophy and Public Affairs*, Vol. 29, 2000, pp. 137–69; A. Williams, 'Incentives, Inequality, and Publicity', *Philosophy and Public Affairs*, Vol. 27, 1998, pp. 225–47; D. Estlund, 'Liberalism, Equality, and Fraternity in Cohen's Critique of Rawls', *The Journal of Political Philosophy*, Vol. 6, 1998, pp. 99–112.

28. Some suppose that the liberal account of citizenship sees citizenship as essentially a contractual relationship (see, e.g., P. Conover, I. Crewe, and D. Searing, 'The Nature of Citizenship in the United States and Great Britain: Empirical Comments on

Theoretical Themes', *Journal of Politics*, Vol. 53, 1991, pp. 800–32). The justice account includes this way of understanding citizenship but is not exhausted by it.

29. Although it is difficult to pin the justice account on individual thinkers, a number of accounts of the rights, duties, and virtues of citizenship which have been developed in the context of liberal responses to communitarian criticism, and in the debate over political or comprehensive forms of liberalism and their implications for civic education, are compatible with it: see, for example, Macedo, *Liberal Virtues*, especially Ch. 7; Galston, *Liberal Purposes*, especially Parts III–IV; E. Callan, *Creating Citizens: Political Education and Liberal Democracy* (Oxford: Oxford University Press, 1997), especially Ch. 2. Stuart White's account of economic citizenship in *The Civic Minimum* is also compatible with a justice account. The reason it is hard to attribute the justice account to particular thinkers with any confidence is because I define it as the view that *all* the rights, duties, and virtues of citizenship are justified by reference to considerations of justice, and this issue tends not to be addressed in these debates. It might be thought that this provides a reason to change the way I define the justice account, for example, it might instead be defined as the view that the rights, duties, and virtues of citizenship are derived *primarily* from considerations of justice, which would allow some of them to be derived from other sources. But I resist this for reasons that will become clearer in Chapter 2, section 2: other sources of rights, duties, and virtues tend to give them different scope, so that they apply to different groups of people, and incorporating them into the justice account obscures that point.

30. Indeed some move to a common good account because they believe that a justice account is too limited: see Tomasi, *Liberalism Beyond Justice*, Ch. 4.

31. See I. Honohan, *Civic Republicanism* (London: Routledge, 2002), pp. 150–4; P. Pettit, *Republicanism: A Theory of Freedom and Government* (Oxford: Oxford University Press, 1999), p. 287.

32. See Honohan, *Civic Republicanism*, pp. 150–4.

33. In practice, it seems to me that common good accounts sometimes combine the different ways of understanding the common good that I have distinguished, and regard them as identifying different aspects of it that have independent weight even though they overlap: in that case the common good is understood as (in part) an aggregate of individual goods, as (in part) the conditions required in general for each person to be able to achieve his or her good, and as (in part) those goods that are partially constitutive of each person's good.

34. See C. Taylor, 'Irreducibly Social Goods', in his *Philosophical Arguments* (Cambridge, MA: Harvard University Press, 1995).

35. For an account of what is meant by a social form, see J. Raz, *The Morality of Freedom* (Oxford: Oxford University Press, 1986), pp. 308–13.

36. Goods which are irreducibly social because they essentially involve interaction with others may of course also depend upon the existence of social forms, so they may be irreducibly social in both ways.

37. In other cases providing these conditions seems to involve going beyond what justice requires, though examples here are bound to be controversial. John Tomasi,

for example, argues that the common good includes the conditions which need to be met before individual citizens can feel at home in their polity, and that promoting these conditions may involve the state going beyond justice by, for example, seeking to counteract some of the potentially non-neutral effects of policies that are nevertheless justified in a way that does not appeal to the truth or correctness of any particular comprehensive moral doctrine. See Tomasi, *Liberalism Beyond Justice*, Ch. 5, especially pp. 85–100.

38. Each citizen having the opportunity to participate on *equal terms* need not exclude the possibility of a differentiated citizenship in which different groups of citizens (perhaps women, or cultural minorities) had different sets of rights. Indeed a differentiated citizenship might be required in order for them to be included on equal terms. See R. Lister, *Citizenship: Feminist Perspectives*, second edition (Basingstoke: Palgrave, 2003), esp. Ch. 3; Kymlicka, *Multicultural Citizenship*; Young, 'Polity and Group Difference'.

39. According to the equal membership account, the value of citizenship depends in part on the relevant collective being able to exercise significant control over its members' conditions of existence. If processes of globalization undermine the degree of control that it is possible to exercise over these conditions, then the value of citizenship is correspondingly diminished.

40. See A. Moore and R. Crisp, 'Welfarism in Moral Theory', *Australasian Journal of Philosophy*, Vol. 74, 1996, pp. 598–613. See also R. Crisp, *Reasons and the Good* (Oxford: Oxford University Press, 2006), Ch. 2; N. Holtug, *Persons, Interests, and Justice* (Oxford: Oxford University Press, 2010), Ch. 6.

41. In *A Theory of Justice*, Rawls maintains that there is a natural duty of mutual respect which is understood as a 'duty to show a person the respect which is due to him as a moral being', which involves 'a willingness to see the situation of others from their point of view' and 'being prepared to give reasons for our actions whenever the interests of others are materially affected' (Rawls, *A Theory of Justice*, p. 337/297; Cf. J. Rawls, *Political Liberalism*, paperback edition (New York: Columbia University Press, 1996), p. 217.) Rawls regards these duties as 'an essential part of any theory of justice' (Rawls, *A Theory of Justice*, p. 108/93), and believes that they can be justified by showing that they would be chosen in the original position (Rawls, *A Theory of Justice*, p. 115/99). But it is not clear that this suffices to show that they are duties of justice in particular (or even that they are duties of citizenship, that is, duties owed to one's fellow citizens). G. A. Cohen, for example, argues that we cannot equate principles of justice with those principles that would be chosen in the original position, for the principles chosen there may serve other values apart from justice (see Cohen, *Rescuing Justice and Equality*, p. 283). An alternative way of grounding a duty of respect of this kind in considerations of justice would be to argue that its fulfilment is required to sustain or promote just institutions. This would make the defence of this duty less robust, however, for it is not clear that universal (or even widespread) fulfilment of it really is required in order for just institutions to be created or maintained. I shall return to these issues in Chapter 6, section 3.

42. Rawls, *A Theory of Justice*, p. 204/179.

43. See Rawls, *Political Liberalism*, pp. 326–7.

44. See Chapter 4, section 5, for further discussion.

45. See Rawls, *Political Liberalism*, pp. 293, 308, 335.

46. See Rawls, *Political Liberalism*, p. 299.

47. Carina Fourie emphasizes the importance of social equality in her doctoral thesis 'Justice and the Duties of Social Equality' (University College London, 2007), but my account diverges from hers in supposing that the value of social equality is partially independent of that of justice.

48. See D. Miller, 'Equality and Justice', in A. Mason (ed.), *Ideals of Equality* (Oxford: Blackwell, 1998), pp. 21–36.

49. G. E. Moore, *Principia Ethica*, revised edition (Cambridge: Cambridge University Press, 1993), p. 79.

50. Moore, *Principia Ethica*, p. 81.

51. Moore, *Principia Ethica*, p. 145.

52. See J. Dancy, *Ethics Without Principles* (Oxford: Oxford University Press, 2004), pp. 170–84.

53. See A. Mason, *Community, Solidarity, and Belonging: Levels of Community and Their Normative Significance* (Cambridge: Cambridge University Press, 2000), Ch. 4, section 3. Of course not all aspects of friendship are analogous with citizenship, for example, friendship has an element of voluntariness that citizenship may lack.

54. Christopher Wellman challenges the analogy between citizenship and friendship, partly on the grounds that there are no duties of friendship (see C. Wellman, 'Friends, Compatriots, and Special Political Obligations', *Political Theory*, Vol. 29, 2001, pp. 224–30.) In his view friendship is of intrinsic moral value, but a good friend is not someone who acts from, or complies with, duties of friendship, but rather someone who is disposed to act, and be motivated to act, in various ways, and to be disposed to various feelings and emotions (Wellman, 'Friends, Compatriots, and Special Obligations', p. 225). Although I agree that being a good friend needs to be analysed, in part, in terms of a responsiveness that flows from the possession of a certain kind of character, it seems to me that part of what it is to be a good friend is nevertheless to be motivated to fulfil various imperfect duties, for example, sometimes and to some degree to come to the aid of one's friends and to support them in various ways when they are in need. Wellman's rejoinder to this idea (Wellman, 'Friends, Compatriots, and Special Obligations', pp. 228ff) strikes me as unsatisfactory: defenders of imperfect duties of friendship are not reduced to saying that we merely have an imperfect duty to develop the disposition to be a good friend.

55. Wellman also challenges the idea that citizenship has intrinsic value (Wellman, 'Friends, Compatriots, and Special Obligations', pp. 222–3). He claims that equal status has no more evaluative significance than the kind of equality enjoyed by those who insure with the same insurance company, and concludes that the weight of the argument in favour of the intrinsic value of citizenship must be borne by the idea that citizens are part of a body which collectively controls their environment. But it is actually the combination of these two ideas that does the

work in the argument: it is the enjoyment of equality of status (including the kind of recognition one enjoys in virtue of being an equal member) within a body that exerts collective control over one's conditions of existence which explains the intrinsic value of citizenship. (This is why I now suggest that we should think of the good of equal membership, at least in part, as an organic whole.) Furthermore, in the particular version of the argument that I am describing in this chapter, the value of social equality, which is partially constitutive of the good of equal membership, also plays some role in justifying the idea that citizenship has intrinsic value

56. Although these are associative obligations they are justified rather differently from those that are grounded directly in the way that people identify with their particular political communities: see J. Horton, *Political Obligation*, second edition (Basingstoke: Macmillan, 2010), Chs. 6–7; 'In Defence of Associative Political Obligations: Part One', *Political Studies*, Vol. 54, 2006, pp. 427–43; 'In Defence of Associative Political Obligations: Part Two', *Political Studies*, Vol. 55, 2007, pp. 1–19. I do not deny that obligations can be grounded exclusively in the subject's identification with his or her particular political community, at least provided we add the condition that the political community that is the object of identification must not be deeply unjust if these obligations are to emerge. (That the political community is not deeply unjust would be an enabler in Dancy's sense: see Dancy, *Ethics Without Principles*, pp. 38–43.) But obligations grounded in this fashion will be contextual in a way that those grounded in the good of equal membership are not, since they will respond directly to citizens' understandings of what it is to be a member of their political community.

57. See the Introduction, section 4.

58. Even if the equal membership account can be distinguished from the justice account, it might seem to collapse into the common good account. For if the equal membership account requires citizens to treat each other as equals in their political activities, then this would seem to require them to give equal weight to each other's interests when they vote and when they argue or campaign for particular political policies. But if that is so, doesn't giving equal weight to each other's interests simply amount to promoting the common good? The equal membership account can take different forms and in some of those forms it may converge to a considerable degree with the common good account. In others, however, it will diverge. Even if treating others as equals in one's political activities involves promoting the common good or its conditions, it is not clear that treating others as equals in one's social interactions requires us to do so: in that context treating others as equals may place various constraints on one's behaviour. For example, it may require not discriminating against others on racial or other grounds, and it may require refraining from acting on racial or other prejudices, but it need not require any general commitment to promoting the common good. Indeed for reasons I gave in section 2 of this chapter, a general commitment to promoting the common good seems to take us beyond the realm of citizenship into the realm of public service. The equal membership account can therefore preserve its distinctive character whilst retaining what is worthwhile in the common good

account. That is why I have suggested that we might regard the equal membership account as the common good account better conceived.

59. See Pocock, 'The Ideal of Citizenship in Classical Times'.

60. D. Miller, 'Bounded Citizenship', in his *Citizenship and National Identity* (Cambridge: Polity Press, 2000), p. 83.

61. See Pettit, *Republicanism*; Q. Skinner, *Liberty Before Liberalism* (Cambridge: Cambridge University Press, 1997), especially Ch. 2; R. Bellamy, *Political Constitutionalism: A Republican Defence of the Constitutionality of Democracy* (Cambridge: Cambridge University Press, 2007); J. Maynor, *Republicanism in the Modern World* (Cambridge: Polity, 2003); C. Laborde, *Critical Republicanism: The Hijab Controversy and Political Philosophy* (Oxford: Oxford University Press, 2008).

62. See D. Miller; 'Constraints on Freedom', *Ethics*, Vol. 94, 1983, pp. 66–86.

63. See M. Kramer, 'Liberty and Domination', especially pp. 43–5; and I. Carter, 'How are Power and Freedom Related?', especially pp. 67–8, both in C. Laborde and J. Maynor (eds), *Republicanism and Political Theory* (Oxford: Blackwell, 2008).

64. See Kramer, 'Liberty and Domination', especially pp. 47–50; Carter, 'How are Power and Freedom Related?', especially pp. 69–71; Q. Skinner, 'Freedom as the Absence of Arbitrary Power', especially pp. 96–100; and P. Pettit, 'Republican Freedom: Three Axioms, Four Theorems', especially pp. 124–5—all in Laborde and Maynor (eds), *Republicanism and Political Theory*.

65. This would of course be denied by republican theorists. See, for example, Bellamy, *Political Constitutionalism*, especially Ch. 4; Pettit, *Republicanism*, Part II; Maynor, *Republicanism in the Modern World*, especially Ch. 6.

66. If judgements about whether the distribution of wealth and income is just rely solely upon whether the inequalities involved will lead to domination, then we are likely to be lead towards a principle of sufficiency. In *Levelling the Playing Field: The Idea of Equal Opportunity and its Place in Egalitarian Thought* (Oxford: Oxford University Press, 2006), I argue that such a principle needs to be supplemented by quasi-egalitarian principles that limit the extent of inequality that is permissible in relation to various important goods. For a defence of the idea that the evil of domination, understood as a person or group being dependent upon a social relationship in which they are subject to arbitrary power, can provide us with the basis for a comprehensive theory of justice, see F. Lovett, *A General Theory of Domination and Justice* (Oxford: Oxford University Press, 2010). Lovett argues that justice consists in the minimization of domination.

2

Justice and Equal Membership Accounts

Competing or Complementary?

So far I have been assuming that the justice account and the equal membership account are competitors—or, at least, I have not challenged the idea that we have to choose between them. But there are a number of reasons that might be given for denying that they are really in competition with each other. First, despite my rebuttal in the previous chapter, it might be argued that the justice account subsumes the equal membership account, so the latter is redundant. Second, it might be argued that even if they can be kept apart, both can be held together, for they justify duties in different but compatible ways. I shall explore each of these arguments in turn, resisting the first but endorsing the second. My overall aim in this chapter is to achieve a better understanding of the relationship between the justice account and the equal membership account and to show how they may complement each other.

In response to the argument that the equal membership account is subsumed by the justice account, I maintain (in section 1) that the plausibility of this idea depends in part on what we should regard as the best version of the latter. Some versions of the justice account suppose that principles of justice apply only to the basic structure of society and that the duties of citizenship are limited to a duty to support and further just institutions (and perhaps also a duty of fair play which requires citizens who enjoy the benefits of a practice to take a fair share of its burdens). These versions of the justice account diverge markedly from equal membership accounts which hold that citizens are under a demanding obligation to treat each other as equals in civil society and beyond. I argue, however, that there is no good reason to confine the application of principles of justice to the basic structure and that, when we remove this restriction, justice accounts may also be able to underwrite a relatively wide-ranging duty to treat fellow citizens as equals. But I maintain that even when in this respect a justice account converges to a considerable degree with an equal membership account, they nevertheless remain distinct because at the very least they ground this duty (and the virtues which enable citizens to fulfil it) differently. This serves to prevent the equal membership account from being subsumed by the justice account.

In section 2, I concur with the second argument: the justice account and the equal membership account may be held together and can complement each other. This is mainly because they are grounded in different considerations. But it is also partly because the standard framing assumptions of the justice account mean that it does not focus exclusively on *citizens* but instead is concerned more broadly with those living together in the same state, subject to the same set of legal, political, and economic institutions. This will include resident aliens, who possess a legal right of residence but lack the status of citizenship, as well as resident citizens. (Fully worked out versions of the justice account can regard differences between residents—for example, whether they are citizens and, if not, whether they are short-term or long-term residents—as normatively significant in so far as these differences provide reasons of justice for ascribing to them divergent moral rights, entitlements or duties.) Since the justice account provides a different grounding for rights and duties compared to the equal membership account, and focuses on a different set of relationships, they should not be regarded as competitors but rather as providing potentially complementary perspectives—or, at least, as providing contrasting perspectives one of which may be better suited in some cases to illuminating a particular issue. Even when the two perspectives are in tension with each other, it would be a mistake to think we have to choose between them; rather we have to find ways of resolving or accommodating that tension.

It would be misleading to paint too rosy a picture of their relationship, however. There is the additional worry that the justice account, properly thought through, comes into conflict with the equal membership account by favouring a principle for determining who should have a say in decision-making processes that is incompatible in practice with the good of equal membership, because realizing that principle would threaten the existence of political communities with relatively stable memberships. In section 3, I explore this issue but conclude that the tension between the justice account and the equal membership account in this context is best resolved by adopting the principle that all those subjected to laws should have a say in them, or at least a fair opportunity to acquire a say in them, which, I argue, can be grounded in considerations of justice as well as its role in supporting the good of equal membership. Furthermore, I suggest that the value of the good of equal membership is itself dependent on justice, since providing resident non-citizens with a fair opportunity to acquire a say in political decision-making and to become citizens is a condition of securing the full value of that good.

1 Justice and the duty to treat others as equals

Does the justice account, properly thought through, subsume the equal membership account? Although, in Chapter 1, I resisted the idea that the equal membership account is redundant, doubts are likely to remain. The equal membership account might be regarded as redundant on the basis that the rights which emerge from it can also be grounded in considerations of justice and the central duty which emerges from it, that is, the duty to treat one's fellow citizens as equals in all one's social and political interactions with them, is simply part of treating them justly. One way of resisting this argument would be to maintain that principles of justice apply only to the basic structure of society and that the duties of citizenship derived from them are exhausted by a duty to support and further just institutions, and possibly a duty of fair play, and the more specific duties these entail. If so, citizens would not be under any general duty of justice to treat each other as equals in civil society and beyond. I have already raised some doubts about the idea that principles of justice apply only to the basic structure, but since this idea has been influential it merits further exploration. I shall argue that principles of justice do apply to personal behaviour as well as the basic structure, but this does not straightforwardly license the conclusion that citizens are under a general duty of justice to treat each other as equals.

Rawls notoriously maintained that the primary subject of justice is the basic structure of society.[1] This is consistent with the idea that there are other, secondary subjects of justice, including the choices people make within a just basic structure, but he also seemed to suppose that the basic structure is the *only* subject of justice.[2] If the basic structure is the only subject of justice, even if the state has a duty of justice to treat its citizens as equals, it would not follow that citizens were generally required to do so as well, as a matter of justice, when they interact with each other in civil society and beyond. If Rawls does limit the site of justice in this way, what are his reasons for doing so?

In order to answer that question, we need some clarification of what he means by the basic structure. Even on this issue, however, Rawls's writings contain some ambiguity. As Arash Abizadeh points out, the basic structure might be understood in at least three different ways, as comprising '(1) the institutions that determine and regulate the fundamental terms of social cooperation; (2) the institutions that have profound and pervasive impact upon persons' life chances; or (3) the institutions that subject people to coercion'.[3] These contrasting ways of understanding what constitutes the basic structure furnish potentially different explanations of why it is supposed to be the only site to which principles of justice apply. It is nevertheless hard to see how the account of the basic structure contained in either (3) or (2) could justify restricting the application of principles of justice to it. As G. A. Cohen argues, it seems purely arbitrary to restrict the application of these principles to institutions that subject people to coercion.[4] Given that non-coercive practices and patterns of choice can profoundly affect persons' life chances, why should they not also be governed by principles of justice, such as the principle that we should treat others as equals in civil society and beyond? But if having a profound and pervasive impact upon persons' life chances is what determines when principles of justice are applicable to an institution, then there is a straightforward argument for applying these principles not only to such institutions but also to practices and patterns of individual choice that are structured by these institutions, or which take place in the shadow of these institutions (such as those practices and patterns of behaviour which are inconsistent with affirming the fundamental equality of persons), that also profoundly and pervasively affect people's life chances.[5]

What reason might we have for restricting the application of principles of justice to the basic structure when it is understood in terms of (1), that is, as comprising those institutions that determine and regulate the fundamental terms of social cooperation? The most promising case is provided by what Liam Murphy calls the division of labour argument.[6] The institutions that determine and regulate the fundamental terms of social cooperation play an indispensable role in securing background justice. Even though the conditions for background justice can be undermined despite no one acting unjustly, there are not any rules which it would be reasonable to require individuals to follow which could prevent or counteract these undesirable consequences.[7] If we want to maximize justice (it is argued), the best way of doing so is to design institutions to secure background justice in so far as possible, and then allow individuals to make whatever choices they want that are permitted by these institutions. This argument is not persuasive, however. For a start, it is not clear that it counts against extending the application of every principle of justice that applies to the basic structure. The application of some of these principles, such as the principle that people should be treated as equals, might be extended so that they govern not only institutions and policy but also personal behaviour without making excessive demands on individuals, for example, people might be regarded as under a general duty to treat each other as equals in all their social interactions, thereby strengthening the hand of those who want to subsume the equal membership account within the justice account. More generally, even if requiring individuals to act in such a way that they do not undermine background justice, or requiring them to act so as to compensate for the way that the actions of others have undermined background justice, would place excessive demands on them, it may be possible to formulate appropriate principles of justice that do not do so because, for example, they allow individuals to pursue their own self interest (or the interests of those to whom they have some special connection) in circumstances when seeking to promote just outcomes or to maximize justice would place unreasonable burdens on them.[8]

But even if principles of justice govern personal behaviour, it does not follow that the *very same* principles that apply to the basic structure should also apply to behaviour that takes place within it, suitably constrained by personal prerogatives.[9] Even if we have a duty of justice, and of citizenship, to act justly, this leaves open the question of what principles this requires us to act upon. A just basic structure must treat those subject to it as equals, and the laws and policies which emerge from legal and political institutions must do so as well, but does acting justly require citizens to treat each other as equals when they encounter each other in civil society and beyond? It is hard to deny that some ways of treating people as equals in civil society are part of what it is to treat them justly, for they involve acting from a principle of non-discrimination that is unambiguously a principle of justice.[10] When employers refuse to hire those from ethnic minorities, rental agencies refuse to let their apartments to them, or shopkeepers refuse to serve them, then this behaviour represents a failure to treat them as equals in a way that violates the principle of non-discrimination and is deeply unjust. When members of ethnic minorities are subject to harassment or racial abuse in civil society or public spaces, they are treated unjustly. Even if these cases do not involve a straightforward violation of the principle of non-discrimination, this principle can plausibly be extended to cover them. Furthermore, the reasons that underpin a principle of non-discrimination may also mean that it would be unjust for someone to demand a higher wage than his fellow workers simply because he comes from a different ethnic group, or use his race or ethnicity as a way of gaining advantages for himself.[11]

But there are also ways of acting that involve a failure to treat others as equals where it is much less clear that the principle of non-discrimination has been violated and where it is also unclear that any other injustice (as opposed to some other moral wrong) has been committed. Consider the following behaviour: when shopping at a supermarket, a person tries to avoid going through a till that is operated by a member of an ethnic minority; when he catches a bus, he would rather stand than sit next to someone from that minority; when choosing a school for his child he selects the one which has the lowest proportion from that minority in it; when a member of that minority buys the house next door to his, he decides to move away; he discourages his child from playing with children from that minority in the neighbourhood; he would never invite a member of that minority into his home, whatever else they shared in common.[12] Each of these forms of behaviour involves ethnic or racial prejudice,[13] and a consequent failure to treat others as equals, but it is not clear that they involve injustice. A principle of non-discrimination, it might be thought, governs a person's behaviour in some areas of civil society, but not in all aspects of her private life, and it is the limited scope of that principle which makes it hard to think that the forms of behaviour I have identified involve discrimination.[14] Nor is it easy to see why we should think these forms of behaviour necessarily involve some other kind of injustice: no one need be made worse off by them and, considered individually at least, the actions described do not seem to trigger what Rainer Forst describes as 'the right to justification' which would entitle members of this minority to demand a justification for the behaviour they experience.[15]

To deny that behaving in these ways is in itself unjust does not mean that one must regard it as morally unproblematic. Indeed an equal membership account can hold that even though, say, discouraging one's child from playing with children from a minority is not unjust, it represents a failure to be a good citizen because it violates one's duty as a citizen to treat fellow citizens as equals. It violates that duty independently of whether it affects their access to the important goods made available by the basic structure or by civil society, and independently of whether it makes them worse off than they would otherwise be. Indeed the fulfilment of this duty can be regarded as realizing a kind of solidarity between citizens that is partially independent of just relations obtaining between them. This conclusion is reinforced by considering cases of cultural or religious insensitivity rather than ethnic or racial prejudice.[16] A person who serves a ham sandwich to a fellow citizen knowing that it would be contrary to his religion to eat it, or a man who tries to shake hands with a fellow (female) citizen knowing that she has religious reasons for avoiding physical contact with men outside her immediate family, fails to treat the other with respect in a way that violates a duty to treat fellow citizens as equals, even though there would be no injustice involved in behaving in these ways.

There does seem to be a strong connection, however, between treating others as equals in one's social relations and promoting just outcomes or avoiding being part of stigmatizing relationships. When the forms of behaviour I have described become commonplace in a society, this expresses, or contributes to the creation of, ethnic, racial, or religious stigma, the victims may suffer from a consequent loss in self-respect, and they may experience involuntary disadvantage, each of which makes the behaviour relevant from the point of view of justice.[17] Stigmatization might be regarded as a kind of accumulative harm:[18] even though, considered individually, none of the actions cause harm, they do so accumulatively because of the meaning and significance they acquire. So it might be thought that citizens have a duty to treat each others as equals in *all* their social interactions precisely in order to avoid being implicated in a pattern of behaviour that stigmatizes and disadvantages some of their fellows and in this way contributes to their experience of domination. As a result it might seem once again that the justice account, properly thought through, must converge with an equal membership account in terms of its implications for the duties and virtues of citizenship.

There is nevertheless a powerful reason for resisting the conclusion that the justice account, properly thought through, must subsume the equal membership account. Whatever the implications of the justice account and the equal membership account, they will remain distinct in terms of the *justifications* they give for at least some duties and virtues of citizenship. A justice account justifies the duty to treat one's fellow citizens as equals in the kind of informal social interactions I have described by reference to the role it plays in promoting and sustaining just institutions and outcomes or preventing racial and ethnic stigmatization, whereas an equal membership account justifies it by its constitutive role in realizing the good of social and political equality, which it regards as non-instrumentally valuable in a distinctive way. Indeed it might be thought that it is an *advantage* of an equal membership account that it does not need to make the justification of a duty to treat others as equals in one's social interactions contingent in any way on the role that the fulfilment of this duty plays in sustaining just institutions, generating just outcomes, avoiding stigmatization, or eliminating involuntary disadvantage. Patterns of behaviour motivated by racial prejudice, such as not sitting next to members of an ethnic minority on the bus or not sending one's child to the local school because it has a high proportion of ethnic minority children, would be morally problematic even in a world in which they did not generate involuntary disadvantage, or did not even express or create ethnic or racial stigma, because human beings were formed psychologically in ways that meant they were unaffected by such behaviour.[19] In other words, when a duty to treat others as equals in one's social interactions is grounded in the good of equal membership, it is more robust than when it is grounded in considerations concerning how justice is best promoted.

Justice accounts are diverse, however, and it might seem that some of them must regard aspects of social equality, or the conditions for its realization, as non-instrumentally valuable components of justice. Consider, for example, the idea that justice consists in non-domination or the minimization of domination.[20] The idea that a just society is simply one in which domination is absent or minimized might appear to threaten the distinction between the justice account and the equal membership account. From the perspective of a theory of justice as non-domination, the violations of social equality I have described may look as if they are simply ways in which members of one group dominate another by exercising arbitrary power over them,[21] and hence unjust in their own terms not merely because of their consequences or wider significance, so appearing to bridge the gap between the equal membership account and the justice account. But even if non-domination or the minimization of domination were by itself to provide us with a fully adequate conception of justice, there would still be reasons for thinking that the value of social equality is partially independent of justice, for the failure to treat others as equals does not always involve the exercise of arbitrary power over them. Imagine a society containing a number of different ethnic groups, none of which have any inclination to wield arbitrary power over each other, and where that society's structures are effective in preventing the arbitrary exercise of power, but where members of each group treat members of the others with disdain, as if they were inferior, in civil society and beyond. This would involve a lamentable failure of social equality, but from the perspective of an account of justice as non-domination (or the minimization of domination) it would not involve any injustice. According to the equal membership account, unlike the non-domination version of the justice account, it would represent a serious violation of the duties of citizenship. Our concern for non-domination and preventing the arbitrary exercise of power captures only part of why we worry about failures to treat people as equals in social interactions, so it can provide us with only a partial understanding of the good of equal membership.

2 Citizens and resident aliens

The equal membership account may differ from the justice account not only in terms of the justification it provides for various rights, duties, and virtues but also the range of virtues and duties it underwrites. There is nevertheless a sense in which we do not have to choose between them. Even though the justice account cannot subsume the equal membership account, it would be odd to suppose that the equal membership account could demonstrate that the justice account is *flawed*, for it could not show that the latter was mistaken about the rights and duties that emerge from considerations of justice. We do not need to choose between these accounts precisely because they are grounded in at least partially distinct values. Nevertheless these accounts cannot straightforwardly be combined to provide a comprehensive theory of the rights, duties, and virtues of citizenship *in particular*. This can be seen more clearly by considering the normative significance that each of them attaches to the distinction between citizens and resident aliens.

For the purposes of this discussion, let me side-step various difficulties in drawing this distinction and simply assume that a resident alien is someone who lives in a state, and has a legal right to reside there, but is not a citizen of it—and indeed is a citizen of some other state.[22] The citizens of a state, I shall stipulate, necessarily differ from resident aliens in at least one respect: they possess some political rights that resident aliens lack. This necessary difference between the rights of citizens and resident aliens may be supplemented in practice by further differences between them in particular states. For example, citizens may have an unconditional legal right of permanent residence that resident aliens lack. Resident aliens' right of residence may be short-term or long-term. Even if it is long-term, it may be for a restricted period of time or require renewal at regular intervals, or if it is permanent, it may be that it can be rescinded under certain circumstances (for example, if she breaks the criminal law or has an extended period of absence from the country). In some states the children of citizens, unlike the children of resident aliens, may be automatically entitled to citizenship of that country regardless of where their parents were living when they were born; and in most states, the citizens of a state, unlike resident aliens living within its borders, have various rights to assistance and support from it when they are travelling abroad. So there is only one necessary difference between citizens and resident aliens but there may be further contingent differences between them.

Justice accounts claim to be analysing the relationship of citizenship in particular, or at least that is how I have represented them so far. In reality, however, their framing assumptions generally mean that they are concerned with the way in which justice is secured by and for those who live together in the same territory, subject to the same legal, political and economic institutions, which includes not just citizens but also resident aliens. Even if justice accounts do not ascribe any fundamental normative significance to being subject to the same legal, political and economic institutions, they may nevertheless suppose that what matters is being involved in the same cooperative scheme for mutual advantage, or belonging to a common scheme that provides it members with aid when in need, yet the groups of people these criteria pick out will generally include resident aliens (and, in certain respects at least, exclude non-resident citizens). This feature of justice accounts is sometimes disguised by the 'idealizing' assumptions they make, such as the assumption that persons are born, live and die in the same state, and acquire the citizenship of that state at birth, then retain it for the rest of their lives; when this assumption is made, there is no distinction to be drawn in practice between citizens and resident aliens.

To claim that justice accounts are generally concerned (whether implicitly or explicitly) with the way in which justice is secured by and for those who live in the same territory, subject to the same institutions, is not to imply that these accounts must deny that residents of different kinds can possess different moral rights and duties. Justice accounts can allow that, in principle, the difference in political rights that citizens possess compared to resident aliens is morally justifiable and can allow that citizens may possess different moral duties from resident aliens—and indeed that long-term residents may possess different moral rights and duties from short-term residents—since there may be reasons of justice that can underwrite these differences. Justice accounts can also acknowledge that citizenship is a particularly valuable status because of the additional rights it provides, and they can ask questions about when resident aliens should be given the opportunity to acquire voting rights or citizenship, and what measures should be taken to prevent them from being exploited. Indeed a fully-fledged justice account of citizenship will incorporate principles to address these issues. But a justice account does not accord citizenship the special significance that the equal membership account does. According to the equal membership account, being a citizen has a particular significance that derives from being a member of a group which makes decisions that importantly affect one's conditions of existence and in which one has equal standing because one enjoys equal opportunity to participate on equal terms and is treated as an equal by fellow members of the group. Resident aliens are not part of the relevant group because, at the minimum, they lack some political rights that citizens possess.

It is the special significance that the equal membership account attributes to citizenship which enables it to justify duties that are owed to fellow citizens *in particular*.[23] In contrast, many of the duties generated by the justice account are likely to bind resident aliens as well as citizens—and these duties might not bind non-resident citizens to the same extent. The justice account may of course underwrite some differences in the duties of citizens compared to resident aliens that relate directly to their different rights. Since resident aliens lack full political rights, such as the right to vote in national elections, they cannot possess a duty to exercise these rights. It is plausible to think that citizens are under such a duty, even if it is conditional in various ways (for example, on being well enough on the day to travel comfortably to a polling booth) or only an imperfect duty, to vote in most elections over the course of their lives. From the perspective of the justice account, however, the most plausible way of grounding this duty is in terms of a more fundamental one to support reasonably just institutions. Yet the duty to support just institutions seems to apply equally to resident aliens, even if it has different implications for resident aliens and citizens that flow from the different rights they are accorded. Indeed it seems to apply to each group as 'insiders', for part of what makes just institutions just is the way in which they give due weight to the interests of *both* citizens and resident aliens.[24]

In response, it might be argued that the duty to support just institutions has more demanding implications across the board for citizens, not just in terms of a duty to vote. This is open to question, however, for it is not clear that the duty to support just institutions is in any other respects more demanding for citizens than for resident aliens. Suppose it were claimed that this duty requires resident aliens to obey reasonably just laws but demands nothing more of them, whereas it requires citizens to keep a watchful eye on government, and speak out against injustice when they become aware of it. This would be hard to defend, at least in relation to resident aliens who have lived in a country for a substantial period of time. Resident aliens lack some political rights that citizens possess, but in liberal-democratic countries at least lack of these rights does not prevent them from being vigilant in these ways. (In our non-ideal world, their obligation to contest injustice may of course be weaker, given the greater risks involved in doing so if they do not enjoy robust protections against deportation.) The idea that long-term resident aliens have a duty to keep a watchful eye on government, and speak out against injustice when they find it, might also be justified in a further way, by appealing to the principle of fair play, on the grounds that the secure enjoyment of various basic liberties, the benefits of which they willingly accept, relies on the presence of such activity.[25] Indeed that justification may in some cases be more robust for resident aliens than it is for citizens, in so far as resident aliens have made a voluntary choice to live under these institutions.[26]

As we have seen, since the justice account grounds many of its specific duties in the more fundamental duty to support and promote just institutions, and resident aliens and (resident) citizens are insiders in relation to the same set of institutions, these duties will tend to bind both groups in the same way and be owed to residents in general. The equal membership account, in contrast, can justify the idea that there are a range of duties that bind fellow citizens in particular and that are owed specifically to each other. However, it might be regarded as a problematic feature of the equal membership account that the special obligations it underwrites are not owed to resident aliens. To assuage some of these worries, it is worth noting that the specialness that the equal membership account attributes to citizenship does not imply that citizens have no obligations to resident aliens—on the contrary, it can acknowledge that they have demanding obligations to them—and it does not imply that fellow citizens have an unconditional right to exclude resident aliens from this relationship. Rather than providing reasons to exclude, the benefits yielded by citizenship give powerful reasons for ensuring that resident aliens have a fair opportunity to become part of it, as I shall maintain in the next section.

The way in which the duties justified by the equal membership are owed only to fellow citizens might nevertheless be regarded as problematic in some cases. For example, since the duty it justifies to treat fellow citizens as equals in all one's interactions with them is not owed to resident aliens, it would not by itself justify any complaint when resident aliens are the victims of the patterns of behaviour I described earlier, for instance, when others refuse to sit next to them on public buses. But it is illuminating again to see the justice and

65

equal membership accounts as complementary, for they cast light on different sorts of relationship. The equal membership account provides us with an account of the rights and duties of citizens in particular, whereas the justice account gives us a more comprehensive account of the rights and duties of justice possessed by residents of different kinds, subject to the same set of institutions. When the justice account and the equal membership account are seen as complementing each other, it need not be troubling that special duties grounded in the good of equal membership are owed only to fellow citizens, for they are supplemented by whatever special duties to residents (including citizens and resident aliens) can be derived from the best theory of justice. These may include an obligation to treat others as equals in a variety of different social contexts, even if this obligation is less wide-ranging than one grounded in an equal membership account.[27] To the extent that it is appropriate to regard resident aliens as future citizens,[28] we should also lament the failure to treat them as equals even when it is not unjust, on the grounds that behaviour of this kind will make it harder for resident aliens to integrate and to *become* citizens of equal standing. Indeed, this may also provide a good reason for others to treat resident aliens *as if* they were already citizens, as equals in civil society and beyond, even when the duties of justice or citizenship do not strictly demand it, since this may facilitate their transition to citizenship and make it easier for them to integrate.[29]

The different foundations of the justice and equal membership accounts, and the way in which they focus in part on different groups, may also generate different views of the importance of the *concept* of citizenship. From the perspective of the justice account, it is conceivable that under some circumstances this concept might lose its point or even begin to obscure the normative landscape. In a world of 'hypermigration' where the majority of citizens in most countries were non-residents and the majority of residents were non-citizens,[30] a justice account might argue, somewhat paradoxically, that we should abandon the concept of citizenship. A defender of that account might think that we should simply disaggregate the various rights, duties, and virtues that citizenship is taken to involve—for example, we might divide up the rights into civil and political rights, social rights, a right of permanent residence (and one's children's right to the same), and a right to diplomatic assistance when travelling abroad. If a clearer view could be obtained of how justice could best be secured for and between the residents of particular territories without invoking the concept of citizenship at all, but simply talking about the different rights or entitlements of different people, including their different rights of residence (that is, whether a right of residence is long-term, short-term, or permanent, and whether it is conditional or unconditional), the various institutional mechanisms for protecting or providing these rights and entitlements, the duties that individuals owe to others who live in the same territory or to different groups of residents, and the virtues they express in their relationships with them, then the justice account would have no further reason to retain it. This is in sharp contrast to the equal membership account. According to the equal membership account, the role of the rights, duties, and virtues of citizenship is to protect, promote or express the complex good of equal membership. From this perspective, abandoning the language of citizenship and disaggregating the rights, duties, and virtues that are constitutive of it, runs the risk of losing sight of the way in which these rights, duties, and virtues combine together to secure or express an important good[31]—one which perhaps has a value that cannot be reduced to the value of its component parts.

3 Justice, equal membership, and the entitlement to a say

I have suggested that one way in which the justice and equal membership accounts complement each other is by focusing on different—albeit overlapping—sets of people: justice accounts focus upon those who live in the same territory subject to the same legal, political, and economic institutions, including resident aliens, whereas equal membership accounts focus on citizens proper. But there are a number of possible sources of tension between the justice account and the equal membership account. Later, in my concluding remarks to this chapter, I shall draw attention to the potential these accounts have to justify conflicting rights and duties. In this section, however, I explore some possible tensions that arise when addressing the question of who is entitled to a say in political decision-making and, more broadly, who is entitled to citizenship, where citizenship is understood as involving not only full voting rights but other rights that, potentially at least, resident aliens do not possess, such as an unconditional right of residence. Addressing these questions throws up the issue of whether considerations of justice and the good of equal membership pull in different directions when we are trying to identify the best principles for governing these matters.

A variety of different principles have been proposed for determining when a person is entitled to a say in the decision-making processes of a polity. I shall focus on those principles that seem to pose the most threat to the good of equal membership, beginning with a principle that is both intuitively appealing and endorsed by many, namely, that anyone whose interests are affected by a decision is entitled to a say in it.[32] This 'all-affected interests principle' stands in need of clarification, however, and faces a charge of incoherence. We need to know what, for the purposes of the principle, is to count as an interest. Does any desire or preference constitute an interest? Does each and every interest matter from the point of view of the principle or only particularly significant interests? If the latter, how are we to draw the line between those interests that are significant and those that are not? Even if we can give normatively persuasive answers to these questions, there is still a potential incoherence at the heart of the principle to which Robert Goodin draws our attention: determining who is entitled to a say in making a decision requires us to identify those whose interests are affected by the decision which is to be made, but whose interests are affected by that decision will depend upon who makes it and what their decision is.[33] It seems to me that the best way out of this difficulty is to distinguish, in the way that David Owen does, between the outcome of a decision and the range of options from which a decision is to be made. We might then say that the all-affected interests principle implies that once a range of possible options has been identified, the class of people who are entitled to a say is constituted by those whose interests would be affected by the choice of any (or none) of those options.[34] To this it might be replied that we have not settled the logically prior question of how a set of possible options is to be identified, and that it is here where the incoherence in the principle arises, for we need someone to identify this set, and the principle can give us no guidance on who should do so. But it seems to me that the appropriate response to this point is to maintain that the principle is not intended to give guidance on *that* question: we have simply to assume that there is a decision to be made, a range of options to choose from, and a mechanism for placing those decisions and options on the agenda.

Even if this constitutes a satisfactory response to the charge of incoherence, the all-affected interests principle seems to have some worrying implications which raise doubts about it. In some (perhaps many) cases, the class of those whose interests are affected by the choice between a range of options will be everyone alive—and perhaps even some who have not yet been born. This might be regarded as simply a radical conclusion that we have to accept and do our best to respect when we design institutions. But the all-affected interests principle has various other implications that are not so easy to swallow. Robert Nozick describes a number of cases where the all-affected interests principle seems to give the wrong answer.[35] For example, he invites us to imagine a case in which a woman receives proposals of marriage from four different men. The decision about which one she should marry clearly affects the interests of all five of them, but it would surely be a mistake to conclude, as the all-affected interests principle would seem to have us do, that the four men should each have a say in it. The decision is hers to make. Nozick also describes the case of Arturo Toscanini, who is in the process of deciding when to retire from his role as conductor of the Symphony of the Air. This decision will have serious financial repercussions for the members of his orchestra, but again it would surely be a mistake to conclude that the orchestra members are entitled to a say in the decision about when Toscanini should retire (or, indeed, whether he should be allowed to retire).

In response to these two cases, it might be argued that it is not decisions about what individual acts should be performed (or allowed) that should be governed directly by the all-affected interests principle, but rather decisions concerning what general rules should apply to the performance of individual acts. But even that leaves open the possibility that the general rule selected by all whose interests are affected by decisions over marriage partners might be one which allowed a majority vote in cases where there are multiple suitors. In order to avoid this problem altogether, it might seem that we need to restrict the scope of the all-affected interests principle in various ways. We might, for example, hold that it is constrained by various individual and collective rights and that it applies only in the space that these rights do not occupy. What is doing the work in the two of Nozick's examples I have described is an underlying appeal to rights of self ownership, which, it might be thought, constrain the all-affected interests principle, in such a way that it applies only when these rights do not settle who should decide. His third example, which concerns the entitlement of the owner of a bus to claim it back when he has lent it to a group of people even though they have over time become dependent upon it, and without giving them any say, appeals to property rights in external objects, and these might also be thought to constrain the application of the all-affected interests principle. (Understood in this way, it would be a mistake to think—in the way that Nozick appears to do—that the all-affected interests principle itself is supposed to determine what decisions should be taken collectively.) But if we restrict the scope of the all-affected interests principle as proposed, it is not clear how much space will be left for it to occupy. In effect it will be hedged in by various principles of justice; its application will be limited to decisions in which matters of justice (or, at least, matters of basic justice) are not at stake. Consequently it will possess far less importance than its defenders have claimed for it.

Restricting the application of the all-affected interests principle to decisions that do not concern matters of basic justice can also seem paradoxical because one obvious way of trying to justify this principle is in terms of its role in promoting just outcomes: the idea would be that when all those whose interests are affected by a decision have a say in it, it is more likely that their interests will be given due weight, and as a result the outcome of decision-making processes are likely to be more just, on balance and over the long term, than any other principle of inclusion. In this light we might draw a distinction between principles of justice that govern the distribution of resources (where 'resources' are broadly understood, so that they include the bodies of individuals and their talents and powers), and principles that govern *who decides* what laws or policies should govern the distribution of resources (which might be justified in terms of judgements about what forms of inclusion, on the whole and in the long run, are most likely to generate just outcomes). Determining whether a law or policy is *legitimate*, that is, whether its enforcement is morally justified all things considered, might then involve a complex balancing of these two sets of principles. Allowing all those whose interests are affected by a decision over a law or policy to have a say in it might in practice generate either a legitimate or an illegitimate outcome. For example, those whose interests are affected by a decision over a law or policy might decide to create various constitutional protections that serve to place a range of individual rights outside of the normal run of majoritarian decision-making, in a way that generates legitimate outcomes. On the other hand, those whose interests are affected by a decision over a law or policy might vote in favour of laws which permit the violation of individual rights, for example, they might adopt a law governing marriage which allows individuals to be married against their will, in which case we might suppose that this outcome is sufficiently unjust that it is illegitimate, even though it emerges as a result of respecting the all-affected interests principle.

This seems to me to be the right way to conceive of the role of the all-affected interests principle, but I do not think that in the end this principle can be justified in the way envisaged. Consider two reasons for worrying about whether institutionalizing the all-affected interests principle is the best way of achieving just outcomes, on balance and in the long run. First, if we care about just outcomes, we might think that what is most important is that when people make decisions they do so on an impartial basis, taking into account the effects of their decisions on the interests of others, regardless of whether these others are involved in the decision-making process. The implementation of the all-affected interests principle is compatible with impartial decision-making of this kind, but we might nevertheless think that in a range of cases the best way in practice of encouraging the impartial consideration of interests is to design institutional structures so that those whose interests are affected by a decision have some court of appeal if they think the outcome is unjust on them rather than by giving all those whose interests are affected a say.[36] Second, we might worry that institutionalizing the all-affected interests principle will reduce the connection that people feel with their decision-making procedures, and perhaps with others involved in them, resulting in less rather than more participation.[37] If different sets of decisions are made by different groups in accordance with the all-affected interests principle, won't individuals identify less with their legal and political institutions than they would to if they were part of a relatively stable body that made collective decisions over a range of different issues? And won't this lack of identification translate into less participation, with the risk of less just outcomes?

This also raises the issue of whether the all-affected interests principle threatens the good of equal membership by failing to underwrite the kind of political groupings which are needed to realize that good, that is, political communities with relatively stable and enduring memberships that make a range of collective decisions that significantly affect their members' conditions of existence. In what follows, I shall refer to these simply as 'bounded political communities' (though it is important here not to be misled by the use of the term 'bounded'). When the all-affected interests principle governs decision-making, different groups will be involved in different sets of decisions: there is no reason to think that the group comprised of those whose members' interests are affected by one decision will be the same as the group comprised of those whose members' interests are affected by some other decision. In response it might be said that, nevertheless, there will be a core group whose members' interests are more affected than others by a range of decisions, and that we should approximate the requirements of the all-affected interests principle by constituting decision-making bodies so that they include those whose interests are most seriously affected by most of the decisions taken by these bodies. But even that seems optimistic given the facts of migration and of global interdependence. The effects of policies often spill over the borders of states in ways that seriously affect others. The idea that we can identify a core group that is differently situated in relation to a wide class of decisions, even in terms of *the degree* to which their interests are affected by those decisions, seems to over-simplify.

Defenders of the all-affected interests principle might simply reply: 'so much the worse for bounded political communities'. They might maintain that the existence of political communities of this kind cannot be defended, except perhaps as an administrative convenience, even if these communities have been the basis of much of our thought about citizenship. But to the extent that bounded political communities are a condition for the realization of the good of equal membership, this response is problematic, for the loss of bounded political communities would also deprive us of this important good. In determining whether a principle for governing who should have a say in political decision-making is defensible, its ability to sustain that good is a relevant consideration; therefore, if a principle is incompatible with the continued existence of bounded political communities, this counts against it.

One alternative would be a principle which held that anyone who is *subject to coercion*, and hence who is subject to the exercise of power, is entitled to a say in the processes that determine how power is to be exercised.[38] Let us call this 'the coercion principle'. In some respects it appears to be narrower than the all-affected interests principle. A decision might affect the interests of a person but not make them subject to coercion, in which case the coercion principle, unlike the all-affected interests principle, would not entail that they are entitled to a say in it.[39] What then does it mean to be 'subject to coercion'? Arash Abizadeh, who defends the coercion principle, distinguishes between being subject to coercion and being coerced: a person is subject to coercion without actually being coerced if they are subject to a coercive threat which does not deter them because, say, they have no desire to do what the threat seeks to dissuade them from doing. But even those not resident in a territory are subject to coercive threats of the form: 'if you seek to enter this territory without permission, you will be coercively prevented from entering or punished if you succeed'; 'if you enter this territory and seek to perform actions of type A, you will be coercively prevented from doing so or punished if you succeed'. In practice, therefore, the coercion principle seems to raise some of the same kind of worries as the all-affected interests principle, since it seems over-expansive: people are subject to coercion by the laws governing territories in which they do not reside, made by states of which they are not citizens, and to which they have no desire to emigrate.[40] If this is so, it is not obvious that giving everyone who is subject to coercion by a law a say in its adoption is likely to produce just outcomes, or that it is consistent with the existence of the bounded political communities that are a condition for the realization of the value of equal membership.

A defender of the coercion principle might try to resist this conclusion on the grounds that those not resident in a state are not subject to coercion by its laws but face merely hypothetical coercion,[41] that is, they would expose themselves to coercion if they were to enter the territory and perform, or attempt to perform, the forbidden act, but are not actually coerced or subject to coercion. But the distinctions between being coerced, being subject to coercion and hypothetical coercion are hard to draw in a way that does not make the coercion principle implausible as a result of the restrictions it places on what is to count as being 'subject to coercion'. Miller, for example, distinguishes between coercion and prevention 'where coercion involves forcing a person *to do* some relatively specific thing, and prevention involves forcing a person *not to do* some relatively specific thing while leaving other options open',[42] and then argues that 'being subject to coercion but not actually coerced' covers only those cases where an attempt to force a person to do some specific thing fails because he nevertheless does that thing. Yet in that case laws do not generally subject a person to coercion, since they do not normally force, or attempt to force, a person to do some specific thing; consequently, the coercion principle becomes implausible if it is understood as specifying a necessary condition for when a person is entitled to say in the determination of a law or policy.[43] The coercion principle faces a dilemma: if being subject to coercion is understood in such a way that one is subject to coercion if it is the case that one would be coerced if one was to perform a particular action in a particular place, then the coercion principle seems unacceptably expansive, whereas if it is understood in such a way that it covers only cases of actual coercion and cases where a substantial threat fails to dissuade one from performing an action, then it is unacceptably restrictive.

In the light of the difficulties faced both by the all-affected interests principle and the coercion principle, an 'all-subjected' principle, which determines who is entitled to a say in decision-making by reference to the relationship that they bear to the commands that are issued by legal and political authorities, should seem attractive. According to this principle, a person is subjected to laws that are prescribed by a *de facto* legal authority either when it issues commands that are directed at her or, at least, that apply to her[44] and it has the capacity to enforce these commands; or when it confers legal rights on her (including various legal powers and immunities) and offers her some means of legal recourse should it fail to respect these rights or to secure them for her. The all-subjected principle can take a number of different forms. I shall consider two versions that are distinguished in terms of whether what matters is being subjected to a *system* of law that is determined by a *de facto* legal authority, or whether what matters instead is being subjected to *individual* laws determined by such an authority. According to the first version, each of those subjected to a system of law are entitled to a say in the determination of any particular law that forms part of that system,[45] whereas according to the second version, each of those subjected to a particular law are entitled to a say in the adoption or otherwise of that law.

The first version of the all-subjected principle might seem problematic, however: if a person's being subjected to a system of law entails that each of the various laws that are part of it must be directed at her or apply to her, then this seems to entail that, in most states, no one is subjected to one. For in most states, at least some of its laws will be directed at resident aliens and not at its citizens, for example, laws requiring resident aliens to register with the local authority in the area in which they live. What this shows, however, is that the most plausible formulation of this version of the principle will hold that a person's being subjected to a system of law entails that *most* of the laws that form part of that system are directed at her or apply to her.[46] (In effect, a person can be subjected to a system of law without being subjected to each and every one of the laws that form part of that system; according to the formulation of the all-subjected principle under consideration, it is being subjected to a system of law that determines whether or not one is entitled to a say in any particular law that forms part of that system.)

The notion of being subjected to a system of law or to individual laws is understood differently from the idea of being subject to coercion. A person is subjected to a system of law—or is 'a legal subject' of it—when most of the laws that comprise it are directed at her (or apply to her) and they are enforceable, whereas a person is subjected to an individual law when the law is directed at her (or applies to her) and it is enforceable.[47] On some understandings of what it is to be subject to coercion, including apparently Abizadeh's, a person is subject to coercion by a law that is issued by some *de facto* legal authority simply in virtue of its being the case that *if* she were to enter the territory within which this legal authority claims jurisdiction, she would then be prevented from doing what that law forbids, but this is insufficient to show that she is *already* subjected to that law according to either version of the all-subjected principle. On other understandings of what it is to be subject to coercion, such as Miller's, a person is subject to coercion by a law only if it either forces her to do some specific thing or attempts to force her to do that thing but fails, whereas she is subjected to a law simply in virtue of it applying to her, even if it does not force her to do anything. Indeed she may be subjected to a law simply because it grants her a right of some kind (for example, a right to a pension, or to diplomatic protection when travelling abroad), without her being subject to coercion at all.

Consider some cases that might be thought to raise difficulties for the all-subjected principle, and that help to clarify what follows from it and where its different versions may diverge. The second formulation is potentially more radical in its implications, but even it seems to be reconcilable with the existence of bounded political communities. First, what do the different versions of the principle imply in relation to laws governing the crossing of a state's borders and the issue of whether non-citizens who lie on the other side of these borders are subjected to these laws? According to the first formulation of the principle, it is implausible to suppose that non-citizens who lie on the other side of the border are subjected to its system of law and policy—only a small fraction of these laws and policies are directed at them or apply to them—so they are not entitled to a say in the particular laws governing who is allowed to cross that border.[48] (The same might also be said of non-resident citizens.) Things look different, however, from the perspective of the second formulation. The particular laws governing the crossing of a state's borders are directed at, or at least apply to, non-citizens who lie beyond these borders. In so far as the legal authority concerned has the capacity to enforce these laws, it follows that would-be immigrants are subjected to them in the relevant way, and hence are entitled to a say in them. Generalized across the state system, this would seem to point in the direction of a regime in which immigration rules and policy are decided by global institutions controlled by a global demos. This strikes me as independently plausible, for such a regime might be thought to best support just outcomes. There is no reason, however, to think that bounded political communities will be unjustifiable or would be likely to wither away were this to happen.

Second, suppose that a state was to pass a law prohibiting those resident in other states from engaging in a particular activity, for example, Britain passes a law prohibiting those resident elsewhere from hacking into its government-associated computer systems. Would this mean, for instance, that those resident in Canada, regardless of whether they were British citizens, were subjected to this law in the sense required to engage the all-subjected principle? It would be implausible to suppose that the passing of this law was sufficient to mean that those living in Canada, regardless of whether they were British citizens, were subjected to the system of British law since it would not be the case that the majority of the laws and policies which form part of that system are directed at them or even apply to them. So, according to the first formulation of the principle, they would not be entitled to a say in the law prohibiting hacking into the British government's computer systems even though it applies to them. In effect they would be subjects of the Canadian rather than the British system of law.[49] The second formulation potentially supports a different conclusion: whether those resident in Canada are entitled to a say in this law would depend upon whether it was enforceable, which in practice would depend on whether the Canadian state was willing to cooperate with Britain in securing the extradition of offenders. Even if they were disposed to do so, however, relatively rare cases of laws such as these would not threaten the very existence of bounded political communities.

Third, there is the issue of what the all-subjected principle implies in relation to tourists and short-term residents, including those on short-term work contracts, and those studying abroad for a short period.[50] Both formulations of this principle seem to imply that members of these groups should have a say in the laws of the country in which they currently reside because they are subjected to these laws in the relevant ways, yet that would seem to pose a threat to the existence of bounded political communities. Here we might take the view that strictly speaking the all-subjected principle has this implication but then argue (as Ludvig Beckman does) that there are administrative reasons connected with due process which mean that a state is entitled to deny tourists or short-term residents the vote if they are unable to complete a fair process of registration in the time required.[51] Alternatively, we might think that these cases provide a reason to amend the all-subjected principle in a way that would better accommodate a commitment to due process, for example, we might suppose that all those who are subjected to a law or policy, or subjected to a system of law and policy, are entitled *either* to a say in it *or* to a fair opportunity to acquire a say in it.[52] This would allow a state to justify requiring people to reside in a state for a minimum period of time—at least the amount of time needed to check that the person is present in the state, and that he is who he says he is—before he was entitled to receive voting rights. Indeed this formulation of the principle *might* be compatible with requiring a longer period of residence before a right to vote was granted. And it might even justify a state denying long standing residents, or permanent residents with a right to remain, a say in decisions provided they had an adequate opportunity to become citizens and thereby acquire full voting rights. So again the all-subjected principle can deal with these cases without implying that bounded political communities are unjustifiable, and without giving us any reason to think that these communities would disappear were that principle to be respected. Given the difficulties faced by the other principles I have discussed, this gives us a powerful reason for favouring it.[53] Indeed, it seems to me that the all-subjected principle is not only well suited to sustaining the good of equal membership, but is also likely to promote just outcomes, especially when it is interpreted as it is in the second formulation.

Although the all-subjected principle seems to provide us with a plausible basis for determining how voting rights should be allocated, it does not by itself provide us with an answer to the question of on what basis citizenship proper should be granted. Potentially at least, citizenship involves not only possessing equal voting rights but also various other rights, such as an unconditional right of permanent residence and the right to pass on one's citizenship to one's children, that resident aliens may lack—and to the extent that they lack these further rights compared to citizens, even if they possess the same voting rights, they lack the equality of status that is integral to the good of equal membership. What principles should govern the acquisition of citizenship? We might think that the answer to this question is obvious: morally speaking, long-term residents are automatically entitled to it. But this raises a host of other questions. Why should long-term residence be regarded as salient for granting citizenship? What is it that gives long-term residency special significance[54] and does it have the same significance in the case of 'irregular' migrants? When should a would-be immigrant be granted employment rights and rights of residency (whether long-term or short-term) in a state? Are states entitled to adopt whatever policy they want on this matter? (Even if immigration policies are to be decided by global or transnational bodies on which would-be immigrants are represented, we might think there are better or worse principles for determining these policies.)

The principles for determining when employment rights and rights of residence should be granted, and for determining when citizenship proper (as opposed to voting rights alone) should be accorded, take us beyond the all-subjected principle. But when the all-subjected principle is in place, and long-term residents are given a fair opportunity to acquire citizenship, it seems to me that whatever additional principles are favoured by considerations of justice, for determining when those who seek entry to a state should be granted employment rights or rights of residence, they will be broadly compatible with sustaining the good of equal membership. Indeed to the extent that these principles can sustain that good, this would count as a further reason in their favour, whereas their incompatibility with that good would count as a reason against them. If employment rights and rights of residence are offered freely, then this will no doubt increase transnational migration. But if voting rights and citizenship are granted to immigrants only after a substantial period of residence, then the good of equal membership itself need not be threatened. It is true that this good would be under threat in a world made up of 'hypermigration' societies of the kind described earlier, in which most residents are non-citizens and most citizens are non-resident.[55] But even if that possibility is left open by what are, on balance, the best principles for determining when voting rights, rights of residence, employment rights, and citizenship proper should be granted, we would need further reasons for thinking that such a world would be the likely outcome of the application of these principles, especially when we take into account the felt need of many people to belong to political communities which, at least to some degree, realize the good of equal membership.

The all-subjected principle and the principles for determining when residents are entitled to citizenship are justified not only by reference to considerations of justice, but also by their role in protecting and promoting the good of equal membership. But this does not collapse the distinction between justice accounts and equal membership accounts; it merely draws attention to the fact that they identify different sources of reasons. Furthermore, in this context justice and the good of equal membership might be regarded as mutually dependent in one respect: when residents are not given a fair opportunity to acquire voting rights or to become citizens of a state, the *current* citizens of that state are to some degree deprived of the good of equal membership, for the value of the social and political equality they realize between them is tainted as a result. The value of a collective body the members of which have equal standing and that makes decisions which importantly affect their conditions of existence (and indeed the value of being a member of such a body) is diminished simply because some are unjustly denied access to the good of equal membership or are unjustly denied voting rights. At a fundamental level, justice and the good of equal membership not only complement each other, but the former is a necessary condition of the latter in its fullest and richest form.

4 Concluding remarks

The justice account and the equal membership account can complement each other in various ways. The equal membership account provides a defence of a range of rights and duties that are part and parcel of being a citizen. The justice account, in contrast, provides a defence of a range of rights and duties that need not be tied to citizenship in particular. Justice accounts can also attribute different rights and duties to resident citizens, non-resident citizens, long-term resident non-citizens, and short-term resident non-citizens, if doing so would provide the best means of fulfilling the requirements of general principles of justice that include all persons within their scope. The justice account and the equal membership account can also complement each other in a different way, because they provide independent grounds for endorsing an all-subjected principle which holds that all those subjected to a law, or a system of it, are entitled to a say in it, or a fair opportunity to acquire a say in it. Indeed the implementation of that principle is a necessary condition of realizing the full value of the good of equal membership.

It is important to emphasize again, however, that there are different versions of both the justice account and the good of equal membership. The extent to which the justice account and the equal membership account diverge, and whether they complement each other, will depend on which particular version of each is endorsed. In subsequent chapters, I shall presuppose a version of the equal membership account that has an unconditional commitment to political equality, that attributes non-instrumental value to social equality as well as political equality, and which allows that a collective the members of which have equal standing and that makes decisions which importantly affect their conditions of existence, and in which each member is treated as an equal in both the sphere of politics and civil society, may have value over and above the value of its component parts. And I shall endorse a version of the justice account that not only supposes that principles of justice apply to personal behaviour as well as the basic structure of society, but which also requires us to counteract the effects of differences in people's social circumstances (such as the families and cultures into which they are born) and differences in their levels of natural endowment (such as the potential to acquire skills and talents with which they are born). These assumptions exclude some versions of both the equal membership account and the justice account, but they do not uniquely identify a particular version of each. When constrained by these assumptions, characteristically at least, the equal membership account has a more robust commitment to social equality than the justice account, whereas the justice account has a more robust commitment to reducing inequalities that are created by circumstances that are beyond people's control.

Whenever justice and equal membership accounts diverge, this raises a question about the enforceability of the rights and duties that emerge from the equal membership account. Put bluntly, if these rights and duties are not grounded in considerations of justice, does the state have any business enforcing them? Social and political equality form an important good that is valuable in itself, so there does not seem to be any general reason for thinking that it would be impermissible to enforce the moral rights and duties that emerge from it. There can be cases, however, in which justice and equal membership accounts come into conflict with each other because they impose incompatible demands on either the state or individuals: what justice requires is different from what the good of equal membership requires, and it is impossible to satisfy both. (As a possible illustration, imagine that the good of equal membership provides us with a strong case for *enforcing* a duty to serve one's political community—by forcing citizens to perform 'caring' work or to do military service since these promote the conditions required for this good to be realized—but such a law would represent an unjust restriction on individual liberty.) In these cases, it might be thought that there is a strong reason, perhaps an overwhelming reason, not to implement or enforce what the good of equal membership requires, which derives from Rawls's idea that justice has a primacy which makes it uncompromising:

> Justice is the first virtue of social institutions, as truth is of systems of thought. A theory however elegant and economical must be rejected or revised if it is untrue; likewise laws and institutions no matter how efficient and well-arranged must be reformed or abolished if they are unjust . . . The only thing that permits us to acquiesce in an erroneous theory is the lack of a better one; analogously, an injustice is tolerable only when it is necessary to avoid an even greater injustice. Being first virtues of human activities, truth and justice are uncompromising.[56]

Rawls's view of justice as the first virtue of social institutions implies that it is impermissible to create an injustice, or even tolerate one, except to avoid a greater injustice. (So, for example, a failure to intervene to guarantee a fully adequate scheme of equal basic liberties would not be permissible unless this was the best way of promoting these liberties in the future, or intervening would lead to more serious violations of them.) But it seems to me that this view about the primacy of justice over-states the case. Justice is an important value—it may even be properly described as the first virtue of social institutions—but it is not the only important value, and there may need to be trade-offs between it and these other values, including the good of equal membership.[57]

The remainder of the book will use the different perspectives provided by the equal membership account and the justice account to cast light on a range of issues, focusing especially on the way in which the duties of citizenship these accounts underwrite may bear upon decisions that have often been regarded as irrelevant to citizenship and as of merely private significance. Sometimes I shall simply draw out the implications of one of these accounts because it provides greater illumination than the other in relation to the issue under consideration. In other cases the divergence between these perspectives is itself instructive: the perspectives may complement each other, or they may be in tension in a way that illuminates the relationship between them. In the next chapter I shall explore an area where it might seem that the requirements of justice and the good of equal membership come apart in a way that creates such a tension, namely, the role that each gives to considerations of personal responsibility, in particular how each addresses the issue of when, and to what extent, citizens should be held responsible for their behaviour, especially when a citizen's choices are particularly imprudent and have damaging effects on his own well-being. Some justice accounts, such as those grounded in a 'luck egalitarian' perspective, may hold the view that when individuals make risky decisions without taking measures to offset that risk, and then experience catastrophic effects on their own well-being, there is no duty of justice to come to their aid. Indeed from this perspective, to tax others in order to provide welfare benefits or medical care for imprudent risk-takers would be to exploit those who refrain from risk-taking or (if they do take risks) protect themselves against possible bad consequences, for example, by purchasing appropriate insurance. From the perspective of the equal membership account, however, allowing citizens to fall below a minimum level is to undermine one of the conditions of social and political equality: citizens cannot enjoy equal standing in the polity—they cannot possess equal opportunity to participate on equal terms in either the political process or in civil society—when their basic needs are not being met.

Notes

1. Rawls, *A Theory of Justice*, p. 7/6.
2. See Rawls, *Political Liberalism*, p. 223.
3. A. Abizadeh, 'Cooperation, Pervasive Impact, and Coercion: On the Scope (not Site) of Distributive Justice', *Philosophy and Public Affairs*, Vol. 35, 2007, p. 319.
4. See Cohen, *Rescuing Justice and Equality*, pp. 136ff.
5. See Cohen, *Rescuing Justice and Equality* pp. 136–7. For relevant discussion, see also A. J. Julius, 'Basic Structure and the Value of Equality', *Philosophy and Public Affairs*, Vol. 31, 2003; Murphy, 'Institutions and the Demands of Justice'; Pogge, 'On the Site of Distributive Justice'; S. Scheffler, 'Is the Basic Structure Basic?' in C. Sypnowich (ed.), *The Egalitarian Conscience: Essays in Honour of G. A. Cohen* (Oxford: Oxford University Press, 2006); Williams, 'Incentives, Inequality, and Publicity'.
6. See Murphy, 'Institutions and the Demands of Justice', p. 257; Abizadeh, 'Cooperation, Pervasive Impact, and Coercion', p. 328.
7. Rawls, *Political Liberalism*, p. 266.
8. This is in effect the response that G. A. Cohen would give to the division of labour argument in the context of personal economic behaviour. He endorses a range of 'personal prerogatives' which allow an individual to depart from what the principles of justice that govern basic institutions would require of her if they were applied directly to her personal economic choices in cases when following these principles would unreasonably constrain her pursuit of her own projects, or prevent her from acting on the special concern she has for particular individuals or groups. For further discussion, see Chapter 5, section 1.

9. That is, we are not thereby committed to monism in Liam Murphy's sense: see Murphy, 'Institutions and the Demands of Justice', p. 254. See also Fourie, 'Justice and the Duties of Social Equality'; S. Shiffrin, 'Incentives, Motives, and Talents', *Philosophy and Public Affairs*, Vol. 38, 2010, pp. 111–42.

10. See, for example, J. Spinner, *The Boundaries of Citizenship* (Baltimore: Johns Hopkins University Press, 1994), pp. 45–8; W. Kymlicka, *Politics in the Vernacular: Nationalism, Multiculturalism, and Citizenship* (Oxford: Oxford University Press, 2001), p. 299.

11. Cf. Shiffrin, 'Incentives, Motives, and Talents', p. 127.

12. Consider also Lawrence Blum's instructive example of a white customer who refuses to put their money into the hands of a black cashier in order to avoid physical contact with her: L. Blum, 'Race, National Ideals, and Civic Virtue', *Social Theory and Practice*, 2007, Vol. 33, pp. 546–51.

13. Elizabeth Anderson draws a distinction between racism and a broader category of racial stigmatization: see E. Anderson, *The Imperative of Integration* (Princeton, NJ: Princeton University Press, 2010), p. 48. I would prefer a three-fold distinction between racist, racially prejudiced, and racially stigmatizing behaviour. Like Anderson, I think that the term 'racist behaviour' should be reserved for occasions of 'serious vice' where an individual is fully conscious of what they are doing. Racially prejudiced behaviour captures individual acts that are motivated, consciously or unconsciously, by ideas that denigrate members of a particular race or presuppose that they are inferior. Racial stigmatization takes a wider perspective, and categorizes individual acts by placing them in a wider pattern of behaviour within a society that has a particular meaning and effect.

14. See Spinner, *The Boundaries of Citizenship*, pp. 45–8.

15. See R. Forst, *The Right to Justification* (New York: Columbia University Press, forthcoming).

16. Joseph Carens's work helped me to see the relevance of these cases, particularly a talk on 'Multiculturalism and Immigration' that he gave at the symposium held in honour of Bhikhu Parekh in London in May 2011.

17. See Anderson, *The Imperative of Integration*, especially Ch. 3, for an illuminating account of the way in which these patterns of behaviour cause injustice in the case of African Americans. Anderson does not seem to believe that individual actions of this kind are unjust in themselves: they are unjust because of the injustices they cause, including stigmatization.

18. See A. Kernohan, *Liberalism, Equality, and Cultural Oppression* (Cambridge: Cambridge University Press, 1998), pp. 71–5.

19. In such a world, might not we simply regard those exhibiting these patterns of behaviour as having odd tastes? I think not, if we have good reason to suppose that their behaviour is motivated by prejudice.

20. See Lovett, *A General Theory of Domination and Justice*.

21. Cf. Anderson, *The Imperative of Integration*, p. 103. In fact Anderson understands 'social equality' differently from me: on her understanding, it is a conceptual truth that violations of social equality are forms of domination. The point I go on to

make applies only on the broader conception of social equality that I am working with, according to which social equality consists in treating others as equals in social interactions. According to this conception, failures of social equality need not involve domination.

22. Understood in this way, resident aliens differ from tourists and visitors. I discuss some of the difficulties in distinguishing citizens from resident aliens in my 'Citizens, Resident Aliens and the Good of Equal Membership', in L. Beckman and E. Urman (eds), *The Territories of Citizenship* (Basingstoke: Palgrave Macmillan, forthcoming).

23. See Chapter 1, section 3.

24. See Chapter 1, section 1.

25. See Dagger, *Civic Virtues*, pp. 98–100, 197.

26. There is also a case for saying that, far from being under fewer duties, resident aliens are subject to additional ones. For example, it might be argued that in some circumstances resident aliens have a duty to *become* citizens when they enjoy the benefits of a reasonably just society, on the grounds that fair play requires them to take part in the political process in ways that are possible only when they enjoy the full range of political rights that citizenship brings with it.

27. It might even be the case that there is a general moral obligation to treat others as equals that goes beyond what justice requires and which is grounded in, or expresses, an obligation to give others the equal respect to which they are entitled in virtue of their equal inherent value. If there is a general moral obligation of this kind, it would not make the obligation to treat one's fellow citizens as equals, grounded in the good of equal membership, redundant. In particular cases, the wrongness of failing to treat a person as an equal may be over-determined—there may be a number of reasons that speak in favour of its wrongness—but if we want a full and complete understanding of the moral wrong involved, then we will need to cite all of these reasons. Furthermore, we should not assume that the force of each reason can be understood in isolation, independently of its relationship to the others. The reasons involved may be holistic in character, interacting with each other in various ways: the fact that a failure to treat another as an equals represents a failure to comply with one's citizenly duties may intensify the wrong that is involved in failing to treat them with the equal respect to which they are entitled as a person (see Dancy, *Ethics Without Principles*, pp. 41–2).

28. See R. Rubio-Marin, *Immigration as a Democratic Challenge: Citizenship and Inclusion in Germany and the United States* (Cambridge, Cambridge University Press, 2000), p. 36. Whether it is appropriate to regard a resident alien as a future citizen will depend to some extent of what right of residence he possesses, that is, whether it is short-term or long-term, and what the appropriate principles are for determining access to citizenship.

29. It might also be the case that some duties of citizenship are grounded directly in the specific identity that a person has as a member of a particular polity, and that these may include obligations to be appropriately welcoming of those who come to live and work in it: see Chapter 1, note 56.

30. See R. Baubock, 'Temporary Migration, Partial Citizenship, and Hypermigration', *Critical Review of International Social and Political Philosophy*, Vol. 14, 2011, p. 684.

31. I argue these points in more depth in 'Citizens, Resident Aliens and the Good of Equal Membership'.

32. For endorsements of the all-affected interests principle, see R. Goodin, 'Enfranchising All Affected Interests, and its Alternatives', *Philosophy and Public Affairs*, 2007, Vol. 35, pp. 40–68; I. M. Young, 'Activist Challenges to Deliberative Democracy', in J. S. Fishkin and P. Laslett (eds), *Debating Deliberative Democracy* (Oxford: Blackwell, 2001), pp. 102–20. For relevant discussion, see also L. Beckman, 'Citizenship and Voting Rights: Should Resident Aliens Vote?', *Citizenship Studies*, Vol. 10, 2006, pp. 153–65; D. Owen, 'Transnational Citizenship and the Democratic State: Modes of Membership and Voting Rights', *Critical Review of International Social and Political Philosophy*, Vol. 14, 2011, pp. 643–45; S. Fine, *Immigration and the Right to Exclude* (Oxford: Oxford University Press, forthcoming), Ch. 2.

33. Goodin, 'Enfranchising All Affected Interests, and its Alternatives', p. 52. Goodin distinguishes between several different versions of the all affected interests principle; the incoherence argument is directed against just one of them, viz. 'the all actually affected interests principle'.

34. Owen, 'Transnational Citizenship and the Democratic State', p. 644.

35. See Nozick, *Anarchy, State, and Utopia*, pp. 268–71.

36. See Owen, 'Transnational Citizenship and the Democratic State', pp. 644–45

37. See D. Miller, 'Democracy's Domain', *Philosophy and Public Affairs*, Vol. 37, 2009, pp. 207–10.

38. See A. Abizadeh, 'Democratic Theory and Border Coercion: No Right to Unilaterally Control Your Borders', *Political Theory*, Vol. 36, 2008, p. 41.

39. The coercion principle might instead be regarded as a refinement of the all-affected interests principle, in effect, as specifying that what matters is one's interest in autonomy, an interest which is compromised whenever one is subject to coercion. Cf. Beckman, 'Citizenship and Voting Rights: Should Resident Aliens Vote?', pp. 158ff.

40. See Fine, *Immigration and the Right to Exclude*, Ch. 2.

41. D. Miller, 'Why Immigration Controls Are Not Coercive: A Reply to Arash Abizadeh', *Political Theory*, Vol. 38, 2010, p. 115.

42. Miller, 'Why Immigration Controls Are Not Coercive', p. 114.

43. See A. Abizadeh, 'Democratic Legitimacy and State Coercion: A Reply to David Miller', *Political Theory*, Vol. 38, 2010, 121–30.

44. We might say that in order for a law to be *directed* at a person, she must be in the class of persons to whom the legislators *intended* the law to apply, but a law might *apply* to a person even if she is not in that class. I owe this idea of a law's applying to a person to Sarah Fine: see her *Immigration and the Right to Exclude*, Ch. 2.

45. For what appears to be an example of the first version, see Ludvig Beckman's 'legal conception of the all-affected interests principle': see L. Beckman, *The Frontiers of Democracy: The Right to Vote and its Limits* (Palgrave Macmillan: Basingstoke, 2009), p. 48.

46. In Fine's terms, she is one of that system of law's 'primary addressees'. See Fine, *Immigration and the Right to Exclude*, Ch. 2.
47. According to this formulation, non-resident citizens would be subjected to a law that denied state pensions to citizens living abroad or which denied them diplomatic protection after they had lived abroad for a certain period.
48. See Beckman, *The Frontiers of Democracy*, pp. 80–2.
49. See Beckman, *The Frontiers of Democracy*, pp. 72–3.
50. Fine, *Immigration and the Right to Exclude*, Ch. 2; L. Beckman, 'Is Citizenship Special? Democracy in the Age of Migration and Human Mobility', a paper presented at the conference on 'The Dynamics of Citizenship in the Post-Political World', University of Stockholm, 26–28 May 2010.
51. Beckman, 'Is Citizenship Special?'
52. Some might object to this refinement on the grounds that the acquisition of voting rights should be mandatory for resident aliens. I shall bracket this issue, however.
53. I have not considered all the available alternatives to the all-subjected principle. For example, there is also Rainer Baubock's stakeholder principle, which ties voting rights to citizenship and holds that 'self-governing political communities should include as citizens those individuals whose circumstances of life link their individual autonomy or well-being to the common good of the political community.' (R. Baubock, 'The Rights and Duties of External Citizenship', *Citizenship Studies*, Vol. 13, 2009, p. 479). I favour instead the (second formulation of the) all-subjected principle for allocating voting rights, but for my purposes here what matters is that the correct principle for doing so should be consistent with the existence of bounded political communities. I have considered but argued against those principles which pose the greatest threat to these communities.
54. For somewhat contrasting answers to these questions, see J. Carens, 'The Integration of Immigrants', *Journal of Moral Philosophy*, Vol. 2, 2005, pp. 29–46; Baubock, 'The Rights and Duties of External Citizenship'.
55. See Baubock, 'Temporary Migration, Partial Citizenship, and Hypermigration', p. 684.
56. Rawls, *A Theory of Justice*, pp. 3–4/3–4.
57. As G. A. Cohen argues, there may also need to be trade offs between justice and other goods such as stability and efficiency: see Cohen, *Rescuing Justice and Equality*, p. 304.

Part II
The Practice of Citizenship: Is there . . .

3

A Duty to Avoid State Dependency?

In recent years it has become commonplace to observe that too much emphasis has been placed on the rights or entitlements of citizenship and not enough on its duties or responsibilities.[1] This point has been made in a particularly forceful way in the context of state benefits, where it has been argued that a culture of dependency has been created that, far from enhancing personal autonomy, has actually diminished it. Although this claim has been advanced mainly by those on the right of the political spectrum, and has been used as an excuse for cutting welfare benefits, it ought to be taken seriously by those on the left as well. Even if reducing welfare benefits is not a just response, various practical measures might be implemented by the state to address this supposed problem; for example, those who are unemployed might be allowed to earn a certain amount of money before it affects their benefits, with the amount of benefit they receive after this threshold has been reached being reduced gradually at a lower rate than their increase in earned income, thereby providing them with incentives to wean themselves off it. But there is also a case, both practically and theoretically, for thinking that a deeper solution is required as well, one that involves citizens internalizing a duty to avoid acting in ways that make it likely that they will need to rely upon state-funded benefits.[2]

I shall refer to this as a duty to avoid becoming dependent upon state aid or a duty to avoid state dependency. Such a duty would have potentially far-reaching implications. It would not only mean that citizens had a duty to seek new employment when they lost their jobs (assuming they were otherwise unable to support themselves), but also a duty to ensure that they had saved adequate resources for their retirement, and a duty to look after their health if they were reliant upon state-funded health care, for example, by eating an adequate diet, exercising regularly, losing weight if necessary, and giving up smoking.[3] (The insistence that citizens were under a wide ranging duty of this kind could again be combined with state policies designed to encourage compliance with it, for example, giving tax breaks for pension contributions, or subsidizing access to leisure activities that involve a degree of physical exertion.) It is best understood as a duty to avoid reliance upon state benefits that are funded through compulsory taxation and provided on the basis of need,[4] rather than as a duty to avoid reliance upon benefits that are given to all citizens irrespective of need or which are given only to those who have elected to contribute in order to acquire an entitlement. So understood, the idea that we have a duty to avoid state dependency can be contrasted with two other duties that we might be thought to be under, one of which is more demanding than it whilst the other is less demanding.

The first is a duty to be economically self-sufficient. This is more demanding than a duty to avoid becoming dependent upon state aid, for it seems to require us to eschew non-market economic reliance on others (including, presumably, members of one's own family). The idea that there is such a duty seems to involve an unappealing ideal of independence that is at odds with various voluntary arrangements that people may enter into to be supported financially in projects that are important to them or have non-market value.

The second is a duty to make a productive contribution to society, grounded in a principle of fair reciprocity. Stuart White defends a duty of this kind and is at pains to distinguish it from one grounded in a principle of strict reciprocity, which would require each citizen to make a productive contribution to society that is equivalent to, or at least proportional to, what she is entitled to claim in return. When a duty to make a productive contribution is grounded in a principle of fair reciprocity, it binds those who claim a share of the social product to make a decent productive contribution, proportionate to their abilities, provided that the institutions that govern economic life are sufficiently fair in terms of the opportunities they afford for making such a contribution.[5] This duty appears to be less demanding than the duty to avoid becoming dependent upon state aid since it seems to allow a person to become dependent on it even if she could avoid doing so, provided she has made a contribution proportionate to her abilities. (The extent to which these duties diverge will depend upon what kind of productive contribution the principle of fair reciprocity requires a person with a given set of abilities to make before she is entitled to elect to draw upon the social product without making any further productive contribution,[6] but unless it entails that the size of this contribution will always be insufficient to justify doing so, they will diverge in some cases.) This is not an objection to such a principle, but it might be thought that it needs to be supplemented by a duty to avoid state dependency.

In this chapter, I shall evaluate the case for saying that citizens (and indeed resident aliens) are under a duty to avoid state dependency in so far as it is within their power to do so. My argument will take place mainly at the level of ideal theory, that is, I shall start from the assumption that society is governed by reasonably just institutions, and that there is a reasonably just distribution of opportunities and resources.[7] I shall for the most part bracket the issue of the extent to which a duty to avoid state dependency might be justified in non-ideal societies. Even if citizens in a just society are under a duty to avoid state dependency, the worst off might not be in an unjust society where they had a smaller share of wealth and income than what they were entitled to, or lacked a fair opportunity to acquire a larger share. Under such circumstances, dependency on the state might serve, partly or wholly, to rectify that injustice. I shall assume, however, that there are limits to how unjust a society can be in terms of its distribution of resources if it provides welfare and health benefits to those who are in need of them through no fault of their own. And even if these benefits are insufficient in practice to enable every citizen to lead a decent life, or distributive justice requires more than sufficiency, the idea that at least the better off in such a society are under a duty to avoid state dependency is plausible—or no less plausible than the idea that citizens in general would be under such a duty in a just society.

It might be thought that a duty to avoid becoming dependent upon state benefits has a clear role in justice accounts which endorse the idea that when people are unable to meet their needs as a result of their own imprudence, they have no entitlement of justice to be looked after. Those who end up in this predicament might be thought to exploit the prudent if they draw state benefits. I begin by considering this view, which, contrary to initial appearances, struggles to make room for a duty to avoid state dependency, for it seems to imply that it would be unjust for the state to come to the aid of those who are responsible for creating their own needs, with the result that such a duty would be redundant so long as the state behaves justly and refrains from doing so. I argue, however, that a justice account informed by this view may nevertheless allow space for such a duty, not least because it can be combined with an equal membership account, which supplies a powerful reason that derives from the good of equal membership to come to the aid of the needy regardless of how their needs arose. In order to underwrite a duty to avoid state dependency in this way, however, we would need to reject the idea that considerations of justice always trump the good of equal membership when the two come into conflict. I then move on to consider two other approaches which can ground a duty to avoid state dependency without having to appeal to the importance of the good of equal membership because they maintain that there is always a reason of justice to look after those who cannot meet their own needs, regardless of whether they are responsible for creating these needs or being unable to meet them.

1 Responsibility and the reason-disabling view

I shall simply assume that when people are unable to meet their own needs through no fault of their own, then there is a reason of justice (or a justice

89

reason, as I shall refer to it) for helping them, and a corresponding *pro tanto* duty of justice to do so.[8] But when people *are* responsible for their plight, does this entail that there is no justice reason to come to their aid, and could the absence of such a reason play a role in grounding the idea that citizens have a duty not to become dependent on the state?

Before addressing this question, let me make some preliminary remarks about responsibility. What conditions have to be met before a person can properly be said to be responsible for her plight in the relevant sense is a matter of dispute. But I shall assume that these conditions can be adequately specified and that they are met when a person has the various capacities necessary for it to be intelligible for us to appraise her behaviour from a moral point of view[9] and where she ends up being unable to meet her own needs in a way that was reasonably avoidable[10]—either because she took a calculated risk when other less risky and reasonable options were available, or because she was negligent, or because she simply chose to place herself in a position where she knew she would be unable to meet her needs. In general at least, we might say that rock climbing is a reasonably avoidable activity, as is drinking excessively (at least for those who are not alcoholics), whereas crossing the road to go to the supermarket or travelling to work are not—though each may be performed in careful or negligent ways. I shall use phrases such as 'is responsible for her plight', 'bears responsibility for her needs', and 'has self-inflicted needs' interchangeably, to pick out the diverse set of cases in which people with the required rational capacities end up with needs that they are unable to meet through acting in ways that are reasonably avoidable.

An individual's responsibility for her plight does sometimes seem to make at least some difference to the issue of whether justice requires us to help her. Suppose, for example, that we have to decide which of two individuals in need we should benefit, one of whom is responsible for her position because she acted recklessly despite repeated advice and warnings from others, whereas the other is simply the victim of brute bad luck (perhaps he was struck by an unexpected flash of lightning). It is hard to believe that this difference between the two of them has *no* bearing at all on the justice of helping one rather than the other. In my view, we should accept that responsibility can make a difference here. The difficulty is how best to capture that difference in terms of the justice reasons we have for helping or not helping those who bear responsibility for their own needs, and the implications of these reasons for the question of whether citizens have a duty not to become dependent on the state.

Consider the idea that there is a justice reason for benefiting a person who is not in a position to lead a decent or satisfactory life but this exists *only* when she is not responsible for her plight. The fact that a person is responsible for her needs removes or 'disables' the justice reason we would otherwise have for aiding her.[11] Let me call this *the reason-disabling view*. When the state is acting justly, it is not obvious that the reason-disabling view has space for the idea that there is a duty not to become dependent on it. Since the reason-disabling view denies that the state has a reason of justice to take care of those with self-inflicted needs, a duty to avoid becoming dependent on it would not seem to have any role to play when it acts justly: if the reason-disabling view is correct, then it seems that the state would not be entitled to provide aid to those who are responsible for creating their own needs and, in the absence of that aid, the idea that there is a duty not to become dependent on the state would be *redundant*.

It is important, however, to distinguish two different versions of the reason-disabling view. The first version maintains that an individual's responsibility for her needs is a justice reason for not helping her which disables our justice reason for coming to her aid, whereas the second version maintains that her responsibility for her plight disables our reason for helping her without *itself* being a reason for not coming to her aid.[12] Although the first version struggles to make space for the idea that citizens have a duty to avoid state dependency, at least when the state is acting justly, the second version may be able to make room for it since it is not committed to the idea that the state acts unjustly when it comes to the aid of those with self-inflicted needs they might reasonably have avoided.

There is in any case good reason to reject the idea that there is a justice reason for not helping someone who is responsible for his plight. For it implies that there is a justice reason for opposing even voluntary charitable schemes for helping those who are responsible for their own needs, yet that seems indefensible. To this it might be replied that when a person is responsible for her plight, she *deserves* to remain needy, so there is a justice reason not to help her.[13] But we need to distinguish between the view that a person doesn't deserve to be helped and the view that a person deserves to remain needy. The former view, which does not entail that there is a justice reason not to help those who are responsible for their plight, has some plausibility, but in general the latter is surely too harsh in its implications. (This is not to deny that there may sometimes be instrumental reasons, unrelated to desert, for being harsh in such cases, for example, to encourage prudence). The idea might be that those who are responsible for their own plight deserve to be punished by being forced to remain needy in much the same way that those who have committed some crime deserved an appropriate punishment for it. But even if one accepts a retributive theory of punishment, it is not clear why we should think that mere imprudence merits punishment—especially not the punishment of being forced to remain needy, which would in some cases be massively disproportionate given that it may result in the death of the imprudent person.

The reason-disabling view might nevertheless maintain that there is a justice reason not to *force* others, through compulsory taxation, to help a person when he is responsible for his plight, even if there is no justice reason not to help him. This position would also seem to imply that a duty to avoid becoming dependent on the state would be redundant when the state is acting justly, but it might seem more plausible than a view which maintains that there is a justice reason not to help those responsible for their plight, since it does not imply any objection to charitable giving. In support of this idea, it might be argued that to force others, through compulsory taxation, to help those who are responsible for their own needs would be to sanction the exploitation of the prudent. Those who do not take risks, for example, will be forced to come to the aid of those who do so when their risk-taking turns out badly. There is some weight to this claim in some circumstances, especially when the risk-takers fail to insure against those risks when they could easily afford to do so, and the others (some of whom may be worse off than the risk-takers) either insure or refrain from taking the risks. But is it *always* the case that forcing others to help those who are responsible for their own needs is to sanction the exploitation of the prudent? To exploit someone is to take unfair advantage of her. Sometimes at least, people take risks which turn out badly for them in circumstances where others routinely take the same risks without any bad consequences. In these cases to characterize them as 'taking advantage of others' does not seem appropriate: everyone is equally reckless, but some are lucky. The idea that there is a justice reason not to force the reckless but lucky to help the no more reckless but unlucky seems misplaced.[14] So whether we have a justice reason not to force others to help those who are responsible for their own needs depends in part upon the choices that these others make.

In practice, of course, a society will consist of some who do not take these risks, some who take the risks but are lucky, and some who take these risks and are unlucky, and it will be hard to separate out the different groups. Under these circumstances defenders of the reason-disabling view might plausibly argue that any potential unfairness can be avoided by forcing each person to purchase insurance which protects him against various forms of misfortune, such as bad health or unemployment. If everyone, including the imprudent, is forced to do so, it is hard to sustain the argument that the prudent are being exploited, provided the size of the contribution a person is required to make varies with her propensity or willingness to engage in risk-taking behaviour. (Unless risk takers, such as smokers—or, at least, those smokers who could choose not to smoke and have reasonable alternatives—pay higher premiums, defenders of the reason-disabling view can argue that smokers will be exploiting non-smokers. The latter could be regarded as subsidizing the health care of the former when smokers foreseeably develop smoking related illnesses.)

When such a scheme is in place, however, it might be denied that those forced to contribute to it have a duty to avoid acting in ways that make it likely that they will become dependent on the benefits provided by it, since they have in effect paid to indemnify themselves against the risks carried by these ways of behaving. It might nevertheless seem that there is some space left for a duty to avoid state dependency to occupy. For it is hard to see how an insurance scheme, properly so called, could allow a person to indemnify herself against each and every way in which she might become needy as a result of her own actions. For example, a person will not be able to insure herself against simply giving up a job on a whim in circumstances when she knows that she will be unable to find an alternative source of income—or, at least, the insurance in this case would have to be set at a rate that would make it unreasonable to purchase. Forms of behaviour of this kind are not a matter of taking a *risk* in the ordinary sense of that term, but rather of choosing to place oneself in a position where one knows one will be unable to meet one's own needs. So some ways in which a person may create needs she is unable to meet would not be covered by these schemes—those where her neediness is a certain or near certain outcome of a choice she makes in full knowledge of the consequences of that choice—and in these cases the issue will still arise of whether there is any reason of justice to force others to come to her aid. Here it could not be argued that others have also gambled but have been lucky, so a defender of the reason-disabling view may maintain, plausibly enough, that it would be unjust to force them to help her through taxation. Again, however, when the state acts justly these cases do not seem to bring into play the idea that citizens have a duty to avoid becoming dependent on the state. So long as the state acts justly, such a duty would be redundant in relation to these cases since (according to the reason-disabling view, when it is developed in the way envisaged) the state could not justly tax its citizens in order to come to the aid of those who have simply chosen to place themselves in a position where they cannot meet their own needs.

There is also another type of case—different from those in which a person takes risks he is insured against that turn out badly and from those in which a person simply chooses to place himself in a situation where he knows he will be unable to meet his own needs. This type of case arises when a person is unable to contribute to a compulsory insurance scheme, perhaps because he has never been gainfully employed, but he takes risks which he would have been insured against had he been able to contribute, and as a result ends up in need. Such cases are trickier, but it is hard for the reason-disabling view to avoid the conclusion that the state has no reason of justice to take care of the person in need, and indeed would act unjustly if it used the proceeds of compulsory taxation in order to do so. So, again, this does not seem to make space for the idea that there is duty to avoid becoming dependent on the state. (Of course, the question would need to be raised of whether in a just society anyone could be in a position where he were unable to contribute to such schemes. Those, for example, who think that everyone is entitled to a basic income may argue that this income will always be sufficient for a person to be able to contribute to these schemes and thereby meet his ordinary needs for food, shelter, and health care.)

So it might seem that there is no place within the reason-disabling view for the idea that there is a duty not to become dependent on state aid, at least when the state acts justly. But I want to suggest that there are nevertheless at least two ways in which such a duty might be given a justified role. First, there may be a variety of reasons in practice for favouring insurance schemes which allow the prudent to be exploited to some degree. Given the practical difficulties involved in accurately determining what risks people take, or are inclined to take, defenders of the reason-disabling view can acknowledge that there is a strong case for not attempting to set premiums in a way that is sensitive to individual propensities to engage in risk-taking behaviour, even though that will permit the exploitation of the prudent, and instead inculcating a duty to avoid becoming dependent upon state aid. There may also be reasons of respect for persons why we should not seek to *find out* whether a person is engaging in risky activities that would require a higher premium because that may require people to indulge in what Jonathan Wolff calls 'shameful revelation' in a way that is humiliating for them.[15] This would provide us with principled reasons for putting in place an insurance scheme that potentially involved some degree of exploitation of those who avoid risk-taking behaviour, in addition to the pragmatic reasons we have for setting insurance premiums in a way that is independent of individuals' propensities to take risks. It might then plausibly be argued that citizens are under a duty to avoid becoming dependent on the state in order to *reduce* the exploitation of those who refrain from risk-taking behaviour.

The second way in which a defender of the reason-disabling view might accommodate a duty to avoid state dependency involves recognizing that there may be reasons that warrant the state coming to the aid of people with self-inflicted needs even when in doing so it acts unjustly. One promising way of developing this approach is through an appeal to the good of equal membership.[16] The good of equal membership seems to provide an unconditional reason to ensure that each citizen's basic needs are met, regardless of how they arise. The good of equal membership consists, in part, of being an equal member of a collective that makes decisions which importantly affect its members conditions of existence, and which provides equal opportunity to participate on equal terms in the political process and in civil society and beyond. Those whose basic needs are not met do not possess an equal opportunity of this sort. The equal membership account in effect provides a reason for ensuring that the basic needs of citizens are met even when these needs are a result of behaviour they might reasonably have avoided and the consequences of which they are not indemnified against.

Invoking the equal membership account in this way also enables defenders of the reason-disabling view to answer one objection that has been levelled against compulsory insurance schemes, namely, that even if these schemes are fair because they preserve equal freedom and can in principle prevent the imprudent from being exploited, they nevertheless deprive their members (both the prudent and the imprudent) of the option of *not* insuring against disasters that may befall them, and for this reason these schemes restrict individual freedom in a way that is objectionably paternalistic.[17] The equal membership account provides a way of countering these charges, for defenders of it can argue that this restriction of individual freedom is justified on the grounds that it is required in order to secure the good of equal membership rather than for paternalistic reasons.[18]

The approach I am envisaging, which involves combining a reason-disabling view with an appeal to the good of equal membership, would give a potential role for the idea that citizens have a duty to avoid becoming dependent on the state. For although there is a reason grounded in the good of equal membership for helping a person to meet her needs even when they are self-inflicted, the reason-disabling view maintains that there is also a reason of justice for not forcing others to help those with self-inflicted needs when this would involve a degree of exploitation, which provides each citizen with a reason to try to avoid placing herself in a position where she becomes dependent upon the state. In order for this position to be coherent, however, it would have to suppose that on at least some occasions reasons grounded in the good of equal membership may take priority over justice reasons, otherwise there would be no cases where a person could avoid becoming dependent on the state but the state could be justifiably required to take care of her if she did. In other words this position must deny the absolute primacy of justice.[19]

It might be argued, however, that there is no real tension between reasons of justice and reasons deriving from the good of equal membership and that the appeal to the good of equal membership is unnecessary in this context. A justice account which incorporates the reason-disabling view may argue that justice consists of a number of fundamental principles, including a principle of liberty which provides us with 'an equal right to a fully adequate scheme of equal basic liberties which is compatible with a similar scheme of liberties for all'.[20] If this scheme of basic liberties includes political liberty, as it does in Rawls's theory, then there will be space for the idea that there is a reason of justice for ensuring that everyone's basic needs are met, irrespective of how those needs arose. Indeed, any theory of justice that, first, has a weighty independent commitment to political liberty, second, acknowledges that a person's ability to exercise her political liberty effectively is deeply impaired when his basic needs are not met,[21] and third, holds that individuals cannot forfeit their right to these basic liberties, or to the conditions required to exercise them effectively, simply by acting irresponsibly, will be well-disposed towards to the idea that there is a reason of justice for ensuring that everyone's needs are met regardless of how those needs arose. (A justice account formed on this basis would involve a complex version of the reason-disabling view: it would hold that some, but not all, of our justice reasons to aid a person who cannot meet her own needs are disabled by her responsibility for her plight.) Framed in this way, a principle of liberty would seem to have the same effect as a principle grounded in the good of equal membership that required each citizen to have equal access to that good—indeed they would be grounded in considerations that are at least partially overlapping—but giving priority to the principle of liberty would be consistent with a commitment to the primacy of justice.

Is the equal membership account therefore redundant in explaining how a justice account that incorporates the reason-disabling view can underwrite a duty to avoid state dependency? It is true that in some versions of the justice account that incorporate the reason-disabling view, there is no need to appeal to the equal membership account in order to defend a duty to avoid state dependency. But if a theory of justice employs the reason-disabling view as part of an *interpretation* of what a commitment to equal freedom requires, it could not then coherently appeal to an *independent* principle of liberty to trump any reasons it claims we also have for not forcing others to aid those who are responsible for their plight. Even if a principle of liberty is grounded independently, those who endorse the reason-disabling view can coherently maintain that the political liberty of those with self-inflicted needs is not unfairly restricted by their inability as a result to be able to exercise it effectively. In these cases, the equal membership account can still play an important role in justifying the idea that there is a duty to avoid state dependency.

2 Reason-balancing and reason-attenuating

The reason-disabling view is not the only way of conceptualizing the impact that a person's responsibility for his plight has upon our justice reasons for helping him. It competes with two other views, which I shall call the reasons-balancing view and the reason-attenuating view. Both of these views find it easier to make space for the idea that there is a duty to avoid becoming dependent on the state. Indeed both can do so without needing to appeal to the good of equal membership—or even to the various pragmatic and principled reasons we have in practice for favouring a compulsory insurance scheme that allows the prudent to be exploited to some degree.

The reasons-balancing view maintains that there is always a justice reason for helping a person who is not in a position to lead a decent or satisfactory life regardless of whether she is responsible for her own plight (and this reason is always of the same strength for a given level of need), but when she is responsible for it, there is either a justice reason for not helping her, or a justice reason for not forcing others to do so, that has to be weighed against it in determining what justice requires.[22] As with the reason-disabling view, the most plausible version of the reasons-balancing view is one which denies that there is a justice reason for not helping a person who is responsible for creating needs she cannot meet, but which maintains that (in some cases at least) there is a justice reason for not forcing others to do so through compulsory taxation, and that this justice reason derives from the fact that forcing others to help potentially involves exploiting the prudent. The reasons-balancing view differs from the reason-disabling view in maintaining that there is always a reason of justice for benefiting someone who is in need regardless of whether she is responsible for her plight, whereas the reason-disabling view maintains that there is a reason of justice for benefiting someone who is in need only when she is not responsible for her plight. (Note that the reasons-balancing view may maintain that the strength of our reason for benefiting a person when she is responsible for her plight increases the worse off she is.)

The reasons-balancing view will support the idea that there is a duty of justice not to become dependent on the state, but again we need to distinguish different cases: first, those where a person takes risks he is insured against that turn out badly; second, those where a person simply chooses a course of action that she knows for certain will mean that he becomes dependent on the state; third, those where a person is unable to contribute to an insurance scheme but he takes risks that would have been insured against had he been able to contribute. In the first type of case, when insurance premiums are set in a way that takes account of different individual propensities to engage in risk-taking behaviour, there is no role for a duty to avoid state dependency, for under these circumstances there is no reason of justice why citizens should not engage in this type of behaviour or receive the insured benefits when things turn out badly. When, more practicably, insurance premiums are set in a way that is independent of individuals' propensity to take risks, there is a role for such a duty on the grounds that those who on average take greater risks are exploiting the prudent who on average take fewer risks. Both the second and third types of case can also make space for the idea that there is a duty to avoid state dependency, since they can argue that in both circumstances there is a reason for the state to take care of those who end up needy that at least sometimes justifies it doing so, but also a reason for people to avoid ending up in this position that derives from the fact that it is unjust (because unfair) for taxes to be extracted from others to pay for care for them.

There is also a further way of conceptualizing the impact that a person's responsibility for his plight has upon our justice reasons for helping him that differs from both the reason-disabling view and the reasons-balancing view but has considerable plausibility. I shall call it the *reason-attenuating view*. Like the reasons-balancing view it holds that there is always a justice reason for benefiting a person who is not in a position to lead a decent or satisfactory life, but in contrast to that view it maintains that this reason is less strong, that is, it is attenuated, when he is responsible for his plight.[23] The reason-attenuating view, like the reasons-balancing view, can allow that the strength of the justice reason we have for helping someone who is responsible for her plight will depend in part upon how difficult and how costly it would have been for her to avoid the predicament in which she now finds herself, which seems more plausible than holding that there is some threshold, namely, whether her predicament was reasonably avoidable, above which we have no justice reason for helping her, which is an implication of the reason-disabling view.

Like both the reason-disabling view and the reasons-balancing view, the reason-attenuating view has two versions, only one of which seems plausible. According to the first version, an individual's responsibility for her neediness is a justice reason for not aiding her which attenuates our justice reason for helping her, whereas according to the second version her responsibility for her plight attenuates our justice reason for helping her without itself being a justice reason for not doing so. For reasons that are now familiar, only the second version is plausible. Again, however, the second version might maintain that there is sometimes a justice reason for not *forcing others* to aid those who are responsible for their own plight, even if there is no justice reason not to help them, on the grounds that in some cases to do so would be to exploit the prudent. As before, the problem of exploitation can be partially resolved by compulsory insurance schemes which require individuals to pay premiums that take account of their propensity to engage in risk-taking behaviour, but this then shrinks the space that a duty to avoid state dependency can occupy in a just state. The space for that duty is increased when, for practical or principled reasons, insurance premiums are levied at a rate that is independent of individuals' propensity to take risks, for under these circumstances those who refrain from risk-taking behaviour are exploited to some degree by those who engage in it. Like the reasons-balancing view, the reason-attenuating view can also underwrite a duty not to become dependent upon the state in cases not covered by these schemes. When individuals are contemplating choosing to put themselves in a position where they know they will not be able to meet their needs, the reason-attenuating view can coherently maintain that they are under a duty not to do so because it can recognize the injustice that would be involved in forcing those who do not behave in this way to help them, but (like the reasons-balancing view, though not the reason-disabling view) it can acknowledge that there would nevertheless still be a duty of justice to come to their aid if they were to choose to do so.

3 Responsibility and the good of equal membership

Like versions of the justice account which incorporate the reason-disabling view, the equal membership account struggles on its own to justify the idea that citizens have an obligation to avoid becoming dependent on the state. The equal membership account implies an unconditional commitment to ensuring that each citizen's basic needs are met, regardless of how they arise, and does not seem to provide us with a reason why citizens should care about becoming dependent upon the state. As I have already suggested, however, when the equal membership account is combined with the reason-disabling view, it can provide a way of justifying the idea that there is a duty to avoid state dependency. Furthermore, the equal membership account can instead be combined with either the reasons-balancing view or the reason-attenuating view to strengthen the case we have for looking after those in need no matter how those needs arose, or to provide an additional reason for doing so that has to be taken into consideration.

But one might wonder whether the equal membership account, like the justice account, has to give personal responsibility some role. Might it be argued that equal status is something that has to be *earned* and that it is something that should be forfeited under certain conditions? If so, how would this affect the claim that there is always a reason, grounded in the good of equal membership, for coming to the aid of those in need, even if they are responsible for their plight? Any argument of this sort would have to explain why the equal status that is intrinsic to citizenship is something that needs to be earned rather than simply accorded, and how it is to be earned. The idea might be that equal status has to be earned through making some kind of positive contribution to society, and that it is justifiable to deprive those who are able to make such a contribution but choose not to do so of full access to the good of equal membership.[24] But even if in some cases there is a justice reason for taking measures that may result in depriving a person of equal access to that good, such as reducing his welfare benefits, my claim has been that this reason competes with the powerful one we have for respecting and promoting the good of equal membership and that *this* reason does not depend on whether or not an individual has made a positive contribution to society. In this context it is important to distinguish not only between justice reasons and reasons which derive from the good of equal membership but also between being a citizen, including possessing the equal status that is intrinsic to it, and being a *good* citizen. Citizens may be under a duty to contribute to the political community to which they belong, and as a result they may fail to be good citizens when they do not comply with this duty. But there would need to be a further argument to show that a person could justifiably be deprived of his equal status—a status required for him to enjoy the good of equal membership—simply by failing to be a good citizen.

Even if equal status is something that we have a powerful reason for granting to citizens rather than requiring them to earn, is it legitimate to suppose that they forfeit it if they make a *negative* contribution to society? Those who are imprisoned because they have broken the law forfeit, at least temporarily, their right of free movement within the state and their right of free association. In this way they are treated for a period of time as lacking equal status with other citizens in the polity. Provided the laws they break are reasonably just and they were given a fair trial, their lack of equal status would seem to be justified.[25] The justice and other reasons we have for depriving people of their liberty when they commit serious crimes overwhelm and perhaps even disable our reasons, grounded in the good of equal membership, for preserving their equality of status. But these reasons could not plausibly be extended to argue that *mere imprudence* was sufficient to warrant depriving people of the welfare benefits or health care that they needed to enjoy the good of equal membership. The fact that people are responsible for creating their needs does not disable the reasons we have, grounded in the good of equal membership, to come to their aid, even if we were to suppose that responsibility of this kind disables our justice reasons for doing so.

4 Concluding Remarks

If an entitlement to state aid is conditional upon not being responsible for one's inability to meet one's own needs, then it can seem that there is little, if any space, for a citizen's duty to avoid becoming dependent upon it, at least when the state is acting justly: either one cannot avoid doing so, in which case such a duty would be irrelevant, or one becomes dependent in a way that is a foreseeable and avoidable consequence of one's own choices, in which case one's entitlement to state aid is called into question and the duty appears to be redundant. There are a number of ways, however, in which the idea that there is a duty to avoid state dependency might be given a defensible role. I have argued that a justice account, even when it holds that in many cases there is a reason of justice not to force others, through taxation, to come to the aid of those who are responsible for their own needs, can make space for a duty to avoid state dependency when it is combined with an equal membership account. Indeed it might seem that combining a justice account which incorporates a reason-disabling view of this kind with an equal membership account remedies deficiencies that each suffers from when considered in isolation. For the reason-disabling view seems too harsh unless it is combined with a commitment to ensuring that every citizen's basic needs are met, of the sort that flows naturally from an equal membership account, whilst the idea that there is an unconditional commitment to meeting every citizen's basic needs might seem to give insufficient weight to considerations of personal responsibility. However, this way of defending a duty to avoid state dependency relies on denying the absolute primacy of justice. The tension between a justice account which incorporates the reason-disabling view and an equal membership account can be resolved in favour of such a duty by supposing that the good of equal membership can sometimes legitimately outweigh considerations of justice.

Notes

1. A. Etzioni, *The Spirit of Community: Rights, Responsibilities, and the Communitarian Agenda* (New York: Crown Publishers, 1993); D. Selbourne, *The Principle of Duty* (London: Sinclair-Stevenson, 1994); W. Kymlicka and W. Norman, 'Return of the Citizen: A Survey of Recent Work on Citizenship Theory', *Ethics*, Vol. 104, 1994, pp. 355–69; L. Mead, *Beyond Entitlement: The Social Obligations of Citizenship* (New York: Free Press, 1986).
2. This is weaker than a duty to *minimize the risk* that one will have to rely on state-funded benefits. But such a duty would be highly demanding—excessively so, in my view—and arguably its internalization would stifle risk-taking behaviour in a way that had undesirable social consequences.
3. Could such a duty be met by opting out of state-funded health care altogether and joining a private scheme? Even if it could be met in this way, it might be the case that in opting out, in unjust societies at least, citizens are violating a further duty (which I discuss in Chapter 5) not to secure unfair advantages. Education raises similar issues since opting out of state-funded schooling may undermine equality of opportunity and be a way of securing unfair advantages for one's child. It might in any case be regarded as implausible to suppose that a duty to avoid state dependency applies to educational provision, for if it did it would seem to entail that we should avoid having children altogether unless we can afford to pay the full costs of their education. Note, however, that this entailment would be endorsed by those who maintain that it is just (in ideal societies at least) to require people to bear the full costs of their choices, including the choice to have children.

4. The concept of a need raises various philosophical worries, but I shall not address them here. For relevant discussion, see D. Braybooke, *Meeting Needs* (Princeton, NJ: Princeton University Press, 1987); R. Plant, *Modern Political Thought* (Oxford: Blackwell, 1991), Ch. 5; L. Hamilton, *The Political Philosophy of Needs* (Cambridge: Cambridge University Press, 2003). Although I do not argue it here, I would prefer to define a person's needs as anything they require to lead a decent (or satisfactory or minimally flourishing) life. This idea also requires elucidation, but understood in this way, a person's needs go beyond what are often understood to be his *basic* needs: see Fabre, *Whose Body is it Anyway?*, p. 31.

5. White, *The Civic Minimum*, Ch. 3.

6. White discusses the basic work expectation that might be laid down, in both ideal and non-ideal societies, in order for the contributive obligation involved in the principle of fair reciprocity to be met. See White, *The Civic Minimum*, Ch. 5, section 3.

7. For those who harbour doubts about the value of this kind of ideal theory, I offer some further reflections in the Conclusion.

8. This view that there is a justice reason for aiding a person who is not responsible for her plight is held in common by a number of different theories of justice, at least provided it is qualified in various ways. Theories which are committed to some strict form of equality (whether of resources, welfare, opportunity for welfare, or some other form of 'advantage'), or which subscribe to a form of equality which permits inequalities when everyone benefits from them or no one loses, imply that there is a reason for aiding those whose basic needs have not been met, so long as this has the effect of making people more equal in terms of whatever measure is being employed. Prioritarian views which hold that we have a justice reason to give priority to benefiting the worse off when other things are equal will entail that we have a justice reason to give priority to those whose basic needs have not been met when we are in a position to do so, at least so long as we could not provide larger benefits to better off people or the same sized benefits to greater numbers of them. Sufficiency views which maintain that there is a justice reason to benefit those who are not in a position to lead a decent life would entail that we have a reason to help those in need when we are able to do so. The idea that there is a justice reason to help those not responsible for their plight would, however, be rejected by some theories, for example, it would be rejected by forms of libertarianism which maintain that provided those in need have no property rights that are being violated, there is no justice reason to come to their aid even if their basic needs are not being met.

9. This is what T. M. Scanlon refers to as the attributability sense of responsibility: see T. M. Scanlon, *What We Owe to Each Other* (Cambridge, MA: Harvard University Press, 1998), pp. 248–9.

10. For relevant discussion, see P. Vallentyne, 'Brute Luck, Option Luck, and Equality of Initial Opportunities', *Ethics*, Vol. 112, 2002, pp. 533–8; K. Voigt, 'The Harshness Objection: Is Luck Egalitarianism Too Harsh on the Victims of Option Luck', *Ethical Theory and Moral Practice*, Vol. 10, 2007, pp. 389–407, at p. 397; S. Segall, *Health, Luck, and Justice* (Princeton, NJ: Princeton University Press, 2010), pp. 19–24.

11. I borrow the language of 'disabling' from Jonathan Dancy: see Dancy, *Ethics Without Principles*, esp. pp. 38–52. Dancy stresses the holistic character of moral reasons, that is, the way in which something which counts as a reason in one context may not (or may count as an opposite reason) in another context where different considerations are present. But it is a complex question what the relationship is between a holism of reasons and the moral particularism that Dancy defends. See S. McKeever and M. Ridge, *Principled Ethics: Generalism as a Regulative Ideal* (Oxford: Oxford University Press, 2006), Chs. 1–2, for distinctions between different forms of particularism and a discussion of the relationship between holism and moral particularism. I discuss the relevance of particularism and holism about reasons for theorizing about justice in 'Justice, Holism, and Principles' *Res Publica*, Vol. 15, 2009, pp. 179–94.

12. For a discussion of how, in effect, these contrasting positions might emerge from different ways of interpreting (what is often referred to as) 'luck egalitarianism', see Segall, *Health, Luck, and Justice*, pp. 14–19.

13. It might also be argued that justice requires that even voluntary giving should be sensitive to the issue of whether a person's needs are self-inflicted, on the grounds that others whose needs are not self-inflicted might reasonably complain that their needs should be given priority. But at best this shows that there is a justice reason to give priority to those whose needs are not self-inflicted, rather than that there is always a justice reason not to help those whose needs are self-inflicted.

14. There is a large literature on the idea of option luck and how it may justify unequal outcomes: see especially R. Dworkin, *Sovereign Virtue: The Theory and Practice of Equality* (Cambridge, MA: Harvard University Press, 2000), pp. 73–7; Vallentyne, 'Brute Luck, Option Luck, and Equality of Initial Opportunities', pp. 529–57; K. Lippert-Rasmussen, 'Egalitarianism, Option Luck, and Responsibility', *Ethics*, Vol. 111, 2001, pp. 548–79; M. Fleurbaey, *Fairness, Responsibility, and Welfare* (Oxford: Oxford University Press, 2008), Ch. 6; G. A. Cohen, 'Fairness and Legitimacy in Justice, and: Does Option Luck Ever Preserve Justice?', *On the Currency of Egalitarian Justice, and Other Essays in Political Philosophy* (Princeton, NJ: Princeton University Press, 2011), Ch. 6.

15. See J. Wolff, 'Fairness, Respect, and the Egalitarian Ethos', *Philosophy and Public Affairs*, Vol. 27, 1998, pp. 97–122; E. Anderson, 'What is the Point of Equality?', *Ethics*, Vol. 109, 1999, pp. 287–337.

16. This is not the only way in which this strategy might be employed, however. It might appeal instead to humanitarian reasons, or to reasons relating to the value of solidarity, understood as arising independently of justice. Shlomi Segall appears to pursue the latter approach: see his 'In Solidarity with the Imprudent: A Defence of Luck Egalitarianism, *Social Theory and Practice*, Vol. 33, 2007, esp. pp. 195–7, and *Health, Luck, and Justice*, esp. Ch. 4.

17. See Anderson, 'What is the Point of Equality?', p. 301; I. Carter, 'Equal Opportunity and Equal Freedom', a paper presented to the workshop on Equality of Opportunity at the ECPR Joint Sessions, Granada, 14–19 April 2005.

18. This is not the only non-paternalistic justification that might be given for depriving members of these schemes of the option of not insuring. If there is a

humanitarian moral obligation to help those in need regardless of whether their needs are self-inflicted, we might be justified in restricting individual liberty in order to avoid being placed in a position whereby we are morally required to act on that obligation. See P. Bou-Habib, 'Compulsory Insurance Without Paternalism', *Utilitas*, Vol. 18, 2006, 243–63.

19. See Chapter 2, Concluding Remarks.

20. Rawls, *Political Liberalism*, p. 291.

21. Rawls, for example, not only gives his principle of liberty priority over other principles of justice, but also requires that each person's political liberty should have a fair value. See Chapter 1, section 3.

22. The reasons-balancing view, as I shall construe it, does not rule out the possibility that a reason of one of these types always outweighs a reason of the other type. But if there is a reason of justice for not forcing others to help a person who is responsible for his needs that always outweighs our reason of justice for helping him, no matter how great his needs, then this version of the reasons-balancing view is likely to have the same practical consequences as the reason-disabling view.

23. I borrow the language of 'attenuating' from Dancy again: see Dancy, *Ethics Without Principles*, p. 42.

24. Lawrence Mead, for example, maintains that in America 'Equality is not so much an entitlement, a status, as an *activity*. To be equal an American must *do* things, not just claim them' (Mead, *Beyond Entitlement*, p. 239).

25. In many states prisoners are also deprived of their voting rights, but it is much less clear that this practice can be justified. It seems to fall foul of both versions of the all-subjected principle that I considered in Chapter 2, section 3. See Beckman, *The Frontiers of Democracy*, Ch. 5, for further discussion.

4

A Duty to Share Domestic Burdens?

Is there a duty to share domestic burdens and, if so, can it properly be regarded as a duty of citizenship? If there is such a duty, does it imply that mothers and fathers should be equally involved in the raising of their children? There is considerable resistance to the idea that duties of this kind could be part of citizenship, some of which arises from the widespread belief that one acts as a citizen in the public rather than the private sphere. In this chapter, I shall examine the implications of both the justice account and the equal membership account for domestic life, focusing in particular on the distribution of domestic burdens and, within that category, on the distribution of the burdens associated with caring for children.

If principles of justice apply to individual choices as well as the basic structure of society, as I have argued they do, it will be hard to avoid the conclusion that the duties and virtues which are justified by these principles have implications not only for people's economic decisions about what careers to pursue, what salaries to negotiate, and whether to take risks that increase their chances of becoming dependent on the state for support, but also for a range of decisions they make about how their family life is to be organized. Indeed I shall argue that parents are under a duty of justice to share the burdens of childcare and that there are grounds for regarding it as a duty of citizenship. But this does not straightforwardly imply that co-parents are under a duty of justice to engage in *equal parenting*, that is, to be equally involved in the raising of their children, for the appropriate principles of justice in this context will require only that each parent should shoulder a fair share of the burdens of childcare, judgements about which will need to take account of burdens experienced outside the family, together with any agreements parents reached before having children concerning how the burdens of raising them should be distributed between the two of them.

The equal membership account can also underwrite the idea that parents have a duty of citizenship to share domestic burdens. Domestic arrangements have relevance for the good of equal membership, and for its associated duties and virtues, since an unequal distribution of domestic burdens tends to undermine social and political equality by depriving those with the higher share of these burdens of an equal opportunity to participate on equal terms in social and political life. Unlike the justice account, the equal membership account provides a reason for valuing the opportunity for equal parenting and for supposing that each parent is under a *pro tanto* duty of citizenship to divide domestic burdens equally if the other requests to be relieved of his or her greater share of them. The opportunity for equal parenting is likely to serve the good of social and political equality better by putting both mothers and fathers of young children in a position where each can, if he or she wishes, participate to some degree in social and political life unencumbered by child-care burdens.

1 Domestic justice

In recent years feminist theorists have drawn attention to the way in which mainstream theories of justice have neglected the domestic sphere.[1] There is no doubt that, historically speaking, labeling the family (and domestic life more generally) as 'private' has served to shield and even legitimize the abuse and exploitation of women, and also children. But in so far as liberal theory has been complicit in their abuse and exploitation, this has been despite rather than because of its fundamental commitments. The idea of equal inalienable rights, to which most forms of liberalism and indeed most versions of the justice account subscribe, must stand opposed to domestic violence and marital rape, whatever the content of the marriage contract that is implicitly or explicitly agreed. If family members possess rights that can be violated not only by strangers, friends, and acquaintances, but also by their fathers and mothers, husbands and wives, sons and daughters, and brothers and sisters, the family cannot be 'beyond justice', and justice accounts must recognize at least some duties and virtues that have relevance in domestic contexts.

Justice accounts must also acknowledge the ways in which practices within the family can potentially undermine equality of opportunity, thereby generating various duties which require mothers and fathers to avoid making decisions which have that consequence. There is, for example, a potential threat to equality of opportunity when parents subsidize the costs of higher education for their sons but not for their daughters, or when families insist that their daughters provide domestic help before and after school hours, preventing them from devoting time to schoolwork whilst their sons are left free to concentrate on it.[2] Again, it would seem that parents have a duty of justice and of citizenship not to disadvantage their daughters in this way that derives from a principle of equality of opportunity. Other issues surrounding the domestic division of labour between men and women are less clear-cut, however. Except in cases where women are unambiguously forced by their husbands or partners to look after their children and do the housework, it will require a longer argument to show that a practice which involves women taking primary responsibility for domestic work results in their exploitation, or is an infringement of their rights or a violation of their equality of opportunity.

As a preliminary, we need to distinguish between domestic work that is unconnected with caring for children (or for infirm or disabled adult relatives that are incapable of looking after themselves); domestic work that is associated with caring for children (or for infirm or disabled relatives) but which can be done in such a way that it does not involve interacting with them, such as preparing their meals or washing their clothes; and taking care of a child (or an infirm or disabled relative) in a way that involves some degree of interaction with them, such as feeding a child, or taking them to school. It might be thought that issues of justice arise in relation to the first two sets of tasks—let us call them 'domestic chores'—but not in relation to the third, on the grounds that, for example, taking care of one's children is part of what it is to act as a parent, or to be a good parent, and that taking care of one's infirm parents is part of what it is to be a good son or daughter. Indeed it might be argued that the activity of caring should be governed by a different ethic— an ethics of care—rather than by considerations of justice,[3] and that we should think about the activity of caring for children or for infirm or disabled relatives in terms of appropriate responsiveness to needs rather than as a burden to be distributed amongst co-parents or other family members. Thinking about caring activities in terms of the responsibilities attached to particular roles, governed by an ethic that is focused on the meeting of needs, seems better able to respect religious and cultural pluralism, since family roles, such as the roles of mother and father, son and daughter, brother and sister, and grandfather and grandmother, and the caring responsibilities that are attached to these roles, may be defined differently in different cultures and religions. Different family forms, and the different roles that are partially constitutive of them, may involve different normative expectations.

But treating childcare, for instance, as a burden the distribution of which raises issues of justice is not to deny that it can be immensely enjoyable and rewarding, that people may disagree about the respects in which it is a burden, or that it may be governed by an ethic that is at least partially independent of considerations of justice. Nor indeed is it to deny that being a good parent involves interacting with one's children in a variety of different ways, thereby realizing a range of what Harry Brighouse and Adam Swift call 'familial relationship goods'.[4] This is all compatible with recognizing the respects in which childcare can also be a burden in a manner that raises issues of justice.

Activities such as getting up to a crying toddler in the middle of the night, making sure they reach school on time each morning clean and nourished, and feeding an over-tired baby in the evening, can justifiably be regarded as burdens under one description, even when they involve rewarding moments and even if they are an essential part of forging a relationship with one's child. It may be that regarding these activities as *merely* a burden is incompatible with genuinely caring for one's child. But it would be an over-idealized conception of what it is to care for one's child which denied that these activities are burdensome at all. That they are burdensome is evidenced by the fact that most parents would prefer to do less of them. Burdens can be fused together with benefits, and shouldering them can be part of the obligations attached to specific roles, but their distribution nevertheless appears to raise issues of justice (and, indeed, poses questions about the relationship between considerations of justice and an ethics of care focused on appropriate responsiveness to needs).[5] Even in the absence of a well worked-out principle of justice to govern the distribution of domestic benefits and burdens, it seems hard to deny that decisions not only about the allocation of domestic chores but also concerning the performance of tasks that are constitutive of childcare raise questions of justice—and that they do so partly independent of the way in which the performance of them may restrict access to the labour market, thereby affecting equality of opportunity.[6] (There may of course be a variety of reasons for resisting the *enforcement* of principles of justice in relation to these decisions, but these reasons would nevertheless presuppose that such principles are in play.) Framing the issues in these terms raises large questions about cultural and religious pluralism to which I shall return, but it seems to make sense to distinguish between on the one hand issues of justice concerning the way in which domestic chores and the burdens of childcare are distributed, and on the other hand the normative expectations attached to various roles within different family forms (such as monogamous families, polygamous families, and extended families), embedded in different religions and cultures, that require responsiveness to the needs of other family members—and which may even run contrary to what justice requires.

There are nevertheless a range of arguments which reach sceptical conclusions about the possibility of adequate principles of justice for governing the distribution of domestic benefits and burdens, at least when these principles go beyond the merely procedural. First, there is the now familiar argument that principles of distributive justice apply *only* to the basic structure of society, and not to any behaviour that takes place within it, such as the personal choices made within families concerning how to distribute domestic benefits and burdens, so there cannot be a duty of citizenship to take any particular share of these benefits and burdens that is grounded in a duty of justice. I raised various problems with this argument in Chapter 2, section 1. I shall not consider it any further here and will simply assume that it cannot be sustained.

Second, it might be argued that any plausible principles of justice to govern the distribution of domestic benefits and burdens will fail to satisfy standards of publicity in a way that raises questions about their adequacy. If there are no adequate principles of justice to govern the distribution of domestic benefits and burdens, there can be no corresponding duty of citizenship that family members are under to bring about a particular distribution. I shall call this 'the publicity argument'. According to the version of it that I shall consider, publicity requires there to be common knowledge of what principles of justice apply, what they entail in particular cases, and the extent to which individuals comply with them. An analogous argument has been used in the context of explaining why Rawls and others might justifiably resist the idea that citizens should apply the difference principle when making personal economic choices concerning, for example, what careers to pursue and what rewards to demand for themselves within those careers. This argument does not conclude that principles of justice are always misplaced when applied to personal behaviour, such as the choices that individual family members make that affect the distribution of domestic burdens, but it does raise questions about the adequacy of principles of justice designed for this purpose when their application cannot be publicly checked.

Third, it might be argued that provided a domestic division of labour is freely adopted by family members (or, at least, by those family members capable of consenting), it cannot be unjust. Consent to domestic arrangements, in other words, is sufficient for them to be just, and hence there is no duty of citizenship to bring about any particular distribution of domestic benefits and burdens. I shall call this 'the consent argument'. From the perspective of this argument, domestic justice is in a way purely procedural: provided that the parties can be said genuinely to consent, then any agreement reached will be just, whatever its content.

Fourth, it might be argued that principles of justice must respect reasonable pluralism, including reasonable religious pluralism. Different religions may reasonably endorse different views about the proper roles of men and women in relation to domestic work; for example, they may hold that women should raise the children whilst men work outside the home, and principles of justice (and any corresponding duties of citizenship to comply with such principles) must respect these different views. I shall call this 'the religious pluralism argument'. In so far as it is distinct from the consent argument—and does not reduce to the idea that when the parties consent to a particular division of domestic benefits and burdens, then this is sufficient for it to be just—it relies on an idea of reasonableness, where the requirements of reasonableness add further conditions that must be met before the distribution of domestic benefits and burdens which arises from any agreement can be just. This is the position that Rawls adopts in response to his feminist critics.

I shall consider each of these arguments in turn in the next three sections. My purpose is to make space for the idea that parents have a duty of justice to share domestic burdens, rather than to give precise content to such a duty or arrive at a particular principle or set of principles of distributive justice that govern domestic contexts. (I shall, however, address some doubts about whether this duty can be properly regarded as a duty of citizenship in particular.) I focus mainly on the burdens of childcare rather than the burdens of caring for elderly or infirm adult relatives, for the latter raise different issues. Any plausible theory of domestic justice will need to acknowledge some differences between these two cases that arise from the fact that the parents of a child brought her into the world, and therefore have a special responsibility towards her, at least until she reaches adulthood. With infirm or disabled adult family members, the issues are somewhat different since it is not clear that other family members have any special responsibilities of justice towards them, though they may fail in their responsibility as, for example, sons and daughters, if they do not provide their parents with the care they need. (A principle of fair play may have some relevance in this context—it might be argued that those who have voluntarily enjoyed their fair share of the benefits of family life have a duty to shoulder their fair share of its burdens—but its relevance will be limited, since children do not choose to be brought up by their parents, even though when they reach adulthood they may choose to sustain a relationship with their parents and that relationship may benefit them in various ways.)

2 The publicity argument

What is publicity, and why might it be thought that it serves as a constraint on (or as a desideratum for) any adequate principle of justice and hence any duties of citizenship that are grounded in these principles? Andrew Williams extracts an account of publicity and its importance from Rawls's writings: principles of justice are public if everyone knows they apply, and they are sufficiently clear and unambiguous that it is possible for everyone to know what they entail in particular cases, and to know the extent to which individuals comply with them.[7] Williams thinks that publicity, so understood, is important for social unity when that is conceived as well-ordered social cooperation.[8] Social unity is valuable for a number of reasons. Not least, it is instrumentally valuable because it increases 'the long term probability of a society conforming with its conception of justice'.[9] Presumably, part of what Williams has in mind here is that when a person accepts a principle of justice, and knows that others not only accept it but also comply with it, he has additional reasons to act in accordance with it himself. For, under these circumstances, he knows that if he complies with the principle he will not thereby place himself in a position where he is being exploited by non-compliers, and he knows that if he does not comply with the principle, he will be free riding on the benefits that widespread compliance with it brings. In other words, publicity promotes just behaviour.

Initially Williams appeared to maintain that publicity, understood in this way, is a *constraint* on any adequate principle of justice. On this basis he seemed to argue that Rawls should resist G. A. Cohen's argument that an 'egalitarian ethos' should govern personal economic choices, on the grounds that such an ethos, whether it is construed widely or narrowly, cannot meet this constraint. For example, such an ethos would have to allow a personal prerogative to depart from what egalitarian justice requires in circumstances where it is particularly demanding—perhaps because it would require a person to pursue a career that would be particularly beneficial for the worst off but which she would find considerably less fulfilling than an alternative—yet it is hard to see how the extent of that prerogative could be defined with sufficient precision to meet the publicity constraint.[10] Williams has since proposed that publicity might be best regarded as a desideratum for principles of justice rather than as a constraint on their adequacy.[11] In any case he believes that Cohen's egalitarian ethos cannot meet the requirements for publicity, but a domestic ethos that governs the distribution of domestic benefits and burdens could do so.[12] If he were correct, the importance of publicity would not place an obstacle in the way of defending principles of justice to govern the distri-bution of domestic benefits and burdens. Doubts can be raised concerning his argument, however; indeed Cohen denies that a defensible domestic ethos can meet the conditions required for publicity when these are understood as Williams proposes.[13] For partly overlapping reasons, I also think that Williams is mistaken.

Let us grant for the sake of argument that publicity, as Williams construes it, is either a constraint on the adequacy of a principle of justice or a desideratum for principles of justice. Could defensible principles of justice governing the distribution of domestic benefits and burdens satisfy the requirements for publicity? On the surface it might seem so. But consider the seemingly plausible idea that justice requires domestic burdens to be shared equally between adult family members, and that these members have a duty of justice to ensure that they take an equal share of them. What this implies is not always obvious, for it will depend on how one assesses the size of different kinds of benefits or burdens. How, for example, do you weigh the burden of getting up to a crying toddler in the middle of night compared to the burden of feeding an over-tired baby before bedtime, given the different preferences parents might have, and the different possible welfare effects of a disturbed night compared to the experience of catering for an over-tired baby? Following Williams' lead, however, we might suppose that parents will know enough about each other's dispositions and sensibilities to understand what these effects would be, and therefore are in a position to make these judgements in a reasonably reliable way. But when there is disagreement between parents concerning whether domestic burdens are being distributed equally, it may be hard for others to adjudicate since they lack the knowledge of each parent's preferences and sensibilities that would be required to make reliable judgements about the size of the burdens that each is being asked to bear.[14] Indeed, making judgements of this kind may take several years of living in close proximity to them.

The problems that arise with measuring the size of burdens would make it difficult to apply the principle that domestic benefits and burdens should be distributed equally amongst family members in a way that would satisfy the requirements for publicity. Focusing on the care of children, however, there are a number of independent reasons for rejecting this simple principle. First, it ignores the fact that one parent may work full time for pay outside the home, yet that must make some difference to the issue of what share of domestic burdens it would be just for the other parent to bear. Even if domestic arrangements are governed by independent principles of justice, and in that sense these arrangements constitute a different sphere, these principles must surely take account of any non-domestic burdens that are being shouldered. (In response it might be argued that burdens need to be equalized in each sphere of activity, but it is hard to see why domestic burdens could not, under some circumstances at least, be justly traded off against other burdens experienced in the job market.) Second, what counts as a fair distribution of domestic burdens may also depend in various ways upon whether one lives in a just society with just social norms. For example, in a society in which women experience widespread discrimination in the labour market, male family members may have an obligation to take on a greater than equal share of domestic burdens in order partially to redress the inequalities of access to jobs, and the various advantages they carry with them, that are experienced by female members of their family. That is, they may have an obligation to take their fair share of the burdens of the inequalities suffered by women.[15] Third, it ignores the fact that one parent might have been willing to play his or her procreative role only if the other agreed to take a larger than equal share of the burdens of childcare, and that is surely relevant when it comes to determining the justice of the distribution of domestic burdens.[16] Fourth, to insist that *all* adult family members must take an equal share of domestic burdens, including the burdens of childcare, ignores the fact that some adult family members may not have been involved in the procreative act or the decision to have a child, even if they are living in the same house as the child. For example, they may be the child's grandparents or adult siblings. It is far from clear that those who were not involved in either the procreative act, or the decision-making process about whether to have children, can have the same responsibilities of justice in relation to childcare as those who were involved in that act or process, whatever socially, culturally, or religiously defined obligations they might be deemed to possess as occupants of particular family roles. Fifth, it ignores the fact that, sometimes at least, a parent may justly 'buy out' their responsibilities, by hiring others to look after their children. We might, with good reason in some cases, regard those who 'sub-contract' childcare burdens in this way as bad parents, but it is hard to see why we should regard them as acting *unjustly* by refusing to take their fair share of these burdens.

However, these reasons for rejecting a simple egalitarian principle that favours the equal division of domestic burdens amongst adult family members would not provide any comfort to those who think that publicity is a require-ment that adequate principles of justice must meet or that it is a desideratum for them, yet believe that principles of justice govern the distribution of domestic benefits and burdens. For any plausible principle of this sort that is capable of avoiding the problems that beset the simple egalitarian principle will find it even harder to meet the requirements for publicity. A defensible principle of justice to govern the distribution of domestic benefits and bur-dens would need to take into account the way in which a parent who possesses particular talents may be able to produce much greater benefits for the worse off (or badly off) in his or her society or beyond by working in the market at the expense of taking on fewer burdens at home. This is likely to create difficulties for publicity that are as great as those which arise in relation to personal prerogatives. If the idea is that *some weight* should be given to the fact that a parent with particular skills could create large benefits for the worse off or badly off by working outside the home, then it will be hard to specify precisely how much weight should be given to this fact (or to the various other facts concerning how great these benefits would be for different amounts of time spent working outside the home), in the way that is needed to satisfy the criteria for publicity. To put the point differently, if co-parents owe special duties of justice to each other to share the burdens of childcare, then those special duties will need to be balanced against other duties that require them to take account of the well-being of others, whether these are general duties owed to everyone or other special duties owed to some smaller constituency, such as fellow citizens.[17]

To this it might be replied that the distribution of domestic benefits and burdens should be governed by general egalitarian principles that give equal weight to the benefits and burdens each person experiences, irrespective of where and how they arise, in a way that does not generate any special duties of justice for or between co-parents. I doubt this is true, since (as I have already noted) when parents choose to have children together, this must surely mean that they at least bear some special responsibility to raise their children or provide the resources necessary to do so. But even if I am mistaken in this respect, principles that gave equal weight to burdens wherever and however they arose would run into the same kind of problems that Williams identifies with satisfying the publicity criteria once they were required to give due weight to personal prerogatives.

I have not surveyed all plausible principles of distributive justice that might be applied to domestic benefits and burdens, nor have I defended any particular one. But in the light of my discussion, it seems to me unlikely that any defensible principle will be able to meet the conditions for publicity as Williams construes them. Does this mean that feminists are wrong to suppose that there are adequate principles for governing them? I think not. Publicity in Williams's sense is not a requirement that any adequate principle of justice must meet. A principle of justice can be fully adequate, *qua* principle of justice, even if it fails to satisfy the criteria for publicity. In this respect I am in substantial agreement with G. A. Cohen's response to Williams's argument. We do have a rough and ready idea of what it is to bear 'a fair share' of domestic burdens, despite the difficulties involved in formulating precise principles that determine what would count as a fair share and which specify under what circumstances (if any) one is entitled to do less than one's fair share. As Cohen illustrates, there are also other contexts where we think justice requires people 'to do their bit', without being able to specify precisely what this involves, and where we can make reasonably reliable judgements about whether people are making a good faith attempt to do their bit even in the absence of such principles, for example, in the context of a war campaign or efforts to conserve the environment. If, in the face of this argument, Williams retreats to the claim that publicity is a desideratum of principles of justice rather than a constraint on the adequacy of such principles, then even if we regard the failure of principles of justice to satisfy the requirement of publicity as a defect or flaw in them, it is not clear that this would provide sufficient grounds to conclude that there are no adequate principles of justice for governing the distribution of domestic benefits and burdens. If the desideratum claim means that, other things being equal, a principle of justice is better, qua principle of justice, when it gives weight to the value of publicity, in due recognition of the role that publicity plays in promoting justice, then this does not entitle us to conclude that principles of justice that do not meet the requirements of publicity must be rejected or that they must be inadequate.[18] A principle may be flawed in one respect but nevertheless fit for purpose.

So the adequacy of principles of justice does not depend in any crucial way on their being able to meet the kind of requirements for publicity that Williams describes, and there may be adequate principles of justice that can be applied in a domestic context which fail to meet those requirements. But we are not yet in a position to conclude that any defensible justice account will need to acknowledge that there are duties and virtues of citizenship grounded in principles of distributive justice that govern the distribution of benefits and burdens in a domestic context. There are a number of other arguments to consider which resist that conclusion.

3 The consent argument

According to the consent argument, when a particular domestic division of labour is freely agreed, then it is just, and hence there are no duties of citizenship to bring about any particular division of domestic benefits and burdens. But a range of questions can be asked about what criteria need to be met before we can legitimately say that a domestic arrangement has received the consent of the parties involved in it, particularly in relation to the existence of alternatives. Suppose that a woman was unable to find work outside the home, whereas her male partner was in paid employment when their first baby arrived. Would this mean that her subsequent agreement to look after their children was such that she could not be said to have consented in the sense required for this arrangement to be just? What if he—for whatever reason—has massively greater earning power in the market compared to her? Is this sufficient for us to say that her agreement to take primary responsibility for childcare and domestic chores does not count as genuine consent? Reflection on these questions suggests that if consent is to confer justice on a domestic arrangement, at the very least each of those involved in the decision should have had reasonable alternatives.

What is to count as a reasonable alternative may of course still raise difficult issues. Even if it is clear that a woman has no reasonable alternative but to take primary responsibility for childcare when her husband has massively greater earning power than her, it is much less clear what we should say about cases where there are significant but not enormous differences in earning power. Nevertheless it would be implausible to suppose that each and every difference in earning power casts doubt on the genuineness of the consent. Similarly the different normative expectations which attach to gender roles may exert a powerful force, but they do not typically mean that women have no reasonable alternative but to comply with them. The social norm that mothers should take primary responsibility for childcare, which, for example, is frequently presupposed in studies of how children are affected by their mothers going out to work when they are still young, means that mothers' decisions are subjected to scrutiny and criticism in a way that fathers' decisions are not.[19] But so long as no other social sanctions or constraints are involved, these practices do not seem to have the consequence that women have no reasonable alternative but to take primary responsibility for childcare.

People's desires can also be manipulated in various ways. A woman, for example, can be indoctrinated to think that her proper role is to stay at home and bring up the children whilst her husband goes out to work, and a man can be indoctrinated to think that his proper role as husband and father is to earn the family income whilst his wife looks after the children. But this is not the standard case. Although gender role socialization is a powerful force, and works in complex and subtle ways in shaping people's desires, it does not typically amount to indoctrination—at least not in societies where men and women receive a reasonable standard of education. Indoctrination, we might say, closes people's minds in a way that compromises their personal autonomy and renders them incapable of genuine choice in some area of their lives. Sex role socialization does not typically take this form, even though it may have shaped men's and women's desires in ways they are unaware of. Since sex role socialization typically falls short of indoctrination, it does not prevent men and women from consenting to a domestic arrangement.

When the adults involved in a domestic arrangement have reasonable alternatives available to them, and have not been subject to indoctrination which makes them unable to agree to any other arrangement, is their consent to it sufficient to ensure that it is just? It is implausible to think so. In a context where there is discrimination against women in the labour market, or when women do not have the same opportunities as men to acquire skills or take up places in higher education, it may be rational for them to agree to stay at home and look after the children even if they have reasonable alternatives. That would seem to be consistent with their genuine consent to this domestic arrangement, but the injustices to which they have been subjected outside the home, and indeed the pressures exerted by sexist social norms governing who should look after children, taints the justice of the arrangement to which they have agreed.[20] To this it might be replied that if women were not subject to discrimination, and that there were no sexist social norms with wider social or cultural currency, then consent to a domestic arrangement would be sufficient to guarantee that it is just. Needless to say, this principle would not have any immediate implications for the domestic division of labour in the societies with which we are familiar, but is it defensible? In my view it derives a considerable amount of its force from an unstated assumption that is being smuggled in with the idea of a consensual arrangement, but which strictly speaking goes beyond that idea, namely, that the parties to a genuinely consensual domestic arrangement are free to leave it, so they can have no reasonable complaint against it if they choose to remain. This is an additional assumption since an arrangement can be voluntary in the sense that the parties to it freely enter into it without there necessarily being any freedom of exit from it. But suppose we were to hold that a domestic arrangement is consensual if and only if the parties freely enter into it and are free to exit from it. Would consent to a domestic arrangement, in the absence of discrimination and sexist norms governing who should take primary responsibility for childcare, be sufficient then to make that arrangement just?

Here we would at least need some clarity concerning when the costs of exiting an arrangement are such that a person lacks the freedom to do so, or when those costs mean that her freedom to leave lacks the kind of normative significance it would require to make that arrangement just. In this context we might think it important to distinguish between the costs that are intrinsic to exit and those which are extrinsic.[21] The intrinsic costs of exit are those which are inseparable from it, for example, one of the intrinsic costs of exiting a domestic arrangement would be of being deprived of the enjoyment of at least some of the particular family relationships that are constitutive of it. Extrinsic costs are those that are contingently connected with exiting an arrangement, but which are (in principle at least) separable from it. It might be thought that only extrinsic costs can be such that they restrict freedom of exit. With domestic arrangements, the extrinsic costs suffered by women who exit them may in practice be especially high.[22] For example, depending on her circumstances and the laws that apply to it, these costs might include being forced to leave her children behind with no possibility of future contact with them, violating a religious commitment which requires her to stay with her husband, ostracism from her community, or having to endure a much lower standard of living (perhaps because as a result of caring for children she lacks the marketable skills required to find a well-paid job and her husband is not required to compensate her for the fact that she has not acquired such skills). Admittedly some of these extrinsic costs of exit would be a product of sexist social norms, so they would not be relevant to the assessment of the consent argument in its 'ideal' form. But even if we filter out those costs that are a product of such norms, the remaining costs may still be high. And even when the remaining costs are not so great that we should regard them as restricting a person's freedom of exit, they may nevertheless be high enough to cast doubt on whether her staying in it is sufficient for the distribution of benefits and burdens it involves to count as just. If the costs of leaving a domestic arrangement are high, she may have a reasonable complaint against that arrangement, of a kind that would count against regarding it as just, despite having the freedom to leave it. Further principles would be required to limit these extrinsic costs if consent to a domestic arrangement from which one enjoys freedom of exit is to stand a chance of conferring justice on the distribution of domestic burdens which that arrangement entails. These reflections lead us to Rawls's view, which I shall discuss in the next section.

4 The religious pluralism argument

In what is perhaps the most sophisticated treatment of these issues from a liberal perspective, John Rawls argues that principles of justice apply to the family in virtue of the role it plays as part of the basic structure of society but they do not apply directly to its internal life.[23] Although it is not entirely clear what he means by this, his view seems to be that principles of justice regulate what happens in the family when its activities affect the basic liberties of family members or their opportunities, but since different views about how domestic life should be organized will emerge from different moral and religious doctrines, any particular domestic division of labour is permissible when various conditions are met. As a result, there is no duty of citizenship grounded in a principle of justice that requires co-parents to take a share of domestic burdens.

Rawls seems to think that there are three conditions that are jointly sufficient for the distribution of benefits and burdens that emerges from any given domestic division of labour to count as just, these conditions being motivated by considerations of the kind raised in the previous section. First, the domestic division of labour must be voluntary, that is, receive the genuine consent of all adults involved in it.[24] Second, it must not be a *product*, in whole or in part, of any injustice, such as, for example, discrimination practiced against women in the job market—which may have the effect of giving couples powerful economic reasons to adopt a division of labour in which the woman stays at home in order to raise the children whilst the man seeks paid employment outside the home. Third, the domestic division of labour must not be involved in *causing* any injustice by, for example, depriving women of pensions because they have not had the opportunity or means to make contributions to a pension fund of their own, or depriving them of their fair share of wealth or income if they split up with their husbands.[25]

Rawls's discussion of the role of principles of justice in relation to the family may seem a coherent response to the difficult challenge of moral, religious and cultural pluralism.[26] It allows cultural and religious groups some freedom to organize their own domestic lives as they see fit, but insists that women's basic liberties and opportunities should be protected as much within the family as they are in any other basic institution (or indeed anywhere else). On closer inspection, however, Rawls's position faces a number of difficulties. There are many considerations in play in his discussion of these issues and it is hard to be sure precisely what role each of them is supposed to play in his argument.

From a cursory reading, it might seem that his main reason for insisting that political principles of distributive justice should not govern the domestic division of labour (when the conditions described above are met) is that this division is part of the internal life of the family. But that cannot really be Rawls's argument. The phrase 'the internal life of the family' cannot be intended to pick out some activity or set of activities which, by their very nature, are beyond or transcend principles of justice. Rawls is clear that there are no such activities. Even if an activity takes place out of public view, at the heart of family life, if it involves the denial of basic liberties or the violation of basic rights, then it is condemned by enforceable principles of justice. If, for example, husbands beat or rape their wives, then this constitutes assault and a violation of their wives' rights. To say that some activity is part of the internal life of the family is not to *give* a reason for why principles of justice do not apply to it, but simply to *imply* that such reasons are available. But what are these reasons in the case of principles that govern the distribution of domestic benefits and burdens?

Rawls's main argument seems to be that there are no principles that could be devised which tell us, for example, who should do the childcare, which could be publicly justified, that is, justified by appeal to public reasons, where a public reason is (roughly speaking) a reason that others can reasonably be expected to share, taking into account the variety of different reasonable moral and religious doctrines at large, that is, moral and religious doctrines that are compatible with the equal status of citizens.[27] Any such principles will inevitably rest upon, or involve denying, some comprehensive moral doctrine, such as a religious view concerning men's and women's proper roles within the household, so cannot provide public reasons. Indeed, Rawls recognizes that family members may be operating with their own principles of justice or fairness in dividing up domestic benefits and burdens[28] but he maintains that these principles are derived from different comprehensive moral doctrines, including religious conceptions of the good. In this sense he is conceding that principles of justice or fairness can apply to the internal life of the family. But, in his view, these principles are not political in the relevant sense because they cannot be justified by public reasons, so they should not be *enforced* by the state and they do not generate any duties of citizenship. Nor, presumably, can they be legitimately used by the state in public condemnation of a particular domestic division of labour.

But Rawls needs to provide us with more argument before he is entitled to conclude that there are no publicly justifiable principles to govern the distribution of domestic benefits and burdens. He needs to show that the various conflicting principles which are, or might be, proposed to govern these benefits and burdens can be grounded in different *reasonable* comprehensive doctrines. After all, it might be part of the teachings of a particular religion that husbands are entitled to beat their wives when they disobey them, yet Rawls would not regard that as a reason for saying that principles of justice that forbid this practice are not publicly justifiable or cannot legitimately be enforced. In Rawls's view, a religion which claimed that husbands had the right to beat their disobedient wives would be unreasonable to that extent. If this is so, why does he not say the same about a religiously sanctioned distribution of benefits and burdens in the household that has as one of its consequence that wives can justly be required to work all the hours they are awake, caring for children and doing the housework, whilst their husbands have substantial amounts of leisure time? For it is hard to deny that there is injustice in a situation where men who perform jobs that are no more physically demanding have substantial amounts of leisure time whilst women have none because their domestic responsibilities take up so much time, or because they work in the job market as well as fulfill these responsibilities—or where women have very little good quality leisure time because they are tired by the domestic work they do, whilst men have a sizeable amount of good quality leisure time.[29] Any reasonable comprehensive moral doctrine must surely acknowledge the injustice in these states of affairs, even if, in Rawls's terms, doing so would require classifying leisure as a primary good.[30]

Indeed, Rawls himself says things which make it hard for him to disagree with this verdict. For example, he considers the charge that the basic cause of women's inequality is their greater share in the bearing and raising of children, and as a result entertains favourably the idea that one way of compensating a woman for this greater burden is to suppose that she is entitled to an equal share in the income her husband or partner earns during their marriage, a principle which has particular significance in the case of divorce.[31] Doesn't this commit Rawls to the idea that the domestic division of labour, and the distribution of benefits and burdens in the household, are subject to principles of justice? Rawls might respond that the potential *causal effects* of the domestic division of labour, such as the economic disadvantages that women may experience when their marriages break down after they have spent a significant proportion of their working lives looking after children, are legitimately governed by principles of justice but that the distribution of benefits and burdens that is *intrinsic* to any given domestic division of labour is just provided that it is voluntary and is not the product of any injustice. In the case I am envisaging, however, women's inequality consists in part in their lack of fair access to leisure. Admittedly lack of fair access to leisure time is not a logically necessary consequence of that division of labour: it is not a conceptual truth that when mothers do all of the childcare and housework, they will end up with no leisure time, or low quality leisure time compared to their husbands. Whether they do suffer in this way will depend, in part, on levels of wealth and the kind of job their husbands do, which, for example, will affect whether they can pay for household help or have access to various labour-saving devices, such as washing machines or dishwashers, and will affect what leisure time, and its quality, is enjoyed by their husbands. Lack of fair access to leisure time is, however, the outcome of that division of labour for many women, given the type of care infants require and the limited support available. And lack of fair access to leisure time is not the kind of causal consequence that could be mitigated by tackling the *economic effects* of the domestic division of labour, for example, by requiring a husband to share his income equally with his wife and give her an equal share of his pension fund should they divorce. If principles of justice are to be employed to counteract the causes of women's inequality, they must surely be applied to the domestic division of labour itself.

Suppose Rawls were to concede that a principle can be publicly justified which would forbid a division of domestic labour when one consequence of it is that men have substantial amounts of reasonable quality leisure time but women have none. It might be argued that there are nevertheless weighty reasons for not *enforcing* this principle, for example, because of the intrusiveness that would be involved in determining whether it had been violated.[32] Could Rawls also resist the idea that family members have a duty of citizenship to ensure that leisure time is shared fairly, and that a state of affairs in which men have substantial amounts of reasonable quality leisure time but women have none can be legitimately subject to *public condemnation* because it violates such a duty? Rawls might argue that when the domestic division of labour is voluntary, this makes a difference which justifies not using this principle even as a basis for public condemnation of those arrangements that violate it, and which precludes grounding duties of citizenship in it. But the voluntariness of an arrangement cannot be sufficient to require us not to use principles of justice in public discussion to condemn it, or not to lament in public debate the failure of those involved in the arrangement to live up to their citizenly duties, or we would have to conclude that consensual marital arrangements in which wives are beaten when they are disobedient should not be subject to public condemnation.

Rawls might argue that in the case of the distribution of domestic benefits and burdens it is the voluntariness of the arrangements, *in conjunction with* the fact that no basic rights or liberties have been violated, which makes the cases disanalogous. In order for this response to be effective, it would need to appeal to the idea that the protection of basic rights and liberties is more important than the distribution of other goods such as leisure time, such that the voluntariness of an arrangement is sufficient to mean that principles of justice governing the distribution of leisure time should not be applied in condemnation of it, unlike the principles governing the basic rights and liberties, which can and should be employed to condemn violations of them. Rawls's rank ordering of principles of justice would give some credence to this argument, so it would not be an ad hoc move. It would, however, raise two further issues.

First, we would need some clarification in relation to fair equality of opportunity. Is the voluntariness of an arrangement sufficient to mean that the principle of fair equality of opportunity should not be used to publicly condemn it? Consider the case I mentioned at the beginning of this chapter in which a family provides its sons but not its daughters with financial and other support to go on to higher education. Is that not a violation of the principle of fair equality of opportunity, and of the duty of justice and citizenship that we are under to live up to that principle, one that should receive public condemnation, even if it were sanctioned by various religious doctrines about the proper role of girls and women that were endorsed by the parties involved? According to that principle those with the same level of talent and ability should have the same chances of success, but if this practice were reproduced across a society, it would tend to mean that girls' opportunities were much less good than those of boys with the same level of talent and ability. Rawls of course recognizes that the family as an institution stands in the way of full implementation of the principle of fair equality of opportunity,[33] but he should surely allow that public condemnation of practices within it that undermine the principle is legitimate. But if he does allow that, then why not also allow for the public condemnation of a domestic division of labour which has as one of its consequences that women are deprived of reasonable quality leisure time whilst men enjoy considerable amounts of it?

Second, the revised Rawlsian position I am envisaging would raise questions about whether it is justifiable to hold that basic rights and liberties are so much more important than leisure time (under relatively favourable conditions, at least) that the voluntariness of an arrangement is sufficient to mean that the distribution of the latter should not be publicly condemned even when it can be shown to be unjust by publicly justifiable principles. Given the profound effects that the division of domestic benefits and burdens may have on the quality of people's lives, it is hard to believe that issues concerning them are in general so much less important than issues concerning the protection of the basic liberties that public condemnation is always illegitimate in the context of the former.

If my arguments against Rawls's position are correct, any adequate account of the duties and virtues of justice relevant in a domestic context will have to recognize that they place demands on individuals that may run contrary to particular religious views about the proper roles of men and women. Even if the consent of those involved in a domestic arrangement has normative significance, it will not determine whether that arrangement is just or not, even when we take into account the provisos that Rawls adds.[34] The variations in the distribution of domestic benefits and burdens that differences in culture and religion can justify are more tightly constrained than he allows. This is not to deny that understandings of what it is to be a good father or mother (or indeed a good son or daughter, or a good grandfather or good grandmother) may be culturally specific and informed by religious views about the proper roles of men and women, such that these roles are defined in a way that requires women and girls to take primary responsibility for childcare. (Of course in practice there are likely to be a number of different understandings of what it is to be a good father or mother in a particular religion or culture, and the normative expectations attached to these roles may consequently be a matter of contest within that culture or religion.) And in some cases being a good mother, for example, or to be widely regarded as a good mother, may require a woman to take on more than her fair share of the burdens associated with childcare. But this merely shows that considerations of justice and fairness, and the equal status of men and women they presuppose, may provide grounds for criticizing the way in which these roles are defined.

Although I have resisted a number of different arguments which purport to show that the domestic division of labour is not subject to principles of distributive justice, I have not made the case for any specific principles to govern the distribution of domestic benefits and burdens, nor have I given specific content to the idea that there is a duty to take a fair share of these burdens. We might anyway wonder whether such a duty can be given precise content given the different factors that are relevant to the issue of whether a particular distribution of domestic benefits and burdens is just: perhaps in practice it is best understood as a duty to do one's bit domestically, in the light of the burdens one experiences outside the family, any agreements one might have reached prior to having children, and the position of women in the wider society to which one belongs, that resists any further, more detailed specification. If so, it might best be regarded as an imperfect duty, even though it is derived from a perfect duty to take one's fair share of domestic burdens. As with other imperfect duties, the virtues will have a key role to play in explaining how it is discharged: the just person in this context is one who conscientiously strives to do their share in the light of the burdens they take on outside the home, and in the light of the burdens which are shouldered by other family members.

There is, however, a *prima facie* difficulty in justifying the idea that the duty to take one's fair share of domestic burdens, or the duty to do one's bit in a domestic context, is a duty of citizenship in particular, for it would seem to bind family members rather than fellow citizens. There seems to be a general principle of justice which requires people to bear at least most of the costs of their choices, subject perhaps to the proviso that they are not left destitute as a result, which typically entails that co-parents have an obligation of justice

123

to bear at least most of the burdens of having children.[35] (Even when parents do not make a deliberate choice to have children, they normally choose to engage in sexual activity in the knowledge that this may be the outcome.) This also seems to be a duty of citizenship since it is owed to fellow citizens. But if, as I have argued, each parent also has a further duty to bear his fair share of the burdens of raising his children, then this would seem to be a duty that he owes to his co-parent rather than to his fellow citizens.

The duty to take a fair share of the burdens of raising one's children might, however, be reconstructed as a duty of citizenship in one of two ways. First, it might be regarded as derived from a more wide-ranging duty of citizenship not to seek or gain unfair advantages for oneself or others, where a failure to take one's fair share of these burdens is regarded as enjoying such an advantage.[36] I shall discuss this important duty further in the next chapter. Second, a parent's duty to take a fair share of the burdens of raising his children might properly be regarded as a duty of citizenship when its violation would deprive his co-parent of equal opportunity in the competition for advantaged social positions, or limit her ability to exercise her political liberties effectively. The equal membership account provides a rather different perspective on these issues, however—one which offers greater support to equal parenting.

5 Familial relationships and the good of equal membership

The issue of how domestic burdens should be distributed creates a potential tension between the equal membership account and the justice account. I shall explain how this tension arises, and then show how a partial reconciliation is possible through acknowledging that each parent has a *pro tanto* duty, grounded in the good of equal membership, to take an equal share of the burdens of rearing their children when his or her co-parent wants to be relieved of their greater share.

When the burdens of childcare are such that one or both parents lack an opportunity, comparable to what others in their society enjoy, to participate in the political sphere or civil society (including paid employment in the market), then the good of equal membership provides a reason for relieving them of some of these burdens. Even if what matters ultimately is a person's overall lifetime opportunity to participate in these spheres, parents who look after their children early on will enjoy less of that opportunity than those who do not. In many societies the group most at risk is of course mothers (though some fathers may suffer in the same way in families in which they take primary responsibility for childcare). Childcare responsibilities often deprive mothers with young children of the time or resources necessary to participate on equal terms in the political sphere and in civil society, whereas state-funded or subsidized nursery care, or laws which require employers to provide paid parental leave for some fixed period of time after the birth of a child, perhaps with the aid of state subsidies, can enable parents to combine work and other commitments with the raising of their children. The equal membership account might also defend a policy of offering companies incentives, such as tax breaks, to encourage them to provide their employees with flexible working arrangements that allow parents to manage their childcare responsibilities so that they have greater opportunity to participate on equal terms in work outside the family.[37]

In this context, however, there is a possible tension between the equal membership account and justice accounts that is analogous to the one I considered in Chapter 3. As we have seen, versions of the latter often suppose that (in general) it is just to require people to bear the costs of their choices, including the choice parents make to have children. These costs include having less time for political activity, and not being able to take on various kinds of paid employment that are hard to combine with childcare, for example, those which require working long hours or extra hours at short notice. Since these barriers are in effect regarded as self-imposed, they are not thought to undermine parents' equal political liberty or their equality of opportunity, or at least not in a way that is unfair (although there is space within this conception for the idea that one parent may unfairly undermine his partner's equality of opportunity or ability to exercise her political liberty by violating his obligation to shoulder a fair share of domestic burdens). From this perspective, it is important to distinguish between those laws and state policies that *allow* or even *encourage* others to bear some of those costs but do not *require* them to do so, and those laws and policies that require some or all of those costs to be borne by others. The latter, unlike the former, would be regarded as a threat to justice. State-funded or subsidized childcare would constitute such a threat, as would state-funded or subsidized parental leave, but not a policy of encouraging employers to provide more flexible working arrangements or to subsidize childcare.

As in Chapter 3 this tension can be reduced, this time by recognizing the scope within justice accounts to externalize some of the costs of childcare, given that even those who do not have children are likely to have to rely upon the next generation for support when they reach old age—at the very least they rely upon the *existence* of this generation when they get old, even if they pay the full costs of any care that they then receive. Justice accounts may also be able to justify externalizing the costs of childcare when the circumstances of family units are such that they fall below the level at which their members can lead a decent life, including children who are in this position through no fault of their own.[38] But this will not entirely resolve the tension. Defenders of the equal membership account will think there is a strong case for externalizing a greater share of the costs of childrearing in so far as this is needed to ensure that neither parent is denied an opportunity to participate in social and political life that is equivalent to what others enjoy. A partial reconciliation might be achieved, however, through domestic arrangements in which each parent has the opportunity to participate equally in the nurturing of their children, from infancy through to their teenage years, that is, the opportunity to engage in equal parenting. Each parent might be regarded as being under a *pro tanto* duty of citizenship to take an equal share of the burdens of raising children if the other desires such an arrangement, with that duty being grounded in the good of equal membership. Even if one parent begins by taking primary responsibility for child rearing, and even if this division of labour was agreed before they had children, there is still a strong reason, grounded in the value of equal membership, for the other parent to provide the primary carer with the opportunity to share these burdens equally should she later decide that she wants greater access to political life or civil society—even though this reason would need to be balanced against any duties arising from agreements reached to the contrary beforehand.[39] For this arrangement is likely to constitute the best way of promoting social and political equality when the burdens of caring for young children are shouldered largely by their parents. The opportunity for equal parenting provides both mothers and fathers of young children with the chance, if they so wish, to participate to some degree in civil society, and indeed in politics, unencumbered by the burdens of childcare.

This will not entirely remove the tension, however, for parents of young children will not enjoy the same lifetime opportunity for participation in social and political life as adults who are not parents, yet any attempt to create opportunities to do so that are more nearly equal through state subsidized childcare would (according to the view under consideration) be unjust. The tension that remains indicates that there may need to be some balancing of justice against the good of equal membership—though in this case at least there seems good reason to resolve it in favour of justice.

Equal membership accounts are concerned about domestic arrangements only in so far as they impact upon access to the sphere of politics and civil society. This might make one wonder about the principled basis for stopping here. If the reason for extending the good of equal membership to embrace social equality as well as political equality is that both are important for equality of status within the polity (understood as comprised of its major institutions, including the family), then the same argument would seem to apply to extending the good of equal membership to include equal standing in personal relationships, including those with other adult family members. This would mark a radical change in our ordinary understanding of citizenship, and create a further important difference between justice accounts and those equal membership accounts which extend the notion in this way, but I do not see any principled reason for resisting it. It would give meaning to the idea of intimate citizenship which is gaining currency within the literature.[40] Treating other adult family members as equals in personal relationships that are played out both in and beyond the home may be as important for a person's equal standing in a polity as treating others as equals in interactions that take place in civil society. So there is room within a suitably extended equal membership account for a commitment to 'personal equality', and for a duty of citizenship to treat other adult family members as equals in one's family life.

What this amounts to is, of course, a difficult issue. But it would seem to stand against any systematic devaluing of the activities of other adult family members, including the childcare they undertake, in so far as this systematic devaluing involves a failure to treat them as equals. And it would seem to be inconsistent with husbands taking the major decisions within the family without any attempt to consult their wives, or with husbands controlling the family income with their wives being required to defer or submit to them inside the home. It may also challenge practices such as husbands insisting that their wives walk behind them in the street, and in principle it may have implications for the psychologically complex arena of sexual relationships, which some radical feminists have supposed are permeated by (or even founded upon) the eroticization of dominance and submission.[41]

There is, however, nothing strictly contradictory in the idea that the good of equal membership consists in social and political equality but not personal equality, except in so far as the latter is instrumental to achieving social and political equality. Someone who insists that the good of equal membership is concerned solely with equality of status in social and political relationships, and with personal relationships only in so far as they affect equality of status in social and political relationships, cannot be convicted of holding a self-contradictory position. Indeed, not only is such a position consistent, it might seem to accord better with our intuitions concerning what it is to act as a citizen. Do we really act as citizens when we strive to ensure that our actions in the domestic sphere are oriented towards achieving equality in personal relationships, even when inequalities in these relationships have no wider impact? Our intuitions might be thought to support a negative answer to this question. Appealing to intuitions can of course be dangerous since they are partly a product of the particular historical circumstances in which we live, including the legacy of women's oppression. But arguably our intuitions—at least when they are drawn from the full range of our reflective experience—and the coherence they exhibit is the only test we have of our moral and political theorizing. And it is possible without inconsistency, and by appeal to intuitions, to resist extending the good of equal membership to cover personal equality. Coherence may go beyond bare consistency, placing additional constraints on our theorizing, but it is not clear that it requires us in every case to be able to give a principled reason for the distinctions we draw, or (in the case at hand) why it should require us to give a reason for limiting the good of equal membership to social and political equality, other than that this fits with the judgements we on reflection make about the proper bounds of citizenship and the demands it makes upon us.

6 Concluding remarks

Principles of justice and the good of equal membership provide us with different perspectives on the duties and virtues that are relevant in domestic contexts. There are compelling reasons for thinking that principles of justice must acknowledge that family members have a duty to take a fair share of domestic burdens, including the burdens associated with childcare, though further reasons are required for regarding this as a duty of citizenship as opposed to a duty that some family members owe to each other. However, there is potentially a degree of tension between the equal membership account and justice accounts on these issues, which has its source in similar considerations to those discussed in Chapter 3. There are reasons of justice for holding people responsible for their choices, and therefore for requiring parents to internalize at least a substantial proportion of the costs of bearing and raising their children, but requiring parents to internalize these costs impacts upon their ability to participate in the political sphere and civil society beyond the family, and therefore affects their ability to enjoy the good of equal membership. This tension provides a powerful argument for endorsing domestic arrangements in which each parent gives the other the opportunity to be involved in equal parenting, and for acknowledging that each parent is under a duty of citizenship to provide the other with that opportunity when he or she wishes to participate more fully in social and political life than the responsibilities as primary carer would allow.

Notes

1. Post-Rawls, one of the best discussions has been S. Okin, *Justice, Gender and the Family* (New York: Basic Books, 1989).
2. This will of course depend upon the precise content of principles of equality of opportunity. If equality of opportunity requires that those with the same level of talent and ability and willingness to use them should have the same chances of success, regardless of factors such as class, race, and sex, then this would appear to

prohibit practices which require girls rather than boys to help with the housework when this significantly affects the time they have available for studying. (For a less demanding view of what equality of opportunity requires, however, see my *Levelling the Playing Field*, pp.134–46.) In the UK at least, it might be argued that this way of burdening girls *promotes* fair equality of opportunity on the grounds that it compensates for the wider societal pressures to which boys are subject that affect their educational success, and which mean that, on average, girls achieve better results at school than boys. But if boys' relative underachievement at school does have social causes, there is an efficiency argument for working to remove the barriers that boys face rather than imposing additional burdens on girls.

3. The idea that there is an ethics of care or responsibility that is distinct from an ethics of justice or rights was first entertained by Carol Gilligan in her book *In a Different Voice: Psychological Theory and Women's Development* (Cambridge, MA: Harvard University Press, 1982). See V. Held, *The Ethics of Care: Personal, Political, and Global* (New York: Oxford University Press, 2005), for a comprehensive consideration of the theoretical issues raised by the literature that has grown up around Gilligan's work.

4. See H. Brighouse and A. Swift, 'Legitimate Parental Partiality', *Philosophy and Public Affairs*, Vol. 37, 2009, p. 46, pp. 53–4.

5. It is hard to deny that both an ethics of justice and an ethics of care are indispensable. Indeed Gilligan herself accepts this conclusion, and supposes that at least a partial integration of the two perspectives is required: see A. Mason, 'Gilligan's Conception of Moral Maturity', *Journal for the Theory of Social Behavior*, Vol. 20, 1990, pp. 167–74; Held, *The Ethics of Care*, pp. 15–17. Neither the value of care nor the value of justice appears to be reducible to the other. A just distribution of the burdens of caring for those who are unable to meet their own needs is morally deficient if it leaves some in need—or indeed if everyone's needs are met but some are not genuinely *cared for* because the morally appropriate motives for looking after them are absent (see Held, *The Ethics of Care*, pp. 32–7); so too a state of affairs in which everyone who is unable to meet their own needs is cared for would be morally deficient if it involved an unjust distribution of the burdens of care. Which of justice and care should take priority when they genuinely come into conflict is an important issue beyond the scope of this chapter.

6. See D. Bubeck, *Care, Gender and Justice* (Oxford: Oxford University Press, 1995). Eva Feder Kittay also raises some important questions about the place of care and 'dependency work' more generally in theorizing about justice, and how such theorizing should address the vulnerability of both 'dependency workers' and dependents, in her *Love's Labor: Essays on Women, Equality, and Dependency* (London: Routledge, 1999), Part Two. The role that a gender-based division of labour within the family has played (and continues to play) in the subordination of women has of course been a pervasive theme in feminist writings. See, for example, C. Delphy and D. Leonard, *Familiar Exploitation: A New Analysis of Marriage in Contemporary Western Societies* (Cambridge: Polity, 1992).

7. Williams, 'Incentives, Inequality, and Publicity', p. 233.

8. Williams, 'Incentives, Inequality, and Publicity', pp. 243ff.

9. Williams, 'Incentives, Inequality, and Publicity', p. 244. Williams thinks that social unity may also be valuable because it is necessary for the achievement of personal autonomy and for the realization of a particular form of community (ibid, p. 244).

10. Williams, 'Incentives, Inequality, and Publicity', pp. 239–40.

11. See A. Williams, 'Justice, Incentives and Constructivism', *Ratio*, Vol. 21, 2008, p. 480; Cohen, *Rescuing Justice and Equality*, pp. 364–8.

12. Williams, 'Incentives, Inequality, and Publicity', pp. 242–3.

13. See Cohen, *Rescuing Justice and Equality*, pp. 359–61

14. See Cohen, *Rescuing Justice and Equality*, p. 359–60.

15. See Chapter 5 for relevant discussion.

16. Those who deny this would seem to be committed to the implausible view that sperm donors incur a responsibility to bear an equal share of the costs of bearing and raising any child which results from consequent artificial insemination.

17. These wider duties may also need to be balanced against the duties a person has as a parent, which may require parents to be actively involved in the care of their children.

18. Cohen denies that we can make sense of the idea that publicity is a desideratum of justice (see Cohen, *Rescuing Justice and Equality*, pp. 364–8), but if it is interpreted in the way I have suggested, then it seems to be coherent.

19. See C. Chambers, *Sex, Culture, and Justice: The Limits of Choice* (University Park, PA: Pennsylvania State University Press, 2008), pp. 125–6; A. Mason, 'Equality, Personal Responsibility, and Gender Socialisation', *Proceedings of the Aristotelian Society*, Vol. 100, 2000, pp. 227–46.

20. See C. Chambers, 'All Must Have Prizes: The Liberal Case for Interference in Cultural Practices', in P. Kelly (ed.), *Multiculturalism Reconsidered* (Cambridge: Polity, 2002), pp. 154–7.

21. For relevant discussion, see B. Barry, *Culture and Equality: An Egalitarian Critique of Multiculturalism* (Cambridge: Polity, 2001), p. 150.

22. See S. Okin, '"Mistresses of Their Own Destiny": Group Rights, Gender, and Realistic Rights of Exit', *Ethics*, Vol. 112, 2002, pp. 205–30, especially pp. 219–20.

23. J. Rawls, 'The Idea of Public Reason Revisited', in S. Freeman (ed.), *J. Rawls: Collected Papers* (Cambridge, MA: Harvard University Press, 1999), p. 596.

24. See Rawls, 'The Idea of Public Reason Revisited', p. 599. Rawls discusses the issue of what is to count as a voluntary choice in note 68 on that page.

25. See Rawls, 'The Idea of Public Reason Revisited', p. 600.

26. For discussion of that challenge, see S. Okin, 'Is Multiculturalism Bad for Women?', and the responses to it, in J. Cohen, M. Howard, and M. Nussbaum (eds), *Is Multiculturalism Bad for Women?* (Princeton, NJ: Princeton University Press, 1999).

27. I shall discuss the notion of a public reason in more depth in Chapter 6, section 1.

28. See Rawls, 'The Idea of Public Reason Revisited', p. 598.

29. See N. Fraser, 'After the Family Wage: Gender Equity and the Welfare State', *Political Theory*, Vol. 22, 1994, p. 598; Lister, *Citizenship: Feminist Perspectives*, pp. 132–6.

30. Rawls himself is undecided on the issue of whether leisure should count as a primary good: see Rawls, *Political Liberalism*, pp. 181–2. However, many of those sympathetic to Rawls's work believe that it needs to be included in any defensible

primary goods metric. See, for example, T. Pogge, *Realizing Rawls* (Ithaca, NY: Cornell University Press, 1989), p. 198.

31. See Rawls, 'The Idea of Public Reason Revisited', p. 600. Okin argues for such an entitlement: see *Justice, Gender, and the Family*, pp. 180–3.

32. But what if someone wanted to make a public complaint about the share of domestic burdens she was required to endure? Could state intervention then be justified? If a spouse or partner reached the point of wanting to bring a public complaint against the distribution of benefits and burdens in his or her household, this would surely signal at least the partial breakdown of the relationships which form the basis of that family, with its break-up being a possible outcome. It is not clear that an appropriate and just response from the state could go beyond inviting the couple to attend mediation sessions.

33. See Rawls, *A Theory of Justice*, p. 301/265, p. 511/448.

34. It might be argued that even though consent (even when these conditions are met) is insufficient to make a distribution of domestic benefits and burdens *just*, it nevertheless confers a kind of *legitimacy* on that distribution, in the limited sense that if the consent to it is unanimous no one has a right to complain against it. (For relevant discussion, see Cohen, 'Fairness and Legitimacy in Justice, and: Does Option Luck Ever Preserve Justice?') But the legitimacy-conferring role of the consent would nevertheless be consistent with supposing that citizens are under a duty of justice and of citizenship to share these benefits and burdens fairly.

35. But we need to distinguish between two different kinds of potential costs of bringing children into the world. First, the entitlements children may have to a share of the world's resources, at birth or when they reach adulthood. (Indeed on some theories of justice they may have an entitlement to an equal share of the value of those resources.) Second, the costs involved in raising children, that is, of caring for them until they are able to meet their own needs. Some theories of justice may treat these costs differently, for example, Hillel Steiner's left-libertarianism seems to imply that costs of the first kind should be met equally by all, whereas costs of the second kind should be met by parents alone. (His theory is complex, however, because it holds that parents appropriate a natural resource—germ-line genetic information—when they create children, so they will be under a duty of justice to compensate others for doing so, at least when that information is valuable because it is the basis for various natural abilities: see H. Steiner, *An Essay on Rights* (Oxford: Blackwell, 1994), p. 247; H. Steiner, 'Silver Spoons and Golden Genes: Talent Differentials and Distributive Justice', in D. Archard and C. M. McLeod (eds), *The Moral and Political Status of Children* (Oxford: Oxford University Press, 2002), p. 186.) The most commonly given reason for justifying sharing at least some of the costs of raising children appeals to the way in which new members of a society create benefits for all. Even those members of the current generation who do not have children will most likely have to rely on the next generation to support them as they reach old age. For relevant discussion, see E. Rakowski, *Equal Justice* (Oxford: Oxford University Press, 1991); R. P. George, 'On the External Benefits of Children', in D. T. Myers, K. Kipnis, and C. F. Murphy (eds), *Kindred Matters: Rethinking the Philosophy of the Family* (Ithaca, NY: Cornell

University Press, 1993); P. Casal and A. Williams, 'Rights, Equality and Procreation', *Analyse und Kritik*, Vol. 17, 1995, pp. 93–116; P. Casal and A. Williams, 'Equality of Resources and Procreative Justice' in J. Burley (ed.) *Dworkin and his Critics* (Oxford: Blackwell, 2004), pp. 150–69.

36. From this perspective, not only would campaigning in public for men to do their fair share of housework count as acting as a good citizen, but also sorting out the division of labour in one's own home so that it involves a fair distribution of benefits and burdens. Compare A. Phillips, 'Citizenship and Feminist Theory' in G. Andrews (ed.), *Citizenship* (London: Lawrence and Wishart, 1991), p. 85; Lister, *Citizenship: Feminist Perspectives*, p. 29.

37. An equal membership account might hold that 'family friendly' legislation and public policy are not enough, however. They might suppose that there also needs to be an ethos which regards it as acceptable for parents to take advantage of these opportunities and unacceptable for their careers to be damaged as a result of doing so.

38. This scope may be even greater in non-ideal theory, for example, when men are unwilling to take their fair share of the burdens of childcare; or when the domestic division of labour is either a product, at least in part, of injustices (such as discrimination against women in the labour market) or plays a causal role in creating injustice (e.g., women's lack of pensions because they have worked at home.) Each of these non-ideal circumstances might mean that it was just in practice to externalize some of the costs of raising children, even if ideal theory held that it is just to externalize those costs only when children, and perhaps their parents, fell below the level at which they could lead a decent life.

39. What if a parent who has less than an equal share of the burdens of childrearing wants to take on an equal share of those burdens so that he or she can also enjoy the benefits? Is the other parent under a duty of citizenship to consent? Although there may be independent reasons for thinking that the other parent should consent to such an arrangement, it is hard to see how there could be a duty of citizenship to do so. (There may be various independent reasons for sharing childcare equally. For example, this might lead to more balanced adults if psychoanalytic theories such as Nancy Chodorow's are correct: see, N. Chodorow, *The Reproduction of Mothering: Psychoanalysis and the Sociology of Gender* (Berkeley and Los Angeles, CA: University of California Press, 1978).)

40. See Lister, *Citizenship: Feminist Perspectives*, p. 128.

41. See A. Dworkin, *Pornography: Men Possessing Women* (New York: G. P. Putnam's Sons, 1979); C. Mackinnon, *Feminism Unmodified: Discourses on Life and Law* (Cambridge, MA: Harvard University Press, 1987).

5

A Duty Not to Seek or Gain
Unfair Advantages?

The justice account maintains that citizens are under a duty to support and to further just institutions. But even in a society where basic institutions and laws were perfectly just, there would be scope for individuals to act unjustly. In Chapter 3, I argued that by acting in ways that make it likely that they will become dependent on the state, citizens may end up exploiting the prudent who refrain from taking such risks, whilst in Chapter 4, I argued that a parent may act unfairly by refusing to take a share of the burdens of caring for his or her children. From the perspective of the justice account, it might be thought that the duty to avoid becoming dependent upon the state, and indeed the duty parents are under to share the burdens of caring for their children, can be derived in part from a more wide-ranging duty of citizenship not to seek or gain unfair advantages for oneself or for others. In this context, the notion of an unfair advantage might be understood broadly so that it includes cases where an advantage is obtained unfairly as well as cases where an advantage is unfair because it arises from taking an unfair share of the available benefits or failing to take a fair share of the burdens.[1]

A duty of this kind might have relevance in a number of different contexts. For example, there are various ways in which a citizen may seek to exploit personal connections in order to secure unfair advantages for herself, or for her family or friends. If she knows a public official who is overseeing a bidding process for contracts or who is in charge of giving consent for building projects, she may try to influence that official using methods which, although they are not against the law or even overtly corrupt, involve an attempt to gain advantages in a way that is unfair because it is not available to others. Parents may be able to use their connections to secure unpaid internships for their children, and then support them financially whilst they hold these positions, thereby providing their offspring with valuable work experience that dramatically improves their chances of success when they come to apply for jobs.

The idea that parents are under a duty not to seek unfair advantages for their children allows us at least to articulate the unease there may be about such behaviour even if in the end we judge that it does not violate that duty.

In unjust societies, there will be even greater scope for a citizen to seek unfair advantages for himself or for others since there will be a wider range of ways of behaving that are permitted by the law but which involve injustice. Note also that, given the way in which I have characterized 'unfair advantage', what counts as such may be affected by the injustices that exist in a society. If, for example, many children are deprived of the opportunity for an adequate education because state-funded provision is so poor, to secure even an adequate education for one's child by sending her to a private school may be to gain an unfair advantage in that society, given the *additional* costs it potentially imposes on those children who come from poorer families and have no choice but to remain in state-funded education.[2] As a result of one's child opting out, the others are deprived of a fellow pupil who might enhance their educational experience, and the decision to opt out means that other parents may be encouraged to do so as well, thereby increasing the disadvantage suffered by those who are forced to attend these schools. In other words, in an unjust society such as the one described, educating one's child privately simply in order to give her an adequate education may exacerbate the injustices in a way that involves gaining an unfair advantage for her because it involves a failure to take a fair share of the burdens of injustice.[3]

The existence of opportunities to act to secure unfair advantage is not merely a practical problem that is created by the difficulty in identifying the myriad forms that corruption may take and with devising legislation to deter corrupt behaviour or to punish it when it occurs. It is a wider issue, partly because it extends beyond cases of corruption to other ways in which people may act unjustly, and partly because there are many instances where we think it desirable for different sorts of reason to allow people the liberty to act in a way that creates injustice. The distribution of domestic burdens is one such case. It was no part of my argument in the last chapter that states should try to enforce a particular distribution of domestic benefits and burdens, for that would involve the kind of scrutiny of family life which is at the very least undesirable because of its effects and the risks it poses, and at worst a violation of a right to privacy that family members possess. There are many other cases. For example, we may think it desirable to allow private schools to operate within a largely state-funded educational system, on the grounds that they promote an important interest that parents have in educational choice because they allow parents to choose schools for their children with a particular educational philosophy, or a curriculum that is distinctive in various ways.[4] It may be important to allow these schools to exist even though we know that some of them will give the children who attend them advantages in terms of their access to higher education and the marketable skills they acquire, thereby undermining fair equality of opportunity—and we know that some parents will choose these schools for their children for precisely that reason rather than because of their conception of what constitutes an intrinsically valuable education.

In this chapter, I shall examine the idea that there is a duty not to seek unfair advantages for oneself or for others, understood in the broad way I have described. For obvious reasons, this duty is most at home within a justice account of citizenship; there is no interestingly different equal membership account perspective on it. If there is such a duty, what it implies will depend upon further elaboration of what constitutes an unfair advantage, and this in turn will be affected by judgements about what constitutes the best theory of justice. I shall assume that justice at least sometimes requires us to counteract the effects of differences in people's circumstances. But I shall not presuppose any particular view of what that involves, preferring instead to draw out the implications of two broadly different approaches, which I call the neutralization approach and the mitigation approach.

1 Specifying the duty

Is the relevant duty a duty not to *seek* unfair advantages, or is it a duty not to *gain* unfair advantages in so far as it is within one's power to avoid doing so? The latter might be more demanding in various respects. The former would seem to allow people to behave in ways that bring with them unfair advantages so long as it was not their intention to benefit unfairly, whereas the latter would not permit them to do so, at least if these advantages were a foreseeable consequence of their behaviour. (For example, even if pupils gain unfair advantages from going to a private school the fees for which are beyond most people's means, parents would not be violating the duty when it is understood in the first way envisaged provided they sent their children to such a school simply because of the distinctive curriculum it offered.) A duty not to gain unfair advantages in so far as that is within one's power would require a person to investigate the source of the benefits he is receiving to ensure that they do not have the kind of causal history which would mean that they constitute unfair advantages, for example, to see whether these benefits are a result of his particular race or sex. This may be both difficult and time consuming.[5]

Indeed the duty not to gain unfair advantages in so far as that is within one's power threatens to be *excessively* demanding. Duties of justice (and of citizenship) need to give appropriate weight to what Thomas Nagel calls the personal standpoint. There are different ways in which this might be done, however.

For example, we might allow individuals to depart from a duty of justice not to gain unfair advantages when requiring a person to comply with that duty would unreasonably constrain her pursuit of her own projects, or would unreasonably prevent her from acting on the special concern she has for particular individuals or groups.[6] Understood in this way, this would provide people with a personal prerogative *to act unjustly*. But this is not the only way in which the personal standpoint might be given weight. We might instead think of justice itself as a compromise between personal and impersonal standpoints, in such a way that a person can exercise a personal prerogative to depart from what the impersonal standpoint would otherwise require of him but nevertheless *act justly*. In his seminal book *Equality and Partiality*, Nagel tends to avoid using the term 'justice' in this context, preferring the language of legitimacy, but he appears to think that adequate principles of justice have to be justifiable from both standpoints, which suggests that he would think of justice as a compromise between the personal and impersonal standpoints in the way I have described.[7] G. A. Cohen acknowledges his debt to Nagel[8] in endorsing a personal prerogative, but seems to regard that prerogative in the first way I described, as morally permitting departures from what justice requires rather than as limiting what justice demands.[9]

The second way of conceiving of the relationship between justice and the demand that the personal standpoint be given due weight strikes me as more plausible because it better preserves our intuitive sense of the importance of considerations of justice: we do not think that considerations of justice can be *routinely* overridden. One way of developing it would be to suppose that duties of justice, and of citizenship, are directly subject to the constraint that they must not make unreasonable demands on people. (The fact that a principle would place unreasonable demands on an individual if it were to govern her behaviour might be thought of as silencing or cancelling the reason she would otherwise have for acting upon it.)[10] There is evidence that Rawls accepts such a constraint: for example, when he specifies our natural duty to support and to further just institutions, he does so in a way that is consistent with, and encourages, the idea that principles of justice should not place unreasonable burdens on citizens: 'first, we are to comply with and to do our share in just institutions when they exist and apply to us; and second, we are to assist in the establishment of just arrangements when they do not exist, *at least when this can be done with little cost to ourselves.*'[11] Our duty to support and further just institutions is not a duty to do everything in our power to bring just institutions into existence, nor is it a duty to do everything in our power to counter threats to just institutions. The idea that principles of justice should not place unreasonable burdens on individuals also seems to be implicit in the passage where Rawls presents the institutional division of labour argument.[12] (If he accepts this constraint, however, then it provides a potential answer to that argument, namely, that principles of justice may nevertheless govern personal behaviour provided they do not place unreasonable burdens on people.)

If we operate with this constraint, what is the most plausible form of the duty under consideration? It is a duty not to seek or gain unfair advantages for oneself or others except when this would generate excessive or unreasonable burdens of compliance, but what does this imply? It implies that we not only have a duty not to seek unfair advantages, but also a duty not to accept benefits (or, at least, not to retain them once we have received them) if we know that they constitute unfair advantages, or to engage in behaviour which we know brings with it unfair advantages for ourselves or for others. Whenever we know that a benefit on offer constitutes an unfair advantage, we have a reason of justice, and a duty of citizenship, not to take it. But we do not have a duty to do everything within our power to determine whether a benefit constitutes an unfair advantage. If, however, we suspect that it may do so, then we have a duty to investigate further, at least if we can do so in a way that does not impose massive costs on us, for example, if we can reach an informed judgement by spending a relatively small amount of time doing some research. (Note also that what counts as an unreasonable or excessive burden of compliance will depend in part on whether one lives in a just or an unjust society: what counts as an excessive burden of compliance in a just society might not do so in an unjust society, where more can reasonably be demanded of the better off. So, for example, to ask the well off not to purchase better health care benefits, for themselves or their children, in a society where the distribution of resources is just may be to make an unreasonable demand of them, whereas it would not be in a society where that distribution is unjust since purchasing those benefits may worsen the health care available to the worst off who already have less than their entitlement.)[13]

In the next two sections, I shall look at what this duty implies in relation to unfair advantages that a person may gain because of her social circumstances, such as the family into which she is born, and unfair advantages that a person may gain because of her level of natural ability. I shall refer to it as a duty not to seek or gain unfair advantages, but I intend it to be understood as incorporating the personal prerogative I have described, and to include a duty not knowingly to accept or retain unfair advantages, together with a limited duty to investigate the nature and source of an advantage if one has reason to suspect that it may be unfair.

2 Advantageous social circumstances

The duty not to seek or gain unfair advantages for oneself or for others bears upon a range of decisions that parents have to make concerning how they bring up and educate their children. There are a variety of ways in which parents can benefit their children educationally: reading them bedtime stories; ensuring that family members eat together at mealtimes, with the children being encouraged to join in the conversation; providing a quiet space for them to do their homework; sitting with them whilst they do their homework and providing them with help when they are struggling; buying books for them to read, and computers and other educational aids for them to use; taking them on trips and holidays that have educational value; purchasing extra tuition to support the state-funded education they are receiving; paying for them to be educated privately in smaller classes and better resourced schools. Whether any (or all) of these benefits constitute forms of unfair advantage will depend, at least in part, upon whether they undermine equality of opportunity.

It is hard to deny that equality of opportunity requires more than non-discrimination. Even if there is no discrimination in the allocation of advantaged social positions, such as jobs and places in higher education, and the best qualified candidates are appointed irrespective of factors such as race, ethnicity, sex, disability, and sexual orientation, equality of opportunity will be in question if those from different social backgrounds have very different chances of obtaining the qualifications required for success in these competitions. The distribution of resources between families is clearly relevant to the issue of whether children born into different families possess equality of opportunity. But even if families have equivalent resources available to them, parents may make different decisions concerning how those resources are allocated and how much time they spend with their children. As a result, individual children may benefit not merely in terms of their educational development but also have advantages over others when it comes to public examinations, university entrance, and the job market. How then are we to determine whether an inequality of access to advantage that is created by differences in children's social circumstances is inconsistent with equality of opportunity, and whether parents might have a duty not to provide a benefit for their child because doing so would violate their duty not to seek or obtain unfair advantages for her?

Consider two broadly different approaches to the issue of what equality of opportunity requires in relation to differences in people's social circumstances, such as the different family environments into which they are born, including differences in the talents, skills, and values of their parents. (As an approximation, we might say that a person's social circumstances are those aspects of their social relationships which are beyond their control.) The first of these I shall call the neutralization approach, the second, the mitigation approach. According to the neutralization approach, equality of opportunity requires us to neutralize the effects of differences in people's social circumstances (except perhaps when this would make some worse off and no one better off), and maintains that these effects are neutralized if and only if they do not create any inequalities in their access to advantage. The neutralization approach can be grounded in different ways. Indeed there are both deontological and teleological versions of it. According to teleological versions, the neutralization approach is concerned ultimately with outcomes, in particular it values outcomes in which levels of access to advantage are unaffected by differences in people's social circumstances. According to deontological versions, in contrast, the neutralization approach focuses on the entitlements that people have to equal treatment, by the state and by others, and maintains that a person's fortunate social circumstances should not translate into an entitlement to greater access to advantage.

The alternative approach, which I shall call the mitigation approach, maintains that equality of opportunity requires us to prevent differences in people's social circumstances from unduly affecting their access to advantage. The impulse behind it is to limit inequalities that are the product of differences in people's circumstances but not to eradicate them entirely. It might be thought that the mitigation approach makes sense only as a practical compromise: when we are unable to neutralize the effects of differences in people's social circumstances we should aim to mitigate these effects instead. Understood in this way, the neutralization approach and the mitigation approach would not be competitors. They would not be mutually exclusive, for theorists may favour mitigating the effects of differences in social circumstances because they believe that in practice this is the closest we can come to neutralising them. This is not the way in which I shall understand these two approaches, however. According to my way of framing the distinction, they are competitors because they differ at the most fundamental theoretical level. Even at this level, however, there is still a problem keeping the approaches apart, for as it stands the neutralization approach is simply a version of the mitigation approach: one which maintains that whenever differences in people's social circumstances create an inequality of access to advantage, they unduly affect it. In order to keep the approaches apart, I shall simply stipulate that the mitigation approach permits differences in people's social circumstances to generate at least some inequalities of access to advantage (and not merely when these inequalities make some better off and none worse off).

My characterization of the mitigation approach is still seriously incomplete, however, for it does not tell us what is to count as 'an undue effect' on people's access to advantage.[14] Indeed, the mitigation approach as specified so far is not really a *theory* of equality of opportunity at all since it gives no guidance on which inequalities of access created by differences in people's social circumstances violate equality of opportunity and which do not. In response, it might be said that the mitigation approach cannot be spelled out any further: it simply requires us to make intuitive judgements concerning when a difference in people's social circumstances creates inequalities of access to advantage that are inconsistent with equality of opportunity because they are too great. But that would be just one version of the mitigation approach. Other versions might provide us with a principle, or set of principles, for determining what kind or degree of inequality of access could arise from differences in social circumstances without violating equality of opportunity. It will then be possible to seek justification for the principles that are advocated by a version of the mitigation approach. We can always ask, 'Why does equality of opportunity permit differences in people's social circumstances to have the degree and kind of impact upon their access to advantage that these principles permit?' and 'Why would allowing these circumstances to have any more impact, or a different kind of impact, violate equality of opportunity?' It may be that a stage is reached where these questions admit of no further answers, and defenders of the mitigation approach will be reduced merely to asserting their view that to allow differences in people's social circumstances to have any greater impact, or a different kind of impact, on their access to advantage would violate equality of opportunity. This does not create any serious disanalogy with the neutralization approach, however. For defenders of it can also be called upon to explain why equality of opportunity does not allow differences in people's social circumstances to create *any* inequalities of access to advantage and their reasons may run out as well.

Even if the neutralization approach and the mitigation approach apply primarily to the basic structure of society, we could use them to flesh out what constitutes an unfair advantage, and then to determine when the decisions parents make concerning what amount of time to spend with their children, or what amount of money to spend on their education, violate their obligation not to seek or gain unfair advantages for their children. When the duty not to seek or gain unfair advantage is given content in this way through the neutralization approach, it might seem to imply that parents have a duty of justice and of citizenship not to engage in any practice, or make any decision, which has the effect of creating greater opportunities for their children compared to others. But in that case the duty not to seek or gain unfair advantage for oneself or others would seem to prohibit parents even from reading their children bedtime stories, even when this practice plays a vital role in their relationship to their child.[15]

In response, a defender of the neutralization approach can point out that the duty not to seek or gain unfair advantage, properly specified, incorporates a personal prerogative: it is a duty not to seek or gain unfair advantages for oneself or others *except when this would generate excessive or unreasonable burdens of compliance*. So understood, the duty would seem to permit parents to read bedtime stories to their child: when this form of interaction plays an important role in their relationship with their child, disallowing them from doing so would place excessive or unreasonable burdens on them. But even when we add the proviso, there are many practices which would seem to be incompatible with the duty not to seek or gain unfair advantage when the notion of an unfair advantage is unpacked in the way that the neutralization approach dictates. In a society in which most children did not have access to computers at home, the duty not to seek or gain unfair advantages for one's children would seem to imply that if a parent could provide such access he or she should not do so even when the proviso is taken into account, and it would certainly imply that purchasing extra tuition for them, or paying for private education for them, would be a violation of that duty. If most families are unable to provide their children with a quiet space at home in which to work, or take them on trips and holidays that have educational value, complying with such a duty might even require parents who are able to do so to refrain. Only a very elastic notion of what constitutes an unreasonable or excessive burden of compliance would permit parents to appeal to such burdens to justify providing their children with these advantages. This gives some reason to worry about unpacking the relevant duty in terms of a conception of unfair advantage that is derived from the neutralization approach.

The implications of the mitigation approach for the duty not to seek unfair advantage are likely to be much less outlandish, and the approach more plausible as a result, although what it requires, even in outline, will depend upon how it is developed, in particular on its account of what constitutes an undue effect. One plausible starting point is the idea that differences in children's social circumstances undermine equality of opportunity when these differences mean that some children are deprived of fair access to qualifications. If this view were to inform the duty not to seek or gain unfair advantage, it would have implications for any decision a parent makes concerning his or her child's education that would undermine fair access to qualifications. Of course, this pushes the problem back to the issue of what is to count as fair access to qualifications, if unequal access to qualifications is insufficient in itself to constitute an unfairness in that access.

Elsewhere I have defended the idea that fair access to qualifications can be characterized in terms of two principles, which I call the basic skills principle, and the educational access principle.[16] The basic skills principle holds that each child should be provided with an education, both formal and informal, that enables him to acquire a set of general and particular skills which will allow him to have an adequate range of options, irrespective of his level of natural endowment, so long as that level permits him to acquire these skills. Whenever some children do not receive such an education but others do, there is unfairness in their access to qualifications. For it is highly unlikely that someone who lacks the general ability to read and write, or who lacks basic numerical skills, could have an adequate range of options when the possibilities on offer in his society are, for the most part, options only for those who are literate or numerate. In a society with a variety of social forms and practices, just as no individual option is necessary in order to have an adequate range of options,[17] no particular individual skill is required, but a person will need a range of such skills, provided in large part through the educational system.[18]

It would be implausible to maintain that the basic skills principle provides an exhaustive account of what variations in social circumstances are compatible with fair access to qualifications, and no plausible version of the mitigation approach could hold that it does so. For if it were regarded as exhaustive, it would allow the different economic resources available to different families to have too deep an impact upon their children's access to qualifications for us to say that the effects of differences in people's social circumstances have been limited in the way that justice requires. Suppose that two children receive a secondary education which enables them to acquire equivalent qualifications, but one child has available to her the economic resources to go on to a higher education which would then permit her to train to become a doctor whereas the other does not. The basic skills principle on its own would seem to leave open the possibility that this state of affairs might be permissible. If the effects of differences in social circumstances and natural endowments on access to qualifications are to be mitigated in the way that equality of opportunity requires, then surely this possibility must be excluded. We need a principle which regulates access to higher education in a way that is not merely formal. My proposal is that any plausible version of the mitigation approach must hold that the effects of differences in social circumstances should never be such that some people can enjoy a level and quality of education which others with equivalent qualifications are denied or which they could enjoy only if they or others made sacrifices that it would be unreasonable to expect. I call this the educational access principle. This principle would place constraints on what effect differences in people's social circumstances can legitimately have on their access to higher education. For it could not be reconciled with a state of affairs in which some, as a result of their fortunate social circumstances, possessed the resources necessary to go on to higher education whilst others with equivalent qualifications, but less fortunate social circumstances, did not possess the necessary resources to do so and could not reasonably be expected to acquire them (for example, if they could not acquire them except by taking out a loan the repayment schedule for which would place massive burdens on them, or without making unreasonable demands on family members, such as asking their parents to cash in their pension funds).

142

Even though the basic skills principle and the educational access principle would apply primarily to the design of the basic structure of society, including public educational institutions, they would also inform the duty not to seek or gain unfair advantage, and have implications for how parents should behave towards their children, what kind of educational environment they should provide for them, and what decisions they are permitted to make to increase their children's chances of educational success. Parental neglect of various kinds may stand in the way of children acquiring the skills they need in order to possess an adequate range of options. In the light of the basic skills principle, when a child is in danger of failing to acquire these skills, his parents may be under a duty to provide more help. Informed by the educational access principle, the duty not to seek or gain unfair advantage would have further implications for the decisions parents make about whether to send their children to private schools or provide them with extra educational support. Parents would violate their duty not to seek or to gain unfair advantage when they chose private schooling, or purchased extra tuition and the like for their children, in a context where the publicly funded educational provision available to them satisfied the basic skills principle but through providing these benefits their children enjoyed a level and quality of education denied to most others.

Understood in the way proposed, mitigating the effects that differences in social circumstances may have on children's access to qualifications would nevertheless permit differences in the kind of support and attention parents were permitted to provide without violating their duty not to seek or gain unfair advantages, even in a fully just society. Different families might make different decisions about how they organized their family lives without violating that duty, for example, they might make different decisions concerning whether to insist that they eat their evening meals together and whether part of their house is designated as a space for quiet study. They might also make different decisions about how they used their wealth and income, for example, whether they bought books, computers, and other educational aids for their children, and whether they took them on educational trips outside the home, without violating this duty. In an educational system where there was public provision of comparable quality, parents might choose private education at primary or secondary school level in a way that did not violate their duty not to seek or gain unfair advantage. If, for example, a school offered a distinctive curriculum, or boarding facilities or after hours childcare that parents (given their career choices) needed, then they could choose it for their children without violating this duty. And in terms of higher education, wealthier parents might smooth their children's passage through higher education by providing them with extra funding without violating the duty.

3 Advantageous natural talents and abilities

The duty not to seek unfair advantages for oneself or others also bears upon a range of decisions that individuals make concerning whether to seek advantages (or knowingly to accept advantages) as a result of their possession of a higher than average level of natural endowment, that is, as a result of being born with a higher than average potential for acquiring skills and talents that are in demand. This issue is at the heart of G. A. Cohen's critique of Rawls's incentives argument.[19] Rawls's argument permits individuals even in a perfectly just society to demand higher salaries to perform work that would benefit the worse off in society, even if the worse off would be even better off were these individuals to choose to perform that work for less reward. In Rawls's framework, individuals do not have a duty of justice or citizenship to apply the difference principle to the economic decisions they make concerning what careers to pursue, how hard they work within the jobs they do, and what salaries to negotiate for doing them. Cohen argues that there are the same grounds for applying the difference principle to personal economic behaviour as there are for applying it to the basic structure of society—both have profound and pervasive effects on people's lives—though he also maintains that when this principle is applied to personal choices, it must take into account labour burdens in a way that Rawls's primary goods metric does not,[20] and that it is subject to a personal prerogative which permits individuals to depart from what it requires when acting from it would unreasonably constrain their pursuit of their own projects.[21]

In response to Cohen, Seana Shiffrin has argued that those who endorse the difference principle, and the reasoning that justifies it, may accept that personal economic behaviour which is permitted by the basic structure is nevertheless governed by considerations of justice without supposing that the difference principle itself applies to that behaviour. In particular, she argues that the idea that natural talents are arbitrary from the moral point of view (at least with respect to shares of wealth and income), which is the basis of one of Rawls's main arguments for the difference principle, should constrain personal economic behaviour: an individual should not seek to gain economic advantage from her possession of a natural talent that is in demand. According to the position Shiffrin identifies and defends, individuals' economic behaviour is subject to some of the same moral constraints as it would be on Cohen's view, but these constraints are defended in a different way that also creates some divergences between her position and his. On her view, an individual is permitted to turn down a job (for example, to work as a medical doctor) when he does so solely because he would prefer to pursue some other career (for example, that of landscape gardener) without any appeal to personal prerogatives, since he is not seeking to gain advantage from morally arbitrary factors such as his natural talent. But he is not permitted to agree to accept the former job on condition that he is given a higher salary that goes beyond what would be required to compensate him for any additional labour burdens, since then he would be seeking such an advantage.

It seems to me that Shiffrin's arguments are for the most part compatible with the duty that I am defending in this chapter when that duty is informed by the idea that people can secure unfair advantages through their possession of higher than average levels of natural talent.[22] But her discussion would benefit from drawing a distinction between a neutralization approach and a mitigation approach, applied this time to the effects of the possession of different levels of natural talent. Cohen is, in effect, a neutralizer: he believes that as a matter of justice different levels of natural talent should not create inequalities of access to advantage. Shiffrin shows that it is possible to be a neutralizer in this regard at the level of basic institutions without being a neutralizer at the level of personal behaviour. But it is also possible to hold that natural talents are arbitrary from the moral point of view without even being a neutralizer at the level of basic institutions. It is perfectly consistent to believe that natural talents are arbitrary from the moral point of view but to think that the effects of different levels of natural talent should be mitigated not neutralized. To hold that natural talents are arbitrary from the moral point of view with respect to advantage (or some aspect of advantage) is equivalent to denying that the possession of a higher than average level of natural talent by itself gives a person an entitlement to a greater than average share of that advantage. But this negative conclusion does not entail the positive idea that each person is entitled to an equal share of advantage or (more pertinently) that differences in their levels of natural talent should not generate any inequalities in their access to advantage.

What mitigating the effects of different levels of natural talent would require at the level of institutional design, and then in the context of personal behaviour when it informs the duty not to seek or gain unfair advantages, will of course depend on what it is for these different levels of natural talent to have an undue effect on people's access to advantage (or some component of advantage, such as wealth and income). But in principle it might permit greater inequalities in that access, and in consequence allow individuals at least sometimes to seek to gain from their possession of a higher level of natural talent when they enter salary negotiations or make choices about what career to pursue. For example, mitigating the effects of different levels of natural talent might require a principle of sufficiency at the level of institutional design, together with a limit on inequalities in the access to various goods that are of central importance to flourishing, such as education, health care, and wealth and income. Elsewhere I have defended the principle that the effects of differences in people's circumstances, including differences in their level of natural endowment, should never be such that some can (substantially before the average retirement age) acquire the resources that are necessary in order to be able to lead a decent life whilst choosing not to work to earn an income, whereas others cannot.[23] This principle, which I labelled the accumulation of wealth principle, would, amongst other things, limit the inequalities of wealth and income that society's basic institutions can justly permit to emerge from differences in people's levels of natural endowment. But it is unlikely to limit to any significant extent people's pursuit of their own economic advantage, except at the extremes, for example, when massive salaries or bonuses are on offer. When informed by the accumulation of wealth principle, the duty not to seek or gain unfair advantages for oneself and for others might imply a duty to be vigilant in relation to what one demands (or accepts or keeps) if one is in a fortunate enough position to command such salaries or bonuses, but it is unlikely to bear upon decisions about what career to pursue or what salaries to negotiate in standard cases.

There are many other ways in which the mitigation approach might be developed.[24] But since the mitigation approach is concerned with limiting the inequalities that result from differences in people's levels of natural endowments, the duties derived from it will affect economic behaviour only in so far as a person's economic choices push up against these limits, so they are unlikely to be as demanding as those derived from the neutralization approach.

4 Conclusion

In this chapter, I have defended a wide ranging duty not to seek or gain unfair advantage that has relevance whenever there are practical difficulties with devising legislation that prevents people from doing so, or moral reasons not to enact such legislation. This duty is likely to grow in importance in unjust societies which allow greater scope for individuals to seek or gain unfair advantages. It is particularly salient in the context of a theory of justice which supposes that justice requires us to counteract the effects of differences in people's circumstances. It is most at home within a justice account of citizenship, which is not to deny that it may also have a place within an equal membership account which maintains (for example) that treating others as equals—recognizing the equal standing of others—may sometimes require limiting the preferential concern one may be inclined to show towards one's children in decisions about their education, and may sometimes require limiting the preferential concern one may be inclined to show for one's own interests when making choices about what salaries or bonuses to demand (or accept or retain) from one's employer. The extent of the demands this duty places on individuals will depend, in part, on whether we adopt a neutralization approach or a mitigation approach to counteracting the effects of differences in people's social circumstances and differences in their levels of natural endowment.

Notes

1. I am using the term 'advantage' in its non-competitive or non-comparative sense in which '[s]omething can add to someone's advantage without him, as a result, being better placed, or less worse placed, than somebody else' (G. A. Cohen, 'On the Currency of Egalitarian Justice', *Ethics*, Vol. 99, 1989, p. 917, note 18.) In some cases, of course, gaining an unfair advantage may also involve gaining an unfair advantage over others.

2. See M. Clayton and D. Stevens, 'School Choice and the Burdens of Justice', *Theory and Research in Education*, Vol. 2, 2004, pp. 115–18. For a different view, see A. Swift, *How Not to Be a Hypocrite: School Choice for the Morally Perplexed Parent* (London: a, 2003), Ch. 8.

3. Clayton and Stevens, 'School Choice and the Burdens of Justice', p. 117.

4. For relevant discussion, see Swift, *How Not to Be a Hypocrite*, pp. 25–30, 128–30.

5. For relevant discussion, see Shiffrin, 'Incentives, Motives, and Talents', especially pp. 137–42.

6. Michael Otsuka expresses scepticism about the existence of such prerogatives in his 'Prerogatives to Depart from Equality' in A. O'Hear (ed.), *Political Philosophy* (Cambridge: Cambridge University Press, 2006), pp. 95–111.

7. See, for example, T. Nagel, *Equality and Partiality* (New York: Oxford University Press, 1991) pp. 178–9.

8. See, for example, Cohen, *Rescuing Justice and Equality*, pp 8–11.

9. See Cohen, *Rescuing Justice and Equality*, pp. 10–11, 71, 391. But contrast p. 389, where Cohen seems to endorse the idea that justice itself is a compromise between personal and impersonal standpoints.

10. In other words it might be regarded as a disabler in Jonathan Dancy's sense: see Dancy, *Ethics Without Principles*, pp. 38–43.

11. Rawls, *A Theory of Justice*, p. 334/293–4, italics added.

12. See Chapter 2, section 1. In that passage Rawls maintains that 'the attempt to forestall [the undesirable consequences of economic choices permitted by a just basic structure] by restrictive rules that apply to individuals would be an excessive if not impossible burden' (Rawls, *Political Liberalism*, p. 266).

13. See Clayton and Stevens, 'School Choice and the Burdens of Justice', pp. 119–20.

14. Both the mitigation approach and the neutralization approach also require some account of how 'advantage' should be understood for the purposes of comparing how well off people are. The main candidates in the literature are primary goods,

welfare, resources, capabilities, or some combination of these. I shall not explore this issue here.

15. For relevant discussion, see Harry Brighouse and Adam Swift's discussion of familial relationship goods in Brighouse and Swift, 'Legitimate Parental Partiality', especially pp. 53–9; S. Segall, 'If You're a Luck-Egalitarian, How Come You Read Bedtime Stories to Your Children?', *Critical Review of International Social and Political Philosophy*, Vol. 14, 2011, 23–40; A. Mason, 'Putting Story-Reading to Bed: A Reply to Segall', *Critical Review of International Social and Political Philosophy*, Vol. 14, 2011, 81–8.

16. Mason, *Levelling the Playing Field*, pp. 134–50. This is, of course, just one proposal. Matthew Clayton defends what is in effect a version of the mitigation approach by employing a conception of unfair advantage that is developed by extending Ronald Dworkin's device of a hypothetical insurance market (see M. Clayton, *Justice and Legitimacy in Upbringing* (Oxford: Oxford University Press, 2006), especially pp. 61–75.) A version of the mitigation approach might also be developed by incorporating prioritarian principles: see note 24 below.

17. Raz, *The Morality of Freedom*, pp. 410–11.

18. By specific skills, I have in mind the following sorts of thing: the ability to work cooperatively with others; the ability to extract the main points from a report; the ability to organize tasks so as to meet deadlines; the ability to understand diagrams or pictorial representations; dexterity in confined spaces.

19. See Cohen, *Rescuing Justice and Equality*, Ch. 1.

20. See Cohen, *Rescuing Justice and Equality*, pp. 16, 98–100.

21. See Cohen, *Rescuing Justice and Equality*, pp. 10–11, 61–2, 70–2, 387–94.

22. Although, unlike Shiffrin, I am treating it as a perfect rather than an imperfect duty. See Shiffrin, 'Incentives, Motives, and Talents', pp. 141–2.

23. Mason, *Levelling the Playing Field*, pp. 147–50.

24. Rather than consisting of quasi-egalitarian principles that limit the extent of permissible inequalities, the mitigation approach might be made up of prioritarian principles. Prioritarianism holds that, when other things are equal (in particular, when benefits are of the same magnitude, and there is the same number of potential beneficiaries), benefiting the worse off matters more than benefiting the better off. When it is regarded as (part of) a theory of justice, it holds that there is a reason of justice to give priority to benefiting the worse off. See D. Parfit, 'Equality and Priority', in A. Mason (ed.), *Ideals of Equality* (Oxford: Blackwell, 1998), pp. 12–13; Mason, *Levelling the Playing Field*, pp. 113–16.

6

A Duty to Offer Only Public Reasons?

Do citizens have a duty to restrict the kind of reasons they offer in public debate?[1] Do they act impermissibly in a public forum if they appeal to religious reasons or, more generally, if they appeal to reasons that are tied to specific moral doctrines or particular conceptions of the good? Are they morally required to offer only 'public' reasons? The justice and equal membership accounts provide different perspectives on this issue. I consider two ways in which the idea that citizens are under a duty to limit themselves to public reasons in public debate might be defended from within a justice account. The first of these approaches grounds the duty in the importance of *legitimacy*, understood as requiring justification to all, and claims that this is best secured by a democratic system in which citizens offer only public reasons in public debate over matters of basic justice, whereas the second argues that it is *unreasonable* for citizens to offer non-public reasons in public debate over these matters because that would be to propose terms of cooperation that they could not reasonably expect their fellow citizens to accept. I also consider the idea that if citizens are to *respect one another* in public debate, then each needs to offer grounds for laws or policies that they can reasonably expect their fellow citizens to endorse. Although a defence of the duty to restrict oneself to public reasons that is grounded in the notion of respect might be developed within a justice account, it is more at home in an equal membership account. I raise objections to each of the three approaches I have identified, but conclude by considering the idea that there might nevertheless be instrumental reasons for recognizing that under some circumstances citizens are under a duty to give only public reasons in public debate, in particular, when compliance with it would promote reasonably stable or just outcomes, or a sense of belonging to the polity.

1 The alleged duty and its scope

In order to assess the case for a duty to restrict the reasons one offers in public debate to public reasons, we need an account of this duty and its scope, including some clarification of what is to count as a public reason and what constitutes public debate. Only then can we determine whether it might be grounded in considerations of justice or in the good of equal membership, or both.

What is a public reason? A public reason is one that we could reasonably expect to be shared by any citizen who held a reasonable moral view or doctrine, that is, a moral view or doctrine compatible with the equal moral standing of their fellow citizens. (Let us also say that a reasonable person is, in part, someone who subscribes to a reasonable moral doctrine.) In a religiously diverse society, reasons that are grounded in a particular religious doctrine cannot count as public reasons. Citizens who do not accept this doctrine could not reasonably be expected to endorse these reasons if that would involve abandoning views to which they reasonably subscribe.[2] If there is a duty to offer only public reasons, citizens are not morally permitted to give reasons that involve an explicit or implicit appeal to religious authority as the ultimate ground for a law or policy, even if these reasons are their main basis for favouring that law or policy. But this does not mean that they are morally prohibited from appealing to a doctrine that has emerged from a particular religious tradition. Provided others who subscribe to reasonable moral views could reasonably accept this doctrine, then its genealogy does not matter. So, for example, someone might appeal to the sanctity of human life in arguing against the legalization of voluntary euthanasia, but provided that they do not defend it by appeal to religious authority, or by appeal to a doctrine that could reasonably be accepted only by those who subscribe to a particular religion, then it might count as a public reason.

I shall simply adopt Rawls's account of the scope of the proposed duty to restrict oneself to public reasons, according to which this duty governs public debate over constitutional essentials and matters of basic justice.[3] The duty might also be extended without strain to govern not only the reasons one gives in public debate over matters of basic justice, but also the grounds on which one decides for whom, or for what, to vote. 'Public debate' is a vague expression, however. Following Rawls again, I shall assume that it covers discussions that take place in the 'public political forum', that is, the discourse of judges, political representatives, government officials and candidates for public office, and by extension the discourse of citizens when they are debating in a public forum what law or policy should be enacted.[4]

Some defences of this duty sanction a range of exceptions. In his defence of public reason in *Political Liberalism*, Rawls allowed that in non-ideal societies citizens might permissibly appeal to non-public reasons when that would best promote the goal of securing a well-ordered and just society.[5] In a later article, he argued that even in ideal societies citizens are morally permitted to offer non-public reasons, provided that they undertake to replace them with public reasons at some point in the future.[6] So, for example, according to this view it would be permissible even in a just society for a person to appeal to the idea that 'we are all equal in the eyes of god' in defending a policy, provided that she acknowledges a commitment to defend it on the basis of public reasons, either then or in the future.

The duty to give only public reasons does not by itself entail a duty to engage in public debate: it is a duty to give public reasons *if* one engages in such debate. Defences of the duty to restrict the reasons one gives in public debate to public reasons are, however, sometimes embedded in a defence of a wider duty to engage in public debate. The defence of such a duty might appeal to the idea that a citizen has a duty of respect or civility to give reasons for the laws or policies he favours, which in turn requires him to be responsive to the objections of others, that is, to defend the reasons he gives in the face of criticism, and a duty to attend to the reasons of others, that is, to listen to what others have to say and try to understand its import even when he is doubtful of its truth. If there is a duty to give reasons for the laws or policies one favours, then so long as one has preferences for particular laws or policies, one is under a duty to engage in public debate. With the exception of section 3, however, I shall focus on the narrower idea that if citizens engage in public debate, then they have a duty to limit the reasons they offer to public reasons. Following others, I shall sometimes call this the reciprocity requirement. I shall examine the resources contained in both the justice account and the equal membership account for grounding it.

2 The liberal conception of legitimacy

Some versions of the justice account maintain that there is a strong connection between the legitimate exercise of coercive political power and the giving of public reasons when debating matters of basic justice, sufficient to justify the idea that citizens have a duty to restrict the reasons they offer in public debate to these reasons. But what exactly is the nature of this connection supposed to be?

According to what might be called 'the liberal conception of legitimacy', it is a necessary truth that the exercise of coercive political power is legitimate if and only if it is *morally permissible* or *morally justified*.[7] Within this conception, however, the substantive claim that is made about the relationship between legitimacy and a duty to restrict oneself to public reasons takes a number of different forms. Consider three of them:

(1) The exercise of political power is legitimate concerning matters of basic justice if and only if it is based on laws and policies that are *justifiable to all reasonable persons* subject to them. In practice, the best means of ensuring that laws and policies on such matters are justifiable in this way is to put in place democratic political procedures and for ordinary citizens and their political representatives to acknowledge and act from a duty to restrict the reasons they offer in public debate on matters of basic justice to public reasons.

(2) The exercise of political power is legitimate concerning matters of basic justice if and only if it is based on laws and policies that are justified by reasons that are actually *endorsed by each reasonable person* subject to them. In practice, the best means of ensuring that it is based on such laws and policies is to put in place democratic political procedures and for ordinary citizens and their political representatives to acknowledge and act from a duty to restrict the reasons they offer in public debate on matters of basic justice to public reasons.

(3) The exercise of political power is legitimate concerning matters of basic justice if and only if the laws and policies that govern these matters are the product of democratic procedures in which only public reasons are treated as relevant. In practice, this requires ordinary citizens and their political representatives to exercise self-restraint, that is, to acknowledge and act from a duty to restrict the reasons they offer in public debate on matters of basic justice to public reasons.

Only (3) ties legitimacy directly to the giving of public reasons. (3), in contrast to (1) and (2), expresses a procedural conception of legitimacy according to which the exclusion of private reasons is partially constitutive of the relevant procedure and hence of legitimacy itself. Both (1) and (2) regard the giving of only public reasons, and the political procedures in which these reasons are to be exchanged, as contingently connected to legitimacy: the restriction to public reasons is regarded as part of the best means of achieving legitimacy.[8]

The formulations of the liberal conception of legitimacy contained in (1)–(3) have different strengths and weaknesses, but they have related features which make it hard for them to justify the requirement that citizens should give *only* public reasons. Consider (1). In order to justify its conclusion that in practice the best way of securing legitimacy is for citizens to restrict themselves to public reasons, it needs to hold that the exercise of political power is legitimate only if it is justifiable to all of those subject to it on the basis of the *same* reasons. The notion of being justifiable to all does not necessarily entail 'justifiable to all on the basis of the same reasons', but unless we interpret it in this way, it is unclear what the connection is supposed to be between it and the exchange of public reasons. If we allow that laws and policies are justifiable to all when they are justifiable to different people on the basis of different reasons, then we allow the possibility that laws and policies might be justifiable to all on the basis of different non-public reasons.[9] For example, some people might endorse the idea that there is a right to religious liberty because they believe that different religions represent different paths to the same god, whilst others endorse that idea because they believe that there is one uniquely correct religion but people must find their own way to it by exercising their own free choice. So the idea that there is a strong connection in practice between a law's being justifiable to all and citizens giving only public reasons in public debate is plausible only if we assume that being 'justifiable to all' means being 'justifiable to all on the basis of the same reasons'. Yet why should we make that assumption? If, for example, what lies behind the liberal conception of legitimacy is a commitment to respecting each person's autonomy—each person's capacity to judge for herself how she should lead her life, what arrangements she will flourish under, or what justice requires—this gives no warrant for making this assumption: why should it matter from the point of view of respecting personal autonomy whether the exercise of coercive power is underwritten by a public reason that can reasonably be accepted by each person, or whether for different people it is underwritten by different private reasons?

Similarly, with (2) why should we rule out the possibility that full legitimacy might be secured when a law is adopted because reasonable people favour it for different private reasons rather than for shared public reasons or because they—or some of them—favour it for different private reasons *in addition* to shared public reasons? (Again, enforcing a law that a person endorses on the basis of his own private reasons would be perfectly consistent with respecting his personal autonomy. Why should *my* personal autonomy be threatened by the fact that I am coerced by a law that other people endorse for reasons different from mine, even if their reasons for endorsing it figure in the explanation for why that law or policy was adopted, provided that I endorse this law for my own reasons?) But allowing this possibility would sever, or at least seriously weaken, the connection between securing legitimacy and a practice of giving only public reasons.

The exclusion of private reasons in (2) becomes even harder to justify if we revise it in order to accommodate better the likelihood of conflict between different public reasons. Suppose, for example, that according to this revised version, the exercise of political power is regarded as legitimate on matters of basic justice if and only if it is based on laws and policies justified by reasons that each reasonable person endorses *and* when reasonable people disagree about the relative weight to attach to different reasons the force of which they each accept, then these laws and policies reflect the balance of reasons favoured by the majority.[10] This avoids a counterintuitive consequence of (2) as it stands, namely, that the exercise of political power would be legitimate when the law which underwrites it is justified by a reason that everyone endorses, even though everyone thinks there are stronger reasons that each also endorses for favouring a different law. But denying the relevance of private reasons to legitimacy now has the rather odd consequence that a law or policy might be legitimate compared to a rival because a majority of reasonable people think that the strongest *public* reasons speak in its favour, even though they would all, on the basis of their different *private* reasons, prefer the rival law or policy which is supported by what they judge to be weaker public reasons.

Although (3) ties legitimacy directly to the exclusion of private reasons, if it is to be defended we need some rationale for doing so. Yet this is hard to provide for now familiar reasons. Why not say that what matters for legitimacy is the existence of procedures which allow the giving of either public reasons or private reasons that are compatible with accepting the equal moral standing of all, rather than the giving of specifically public reasons? In response it might be said that the formulation in (3) brings into play a broader notion of what is required to respect one's fellow citizens in public debate concerning matters of basic justice (or to treat others as equals in that context), namely, that it requires restricting oneself to public reasons. The connection to legitimacy, understood as the morally permissible (or morally justified) exercise of coercive political power, is tenuous here but this argument nevertheless has independent force as a potential justification for the idea that citizens are under a duty to restrict themselves to public reasons in public debate. I shall examine it in the next section.

3 Being respectful

The duty to give only public reasons might be defended by appealing to an ideal of respect for persons as citizens, independently of any supposed connection to the legitimate exercise of political power: the idea would be that treating fellow citizens as equals in the political process requires showing them respect in that process, which in turn requires the restriction to public reasons. When the argument proceeds in this way, the duty to give only public reasons might be regarded as part of a wider duty to *engage* in public debate: according to this view, respect for one's fellow citizens requires not only that a person limit herself to public reasons *if* she engages in public debate, but also that she engage in that debate, listening attentively to the arguments of others and responding to them, defending her position in terms that they too can accept. It is not always clear whether the duty to give only public reasons is being located in a wider duty of this kind: indeed it seems to me that Rawls veers between a narrower and a wider view of what the duty of respect or civility entails.[11] When it is understood as entailing a duty to engage in public debate that involves listening attentively to the arguments of others and giving only public reasons in response, it is more plausibly located in an equal membership account, for it seems to go beyond what could be justified by reference to considerations of justice alone.[12]

Could a duty to engage in public debate in this manner be justified by appealing to the idea that we have a duty to show respect to our fellow citizens in the political process, in effect expressing our duty to treat them as equals in that process—a duty that is justified by, and partially constitutive of, the good of equal membership? It is not clear how it could, for why should we think that there need be anything *disrespectful* in a blank refusal to engage in public debate at all? Citizens may have other things to do, in accordance with their own conceptions of the good; their decision not to participate in public debate may simply reflect a different set of priorities rather than involve any necessary disrespect, even when the issues involved are important to them or to others. More generally, it seems to me that a democratic society in which ordinary citizens vote but do not debate their policy preferences even on matters of basic justice need not signify any failure of respect, even if we regard it as deficient in other ways.[13]

Citizens may, however, occupy roles which require them to participate in public debate, for example, they may be political representatives in a legislative, or Supreme Court judges. What then does respect for one's fellow citizens require of those who *do* engage in public debate, whether as ordinary citizens or as occupants of specific public roles? In particular, does it require a citizen to limit himself to public reasons? If so, why would it be disrespectful to give reasons that one thought that only some of one's fellow citizens would find persuasive, focusing in effect on the particular moral doctrines to which they subscribed and the implications of those doctrines? Or indeed, why would it be disrespectful simply to give one's own private reasons without any expectation that they will be shared by others? David Archard distinguishes between a maximal and a minimal specification of the obligation of civility that might be thought to govern respectful debate between citizens. According to the minimal interpretation 'I am required to give you what are the reasons for my political actions and which you can in principle recognize to be my reasons', whereas according to the maximal interpretation 'I am required to give you reasons for my political actions which you can in principle accept as good reasons'.[14] We need a justification for favouring the maximal interpretation over the minimal interpretation.[15] Even if the minimal interpretation is too weak, there are other positions available between it and the maximal interpretation, for example, one which restricts the kind of reasons that are compatible with respecting one's fellow citizens, so that, for example, racist or sexist reasons are excluded.

Nor is it clear that the very idea of respect for one's fellow citizens requires a citizen to *respond* to the arguments of her fellows if or when she offers her own reasons. If a citizen gives her own reasons for her policy preferences but refuses to respond to the arguments of others because she believes they are not worthy of serious consideration, or because she believes they are incapable of reasoning correctly about what justice requires, then this is disrespectful (except perhaps when she is confronted by racist or other reasons that deny the fundamental equality of persons). If a citizen engages in public debate but takes some of his fellow citizens' reasons less seriously simply because of who they are, then he is surely treating them with disrespect, except perhaps in special circumstances where they occupy roles or positions which call into question their entitlement to make the arguments they do.[16] But a citizen who participates in public debate simply by giving her reasons for her policy preferences is not necessarily disrespectful when she refuses to respond to the arguments of her fellow citizens if she does so even-handedly and does not ridicule their arguments.[17]

It might be maintained, however, that even if there need be no *disrespect* involved in giving one's reasons but not responding to the reasons of others, it does not follow that this is a *respectful* or civil way of participating. Perhaps there is some middle ground between not being disrespectful and being respectful that would be occupied by a citizen who presented his reasons but didn't respond to the arguments of others despite requests to do so: he is not showing respect for his fellow citizens but nor is he necessarily being disrespectful to them. This description is plausible in some cases, but it is not clear that a citizen who takes part in public debate by giving his own reasons but not responding to the reasons of others *must* fail to be respectful or civil. If he has some understanding of the impact of different policies on the ways of life of his fellow citizens, and of the reasons that they have for favouring different policies, and in the light of this tries to accommodate their policy preferences by adjusting his own, then surely he could be showing respect to them even if he votes without giving his reasons for his policy preferences, or gives those reasons but without responding to their arguments.

Is respecting one's fellow citizens then purely a matter of how one engages in public debate when one does so, rather than the *content* of the reasons one gives and how they might be justified?[18] I think it would be mistaken to suppose that respect for one's fellow citizens is concerned solely with the manner in which one engages with them. Even if we reject the idea that treating one's fellow citizens as equals in public debate requires limiting oneself to public reasons, we would nevertheless have to place some limits on what kinds of reasons are consistent with it. Treating one's fellow citizens as equals, for example, excludes giving racist or sexist reasons. This raises difficult questions, however. Are some reasons inherently disrespectful because they are inconsistent with treating all of one's fellow citizens as equals? How should we determine what is to count as such a reason? Do homophobic reasons fail to treat gays and lesbians as equals—including reasons of this kind which play a role in religious practices and have a basis in religious texts? Does arguing that mothers who are carrying foetuses with Downs Syndrome should have a right to an abortion represent a failure to treat those citizens who carry that syndrome as equals?

These questions are hard to answer satisfactorily, but it seems clear that some reasons may be such that offering them in the context of public debate violates a duty to treat fellow citizens as equals that can be grounded either in considerations of justice or in the good of equal membership. For example, racist, sexist, or homophobic reasons often express contempt for groups of citizens, and in this way violate a duty of respect that is equally at home in either a justice account or an equal membership account. Other reasons, however, may fail to treat others as equals without necessarily expressing contempt for them, or even disparaging them, and in these cases it is not clear that any duty of justice is violated in offering them in public debate, though doing so would offend against the good of equal membership. So, for example, it might be argued (controversially, of course) that defending an abortion policy which allows abortion on demand for those carrying a foetus with an abnormality, on the grounds that the lives which are led by those with this abnormality are less fulfilling, represents a failure to treat those with this abnormality as equals, thereby offending against the good of equal member-ship, but without expressing contempt for, or disparaging, those with these disabilities, and without therefore violating any duty of justice.[19] Ways of arguing that fail to treat fellow citizens as equals but which are not unjust in themselves are still morally objectionable since they violate a duty that is grounded in the good of equal membership—and even when the victims are not fellow citizens but resident aliens, the presence of these arguments in public debate may make it harder for them to make the transition to citizenship. (A justice account may also hold that forms of disrespect that are not serious enough to count as unjust in themselves can promote unjust outcomes, for example, by contributing to the stigmatizing of a group, and so it might object to them on these grounds.)

But these difficult issues concerning what is to count as a disrespectful reason, and whether the giving of a disrespectful reason that fails to treat fellow citizens as equals is automatically unjust, do not need to be resolved in order to show that respect for persons as citizens does not require a practice of public reason, for we have not found an argument for thinking that a failure to engage in public debate, or a failure to limit oneself to public reasons when one does so, necessarily represents a failure to treat one's fellow citizens as equals. The requirement that citizens restrict themselves to public reasons can seem plausible because we do suppose that certain kinds of reasons are disrespectful or otherwise inappropriate in public debate, for example, reasons that appeal to racist or sexist ideas, or to naked self or group interest, and it is tempting to think that the reciprocity requirement provides us with the best explanation of why reasons of these kinds are objectionable. But it seems to me that this requirement draws the line between objectionable and appropriate (even if contestable) reasons in the wrong way and in the wrong place. We can explain why the appeal to, say, racist and sexist ideas, or indeed the pursuit of self or group interests in public debate without any regard to the interests of others, is objectionable without invoking it.

4 Being reasonable

Even if restricting oneself to public reasons in public debate is not a requirement of treating one's fellow citizens with respect, as equals, could it be a requirement of reasonableness? It might be argued that we behave reasonably in public debate only when we propose (or at least, aim to propose) fair terms of cooperation. Being reasonable is not merely having reasons for behaving in the way that one does. Rawls, for example, says that 'Persons are reasonable in one basic aspect when, among equals say, they are ready to propose principles and standards as fair terms of cooperation and to abide by them willingly, given the assurance that others will likewise do so'.[20] By extension, we might suppose that people behave reasonably only if they restrict themselves to public reasons when they are involved in public debate over constitutional essentials or matters of basic justice. For it might be held that only then can they be genuinely motivated by a desire to propose fair terms of cooperation, on the grounds that these terms can be fair only if they are such that others too can reasonably be expected to accept them. In this way a defence of the reciprocity requirement by appeal to the importance of reasonableness might be mounted from within a justice account.

It is plausible to think that we act reasonably in public debate only if we propose, or try to propose, fair terms of cooperation, but it is not clear what are to count as 'fair terms of cooperation'. Properly inclusive democratic procedures might be thought to constitute fair terms of cooperation, and in that case being reasonable in the context of one's role as a citizen might merely require a willingness to defend such procedures and abide by the outcome of them (given the assurance that others will do so as well). This would fall short of the idea that citizens are unreasonable unless they are willing to restrict themselves to public reasons in public debate. Even if any plausible attempt to specify 'fair terms of cooperation' must also include reference to measures that protect non-political liberties as well (such as religious liberty), it does not follow that it would be unreasonable to refuse to abide by the reciprocity requirement in arguing for these measures.

Rawls maintains that in order to be reasonable, citizens must acknowledge, and give due weight to, 'the burdens of judgement', which make possible reasonable disagreement of various kinds. Although these burdens may mean that it would be unreasonable for citizens to propose that the coercive power of the state be used to enforce conformity with a particular moral doctrine, for example, by punishing those who do not practice a particular religion, it does not follow that it would be unreasonable for them not to abide by the reciprocity requirement. Citizens might, for instance, appeal to religious reasons in support of religious freedom, or appeal to religious reasons to justify an exemption from a general requirement, whilst nevertheless giving due weight to the burdens of judgement.

In order to make progress on the issue of whether it is unreasonable not to abide by the reciprocity requirement in public debate, we may benefit from standing back from abstract claims about what constitute fair terms of cooperation, looking instead at how this requirement plays out in relation to particular issues of law and policy that have been a matter of public debate. In this way we can assess whether in these cases it provides us with a plausible account of what it is to behave reasonably in public debate. Consider an issue that is frequently discussed in the literature on multiculturalism and which appears to raise a matter of basic justice: Muslim girls in French schools have demanded the right to wear headscarves in class, in the face of regulations which prohibit the ostentatious display of religious symbols in state funded schools.[21] Now consider two ways in which citizens might try to defend this right.[22] First, they might give a religious reason, by arguing that not wearing a headscarf in class would offend Allah. Second, they might give a public reason argument. For example, they might claim that the girls' religious commitments require that they wear headscarves, and that refusing to allow them to do so would be to place a disproportionate burden on them, or they might argue that there should be the maximum feasible accommodation of diverse ways of life compatible with individual rights. Why should we regard the giving of reasons of the first kind as a display of unreasonableness? Of course, it would be unreasonable to expect others (non-Muslims, for example) to share the view that it is offensive to Allah for the girls not to wear headscarves, but they need not expect this of others. This religious reason might nevertheless be the reason why the girls want to wear the headscarves, and one that they believe they are justified in asking their fellow citizens to accommodate. We might not think that offering religious reasons is the most effective way for them to argue their case, or the most effective strategy for persuading others of the merits of an exemption from general requirements, and we might doubt whether these reasons could actually justify such an exemption, but it is hard to see why we must regard it as unreasonable for them to offer reasons of this sort and to be unwilling to search for public reasons.[23]

In setting out how they see things, that is, by giving their reasons why they think that girls should be allowed to wear headscarves at school, they need not be involved in a strategic manoeuvre, or be pressing the interests of the group to which they belong in a way that is unreasonable. They may reasonably think that others should take account of these reasons, by accommodating them in some way or compromising. They may reasonably think that the accommodation or compromise they are seeking is consistent with the common good even if it is not required by that good. And they may regard this accommodation or compromise as a way in which others can recognize them as fellow citizens even if they are not demanding it on that basis. It is tempting to think that a person who seeks such a compromise or accommodation must be appealing to a public reason if her behaviour is to be reasonable, that is, to a public reason rooted in a principle concerning when people should accommodate reasons that they do not share or compromise in the face of them. But again that need not be so: she may simply be appealing to her own (perhaps even religiously grounded) view of when reasons should be accommodated or a compromise made without any reason for thinking that her view will be shared. Her opponents may in the end decide that given the strength of feeling over the issue they should indeed compromise; they may even refer to their own principles for determining whether and when they should compromise.[24] Alternatively, they may accept her demand because it falls under some other general principle of justice they endorse, for example, the principle that groups should be exempted from a requirement when that requirement places disproportionate burdens on their members. (If they see things in these terms they would not have to suppose that they were making a compromise.) But neither of these reasons for accepting her demand would entail that the demand itself was invoking, even implicitly, some principle which might be thought to satisfy the reciprocity requirement.[25]

5 Instrumental and contextual arguments

Several of the attempts to justify a duty to restrict oneself to public reasons in public debate that I have so far considered regard the fulfilment of such a duty as a conceptually necessary condition of something else that is non-instrumentally valuable, whether legitimacy, respect for persons, or reasonableness.[26] In my view, these claims are much too extravagant. But it might be argued that the relevant duty can be justified on a variety of instrumental grounds because its fulfilment has a number of good effects, for example: the promotion of stability (or the stability of reasonably just institutions) or a sense of belonging to the polity—perhaps even that it fosters the former because it promotes the latter; or that decisions which are the product of a process which involves the exchange of public reasons are likely to be wiser or more just; or that public debate that observes the reciprocity requirement is likely to make people's preferences less selfish and more oriented to the common good.[27] These attempts to justify a duty to give only public reasons, some of which appeal to its by-products, might be more effective than the proposals I have so far considered. Those which maintain that a duty to restrict oneself to public reasons is justified in terms of the role it plays in sustaining just institutions, or just outcomes more generally, would fit naturally within a justice account. (Of course, parallel arguments would be possible within an equal membership account, since a duty to restrict oneself to public reasons might be justified in terms of its role in sustaining the conditions required for social and political equality.)

It is ultimately an empirical issue whether the widespread fulfilment of a duty to give only public reasons promotes values such as a sense of belonging or just outcomes.[28] But in the case of the latter at least, it might be thought that it is a safe bet. For even if the *legitimacy* of the exercise of coercive political power does not depend upon its being grounded in principles that are justifiable to all, it might be thought that the *justice* of laws and policies which govern fundamental matters depends upon these being grounded in principles that are justifiable to all. If that is so, it might seem that a practice of giving only public reasons in public debate, and voting on the basis of public reasons, is much more likely to lead to the adoption of just law and policy than one that involves giving both public and private reasons. It is not my purpose in this book to argue for any particular theory of justice, or to take a stand on debates between, say, political liberals and liberal perfectionists. But even if any adequate principles of justice must be justifiable to all, it is again unclear why they need to be justifiable to all on the basis of shared public reasons rather than different private reasons (provided those private reasons are compatible with the equal moral standing of persons). And even if it were possible to show that justice rather than legitimacy requires principles to be justifiable to all on the basis of shared public reasons, we should at least entertain the idea that a practice of citizens restricting themselves to public reasons in public debate might not always be particularly well suited to promoting or sustaining reasonably just institutions.

Under some non-ideal circumstances even Rawls would allow participants to offer non-public reasons in public debate, for example, when this constitutes 'the best way to bring about a well-ordered and just society in which the ideal of public reason could eventually be honored'.[29] Institutions that stifle rather than foster public deliberation might also do rather better at promoting reasonably stable institutions, that are close to being as just as it is feasible for them to be, in deeply divided societies when deliberation is unlikely to lead to greater convergence.[30] In such a society opposing parties might 'greet each other not with a fraternal embrace, nor even a businesslike handshake, but rather with a nod of mutual acknowledgement, initially grudging, that they will occupy the same society—reluctantly but inescapably—for the foreseeable future'.[31]

Political liberals might nevertheless argue that in ideal societies, governed by principles of justice that are justified by reasons acceptable to all, a practice of exchanging only public reasons is most likely to sustain just institutions. Even this is not obviously true, however. For even in what, from the perspective of political liberalism, would count as a reasonably just society, a practice of deliberation which allowed citizens to employ arguments that violated the reciprocity requirement might do rather better at sustaining just institutions, partly through avoiding alienation and fostering a sense of belonging to the polity, than one which insisted on complying with that requirement, because citizens would then be able to give the full and complete reasons for why they wanted a particular law or policy enacted.[32] Indeed the civic virtues necessary for sustaining reasonably just institutions could be different in different cases. In some cases, these virtues might include a willingness to engage in a practice of public reason that involves the reciprocity requirement, whilst in other cases a willingness to give full and complete reasons for one's policy preferences (or even an unwillingness to engage in public debate at all) could be more conducive to sustaining such institutions.

What is required by respect for persons as citizens, or indeed reasonableness, may also vary with circumstances, including the history of the relations between citizens.[33] Refusing to engage in debate, or to restrict one's reasons, need not involve a failure to take seriously the reasons of one's fellow citizens, or involve treating them as inferior, and it need not involve supposing that they will or should find one's reasons authoritative.[34] What it is to respect one's fellow citizens or to be reasonable, and civic virtue itself, is more contextual than the abstract arguments that I considered in sections 2–4 of this chapter would allow. One possible reply to this would involve insisting again on the importance of the distinction between ideal theory, which applies only to societies that are already substantially just, and where any historical injustice has been rectified, and non-ideal theory which applies to those societies which are tarnished by injustice. When a society is substantially just in terms of its institutions, then reasonable and respectful behaviour (it might be argued) will require citizens who engage in public debate to abide by the requirements of public reason, and those requirements will best sustain just institutions, law, and policy. But when a society is unjust, what counts in public debate as reasonable behaviour, for example, from those who are marginalized, will be very different from what counts as reasonable or indeed respectful behaviour in a society that is fully inclusive.[35]

I think it is true that what counts as respectful or reasonable behaviour will depend in part upon whether a society is just or not, and what kind of injustices have left their mark. But it seems to me that even when a society is basically just, what counts as reasonable or respectful behaviour will still depend in part upon its particular circumstances. Deeply divided societies of the sort I had in mind are usually non-ideal in character because they have a history of serious injustice, the legacy of which means that they may function better without any strong commitment to rational dialogue, provided citizens are disposed to cooperate with each other, and regard their institutions as authoritative. But, in principle at least, deeply divided societies need not have a legacy of injustice to deal with; they may simply contain people who are content to live in the same state (perhaps they share the same geographical space but lead largely separate lives), but think that what divides them is so great that there is little chance of converging on law and policy, and would rather let democratic institutions which simply aggregate brute preferences decide things rather than risk the antagonism that might surface through the kind of genuine engagement which would serve to highlight their differences. And there need be nothing unreasonable or disrespectful in that.

6 Concluding remarks

Although under some circumstances a duty to restrict oneself to public reasons in public debate might be justified from within a justice account, neither the justice account nor the equal membership account provides a way of grounding a duty to do so that bears upon all times and places. Both the justice account and the equal membership account can acknowledge the existence of reasons that are inherently disrespectful, and which when offered in public debate represent a failure to treat some as equals. The clearest examples are racist and sexist reasons, but homophobic reasons are also of this kind, as are reasons which appeal to individual or group interests without giving any weight to the interests of others—and there may be other such reasons as well. The giving of reasons of this kind violates a duty grounded in the good of equal membership to treat fellow citizens as equals. It may also violate a duty of justice not to treat others with contempt, or violate a duty to support just institutions, because such a practice may contribute to undermining these institutions or to creating unjust outcomes, perhaps by stigmatizing a group. This is an area where the justice and equal membership accounts complement each other, potentially providing different but mutually consistent perspectives on the duties of citizens.

Notes

1. This chapter draws upon my 'Public Justifiability, Deliberation, and Civic Virtue', *Social Theory and Practice*, Vol. 33, 2007, 679–700.
2. It is hard to unpack the Rawlsian idea of a public reason without an overdose of the term 'reasonable'. I agree with James Bohman and Henry Richardson that this notion of a public reason relies on a substantive conception of reasonableness: see J. Bohman and H. Richardson, 'Liberalism, Deliberative Democracy, and "Reasons that All Can Accept"', *Journal of Political Philosophy*, Vol. 17, 2009, pp. 259–60. But in my view its content is derived from nothing other than the idea that it is not reasonable to expect someone to accept a reason when it is grounded in a particular moral doctrine that he, without inconsistency, rejects, whilst it is reasonable to expect someone to accept the force of a reason when it is consistent with the fundamental equality of citizens and does not rely upon a moral doctrine that he, without inconsistency, rejects.
3. See Rawls, *Political Liberalism*, pp. 214–15. In what follows I shall use 'debate over matters of basic justice' as shorthand for 'debate over constitutional essentials and matters of basic justice'. This restriction on the scope of public reason to matters of basic justice has been challenged by some who argue that it should apply to public debate over any issue that raises a question of justice: see J. Quong, 'The Scope of Public Reason', *Political Studies*, Vol. 52, 2004, pp. 233–50; Quong, *Liberalism Without Perfection*, pp. 273–87.
4. See Rawls, 'The Idea of Public Reason Revisited', pp. 575–7. See also Rawls, *Political Liberalism*, p. 215; A. Laden, *Reasonably Radical: Deliberative Liberalism and the Politics of Identity* (Ithaca: Cornell University Press, 2001), p. 101.
5. See Rawls, *Political Liberalism*, p. 250.
6. See Rawls, 'The Idea of Public Reason Revisited', p. 591.
7. Note that the view that the exercise of coercive political power is legitimate if and only if it is morally justified allows that power may be legitimately exercised in enforcing or implementing laws or policies that are unjust (or morally unjustified, all things considered), since claiming that the exercise of power is morally justified is not the same as claiming that the law or policy which is being enforced or implemented is itself just or morally justified. So this conception of legitimacy allows space for the commonsense idea that there can be unjust laws and policies that it is nevertheless legitimate to enforce because they are a product of legitimate procedures.

8. Sometimes Rawls seems to accept (1). For example, he says: 'political power is legitimate only when it is exercised in accordance with a constitution (written or unwritten) the essentials of which all citizens, as reasonable and rational, *can endorse* in the light of their common human reason' (J. Rawls, *Justice as Fairness: A Restatement* (Cambridge, MA: Harvard University Press, 2001), p. 41, italics added; cf. Rawls, *Political Liberalism*, p. 137). But he also comes close to offering a version of (2) in places where he seems to maintain that the exercise of coercive power in matters of basic justice is legitimate only when the law or policy that sanctions it is actually *endorsed* for public reasons. For example, he says that 'our exercise of political power is proper only when we sincerely believe that the reasons we offer for our political action may reasonably be accepted by other citizens as a justification of those actions' (Rawls, *Political Liberalism*, p. xlvi; cf. pp. 226–7), and that 'when, on a constitutional essential or matter of basic justice, all appropriate government officials act from and follow public reason, and when all reasonable citizens think of themselves ideally as if they were legislators following public reason, the legal enactment expressing the opinion of the majority is legitimate law. It may not be thought the most reasonable, or the most appropriate, by each, but it is politically (morally) binding on him or her as a citizen and is to be accepted as such. Each thinks that all have spoken and voted at least reasonably, and therefore have followed public reason' (Rawls, 'The Idea of Public Reason Revisited', p. 578).

9. See Quong, *Liberalism Without Perfection*, pp. 263–5; G. F. Gaus, 'The Place of Religious Belief in Public Reason Liberalism', in M. Dimova-Cookson and P. Stirk (eds), *Multiculturalism and Moral Conflict* (London: Routledge, 2010), pp. 25–6. I shall refer to non-public reasons as 'private reasons' in what follows.

10. This is close to Rawls's formulation, though he would add that in order for the exercise of political power to be legitimate, citizens must vote in accordance with their sincere view of what law or policy is best supported by public reasons: see Rawls, *Political Liberalism*, lv–lvi.

11. Rawls holds that the duty of civility requires citizens to '*be able* to explain to one another on . . . fundamental questions how the principles and policies they advocate and vote for can be supported by the political values of public reason' (*Political Liberalism*, p. 217, italics added), which falls short of an obligation to participate in public debate. But he then adds that citizens should be 'ready to explain the basis of their actions to one another in terms each could reasonably expect that others might endorse' (*Political Liberalism*, p. 218; see also, Rawls, *A Theory of Justice*, p. 337/297), which comes close to attributing to them an obligation to participate in public debate.

12. In Rawls's view, the duty to treat others with respect is a natural duty that is justified on the grounds that it would be chosen by the parties in the original position (Rawls, *A Theory of Justice*, p. 115/99). But this raises the question of whether all the principles that would be chosen there are principles of justice in particular. G. A. Cohen, for example, argues that the principles chosen in the original position may serve other values apart from justice. See Cohen, *Rescuing Justice and Equality*, Ch. 7. A duty to engage in public debate might be grounded in a

duty to support and promote just institutions (see Chapter 1, section 1) rather than a duty to treat others with respect, but at best it would then be an imperfect duty and the duty to give only public reasons in that debate would require separate justification.

13. See T. Christiano, 'The Significance of Public Deliberation', in J. Bohman and W. Rehg (eds), *Deliberative Democracy: Essays on Reason and Politics* (Cambridge, MA: MIT Press, 1997), pp. 253–4. Christiano thinks that there is nevertheless something potentially valuable missing from such a society, namely, citizens going through 'the learning process that discussion among differently situated persons with different points of view affords' (p. 254). This might also explain the disrespect that is generally involved in barring some from public deliberation, or taking their arguments less seriously than those of others. In that case there is a kind of inequality in the cognitive conditions for decision-making that is disrespectful to those who suffer under it (see p. 256).

14. D. Archard, 'Political Disagreement, Legitimacy, and Civility', *Philosophical Explorations*, Vol. 4, 2001, p. 217.

15. There are notions of sincerity that might seem to provide support for the maximal interpretation of the duty of civility and for the idea that it is disrespectful not to restrict oneself to public reasons: see Quong, *Liberalism Without Perfection*, pp. 265–6; G. Gaus, *Justificatory Liberalism: An Essay on Epistemology and Political Theory* (Oxford: Oxford University Press, 1996), pp. 139–40. But in the ordinary sense one can be sincere in defending a law or policy simply by offering what one genuinely believes to be good reasons for adopting that law or policy, without even thinking that others will count them as reasons. It is hard to see why one would adopt a stronger notion of sincerity that required a person to restrict herself to public reasons unless one had independent grounds for thinking that respect for others required self-restraint of that kind.

16. For example, it is not obvious that it is disrespectful to refuse to take seriously the arguments of a representative of a government when he criticizes 'terrorists' for killing innocent people if his government is itself involved in killing civilians. For relevant discussion, see G. A. Cohen, 'Casting the First Stone: Who Can, and Who Can't, Condemn the Terrorists?', in A. O'Hear (ed.), *Political Philosophy* (Cambridge: Cambridge University Press, 2006).

17. Someone who refuses to engage with another as an 'intelligent reasoner' need not be treating him with disrespect, for that refusal need not be understood as an implicit denial that he counts as such: cf. Bohman and Richardson, 'Liberalism, Deliberative Democracy, and "Reasons that All Can Accept"', p. 269.

18. See Bohman and Richardson, 'Liberalism, Deliberative Democracy, and "Reasons that All Can Accept"', pp. 269, 272.

19. For relevant discussion, see S. Burtt, 'Is Inclusion a Civic Virtue? Adoption, Disability and the Liberal State', *Social Theory and Practice*, Vol. 33, 2007, pp. 557–78.

20. Rawls, *Political Liberalism*, p. 49.

21. For a comprehensive analysis of this issue, and the theoretical bases of the arguments that have been brought to bear on it, see Laborde, *Critical Republicanism*.

22. See Laden, *Reasonably Radical*, pp. 104–7.

23. See W. Galston, 'Diversity, Toleration, and Deliberative Democracy: Religious Minorities and Public Schooling', in S. Macedo (ed.), *Deliberative Politics: Essays on Disagreement and Democracy* (New York: Oxford University Press, 1999), esp. pp. 43–7, for relevant discussion.

24. See R. Bellamy, *Liberalism and Pluralism: Towards a Politics of Compromise* (London: Routledge, 1999), Ch. 4; S. May, 'Moral Compromise, Political Reconciliation, and Civic Friendship', *Critical Review of Social and Political Philosophy*, *Critical Review of International Social and Political Philosophy*, Vol. 14, 2011, pp. 581–602.

25. As a further illustration of how private reasons might reasonably be brought to bear on what can be regarded as a matter of basic justice, consider the issue of whether Hindus should be allowed to cremate their dead in the open air. In favour of a policy of allowing this practice, Hindus might appeal to public reasons: that open air cremation is no threat to anyone provided that it is conducted with the proper safeguards, and that if Hindus are forbidden from doing so, their right to freedom of religion is violated. But without being unreasonable, they might instead defend open air cremation simply on the grounds that unless a person's body is cremated in this way she will suffer a bad death that hampers her chances of a beneficial reincarnation, and her soul will be enslaved in an 'endless earthly entrapment'. (These were among the reasons that Davender Ghai gave in the UK for opposing an interpretation of the UK Cremation Act of 1902 to which Newcastle-upon-Tyne City Council had appealed in banning open air cremations. In February 2010 he won his case at the Court of Appeal: see <http://www.independent.co.uk/news/uk/home-news/davender-ghai-wins-funeral-pyre-battle-1895116.html>, accessed 14 June 2011.)

26. The exceptions are positions (1) and (2) in section 2, which maintain that the best means in practice of ensuring that the exercise of political power is legitimate involves citizens restricting themselves to public reasons in public debate.

27. See J. Elster, 'The Market and the Forum: Three Varieties of Political Theory', in J. Bohman and W. Rehg (eds), *Deliberative Democracy: Essays on Reason and Politics* (Cambridge, MA: MIT Press, 1997), p. 12. See also Christiano, 'The Significance of Public Deliberation', pp. 244–58; I. O' Flynn, *Deliberative Democracy and Divided Societies* (Basingstoke: Palgrave Macmillan, 2006), pp. 84–93.

28. Cass Sunstein discusses some of the empirical evidence that bears upon this issue in his 'The Law of Group Polarization', *Journal of Political Philosophy*, Vol. 10, 2002, pp. 175–95.

29. Rawls, *Political Liberalism*, p. 250.

30. Examples here are hard to find, for obvious reasons. But Malaysia at least might be regarded as a polity which has managed to secure a reasonable degree of stability through discouraging public debate, even though serious doubts can be raised about whether Malaysian society is as just as it might feasibly be.

31. M. Osiel, *Mass Atrocity, Collective Memory, and the Law* (New Brunswick: Transaction Publishers, 1997), pp. 43–4. (Quoted by S. May, 'Moral Compromise, Political Reconciliation, and Civic Friendship', p. 600, note 12.)

32. Note also that in some circumstances public deliberation might undermine a sense of belonging but promote just outcomes, and vice-versa. Some of the evidence

to which Sunstein appeals suggests that just outcomes are more likely to emerge when enclaves are not 'walled off' from competing views (see his 'The Law of Group Polarization', p. 191), but it may be that the friction created when different enclaves come into contact with each other will undermine rather than promote an overall group identity or sense of belonging.

33. See Blum, 'Race, National Ideals, and Civic Virtues'.
34. Cf. Laden, *Reasonably Radical*, pp. 114, 129.
35. See Young, 'Activist Challenges to Deliberative Democracy'.

7

A Duty to Integrate?

It is often supposed that immigrants, whether citizens or resident aliens, are under a duty to integrate.[1] The grounds for making this claim are unclear, however. In this chapter I shall examine some possible bases for such a duty, exploring the issue primarily through the lens of the justice account since it seems to me that this account brings it properly into focus. But I shall also introduce the equal membership account because it highlights distinctive reasons for valuing integration or, at least, for worrying about its absence.

This issue is one that has preoccupied political leaders as well as political theorists. In a number of countries, politicians and official reports have claimed that immigrants are under a duty to integrate. In a speech delivered in December 2006, Tony Blair maintained that immigrant groups in Britain were under a duty to integrate and he outlined a number of measures designed to illustrate its practical implications.[2] The French model of national integration has supposed that integration will occur through 'daily exposure to, and participation in, French society', but that model has nevertheless placed demands on immigrants which can be expressed in terms of the idea that they have a duty to integrate, for example, the requirement that Muslim girls refrain from wearing the hijab in schools.[3] In a speech delivered in March 2009, Jason Kenney, Canada's Minister of Citizenship, Immigration and Multiculturalism, affirmed the idea that immigrants are under a duty to integrate, arguing that although Canada has a responsibility to make it easier for them to do so, they also need to make an effort.[4]

But why should it be supposed that immigrants are under a duty to integrate? It might be argued that it was their choice to settle in a new country, so they are under an obligation to adapt in whatever ways are necessary for them to be able to play a full and active role in its life. In this respect immigrants are sometimes thought to be in a different position to national minorities that have a long history of settlement within a territory.[5] This argument has some credibility, but it is limited in terms of its scope. For a start, it is not clear that it applies to those who were forced to leave their countries of origin, either from economic necessity or because they were being persecuted, especially if they had no choice in practice about where to flee. Furthermore, it does not have any clear implications for second (or later) generation members of immigrant groups who made no such choice, and have ended up as part of a minority within a society as a result of decisions made by their family when they were children or before they were born. If the idea that immigrant groups in general are under a duty to integrate is to be defended, the argument for it will have to be grounded in the needs or interests of the polity to which they now belong rather than any choice they made to move there. Given that those needs and interests may vary depending upon the specific circumstances of the polity, the obligations that immigrants (and indeed citizens more generally) are under in this respect may vary from one polity to another, and change over time.[6]

I shall begin by considering the distinction that is often drawn between assimilation and integration and its supposed normative significance. I shall then examine in some depth two different arguments that might be mounted from within a justice account for the idea that there is a duty to integrate, each of which makes claims about the conditions that are required to create or sustain a reasonably just society: the first argument appeals to the importance of social or community cohesion in doing so, the second to the importance of sharing a national identity. These arguments are best understood as deriving a duty to integrate from the duty to support and to further a just society, with the latter requiring residents to promote the conditions that are needed to create or sustain such a society. (This in effect involves an extension of the duty to support and to further just institutions, so that it becomes a duty to support and further a just society. But once we accept that principles of justice apply not only to the basic structure of society but also to practices that profoundly affect people's lives, and we acknowledge that these practices may play an important role in securing justice for their participants, then this extension seems warranted.)

I argue that when levels of trust in a society are low and threaten its ability to create and sustain just institutions and practices, a duty to integrate might be justified in terms of the importance of community cohesion in increasing these levels, but in that case it would bind not only immigrants and minority groups but also those in the majority group who were born in the country. When levels of trust are sufficiently high for reasonably just institutions and practices to be created and sustained, it is less clear that such a duty can be justified in this way. I question whether sharing a national identity has anything to do with integration, properly understood, but then consider whether the importance of such an identity might justify a policy of assimilation and a corresponding duty to assimilate. This again raises empirical issues about the precise relationship between, on the one hand, the creation and maintenance of reasonably just institutions and practices and, on the other, sharing a national identity, but I suggest that a shared sense of belonging to the polity, which I distinguish from a shared national identity, might be equally effective in doing so, casting doubt on whether a duty to assimilate can be justified in these terms.

I conclude by considering the rather different perspective that the equal membership account offers on these issues. It may regard lack of integration as a product of everyday choices that people make, such as where they should live, or where they should send their children to school, which, even if they are not unjust, involve prejudice and signal a failure to treat members of immigrant groups as equals. As a result this account will be troubled by the presence of different groups (whether defined by culture, race, religion, or ethnicity) co-existing in a society without interacting much with each other. When lack of integration has its source in the failure of some to treat others as equals, and these violations of social equality can be tackled in part by bringing different groups into greater contact with each other, then this may serve to ground a duty to integrate, together with a range of integrationist policies. (Of course, a justice account may also have a distinctive role to play in this context: in so far as lack of integration is a product of unjust forms of prejudiced behaviour or deprives minorities of fair access to a range of goods, then members of the majority group may be under a duty to integrate, grounded in the importance of countering these forms of injustice rather than in the need to promote the mutual trust that is crucial for just institutions and practices.)

1 Integration versus assimilation

In Britain at least, the idea of integration has often been introduced by way of a contrast between it and assimilation, with the purpose of explaining how and why a policy of integration can be just and a duty to integrate defended, unlike a policy of assimilation and a corresponding duty to assimilate. Tariq Modood argues that integration, unlike assimilation, is a two-way process. Whereas assimilation requires minority groups to change their practices in order to fit in with the majority group's way of doing things, integration involves a process of *mutual* adjustment.[7] He draws the conclusion that if there is a duty to integrate it must bind not only minority groups but also the majority, and that the former 'cannot alone be blamed for failing (or not trying) to integrate'.[8] It seems to me that Modood's account of integration would benefit from further refinement. Assimilation in its most general sense is best understood as a process in which minority groups change their practices, or aspects of their behaviour (such as the language they use at home or in public), or their values—or indeed some combination of these—so as to become more like members of the majority group, and a policy of assimilation is one which is designed to bring about that outcome.[9] So a policy of assimilation is directed towards minority groups, and a process could not count as one of assimilation unless members of these groups changed their practices, behaviour, or values. Integrationist policies, in contrast, involve a specific purpose and are not necessarily directed towards minorities: they aim to persuade members of one or more groups (whether a minority or the majority) to change or adapt some or all of their values, practices, or behaviour so that the lives of members of different groups become more entwined—in effect so that they lead more of their lives *together*. If this is the distinction, we need to ask why an integrationist policy might be regarded as preferable to one of assimilation, and why the idea that there is a duty to integrate (but not a duty to assimilate) might be regarded as defensible.

It is sometimes supposed that whilst integrationist policies may be permissible, assimilationist policies are always unjust: the state is not entitled to pursue a policy of assimilation, or to demand that immigrants assimilate, but it may be entitled to pursue a policy of integration and demand that they integrate; immigrants have a right not to be subjected to assimilation policies but may be under a duty to integrate. But when the distinction is drawn in the way I am proposing, it would be problematic to assume that assimilation policies are always unjust. In a society where the majority group by and large respects individual rights and endeavours in good faith to provide equality of opportunity (and any failures to do so go against the grain of its practices), but where the violation of these rights or inequality of opportunity is a central part of some aspect of a minority group's way of life, a degree of assimilation might be *required* as a matter of justice.

In practice, of course, things are unlikely to be that clear-cut.[10] Members of a majority group are likely to be involved in their own rights violations in a way that can be traced back to widely-held and deeply rooted attitudes within it, such as those that are part of racist and sexist ideologies. Even when some members of a minority group are behaving in a way that unambiguously involves rights violations, that form of behaviour may be at the margins of its practices rather than at the heart of them and be at odds with the norms that govern these practices. There may nevertheless be a kind of continuity between a group's practices and values and this sub-group's way of behaving such that a demand for assimilation is not inappropriate. Consider, for example, so-called honour killings. Even when these killings are condemned by the norms which govern the mainstream practices of a particular group, they may be made intelligible by its sexual morality and its dominant attitude towards women in such a way that a demand for assimilation in this context has a point. In response it might be said that the demand, properly formulated, is not for assimilation, but simply for respect to be given to individual rights.

There is some truth in this: at root the requirement is to respect individual rights, but it is not misconceived to demand that those who are involved in the violation of individual rights, and who in doing so act from beliefs and values which sanction their behaviour, should assimilate, that is, change their behaviour (though not necessarily their beliefs or values) so that it becomes more like that of others in their society—including other members of their own cultural or religious group.[11]

When assimilationist policies go beyond the goal of ending rights violations or promoting equality of opportunity is there at least a presumption that they are unjust? There are of course clear examples of assimilationist policies that would be unjust because implementing them would itself violate individual rights. For example, laws which forbid the speaking of a minority language in public places would be unjust for this reason. But we need to distinguish coercive assimilationist policies of this sort from non-coercive policies, such as those which simply provide incentives for minority groups to change their practices.[12] For example, the state may provide funds for festivals, carnivals, and processions that have meaning and significance for the majority group, in the hope that by funding them members of minority groups will be attracted to join in as well. It is not obvious that such a policy need be unjust.[13]

Even if it is not always the case that assimilation policies are unjust, it might be thought that a policy of integration is nevertheless preferable, that the state is entitled to pursue such a policy, and that immigrants—or indeed citizens more generally—are under a duty to integrate. When, however, the contrast between assimilation and integration is drawn in the way that I have suggested, they are no longer mutually exclusive. One and the same policy can be both assimilationist *and* integrationist, for it might be directed towards minority groups in an attempt to get them to change their behaviour to become more like that of the majority group so that they live more of their lives in contact with members of that group. Furthermore, we do not have to make a general choice between integrationist and assimilationist policies since in principle it might be the case that an assimilationist policy is justified in response to some of a minority's (or sub-group's) practices, whereas an integrationist policy is justified in response to other practices of either the majority or a minority. Indeed, if we are properly to evaluate proposals for assimilationist and integrationist policies, and for the idea that there is a duty to integrate, we would benefit from placing them in a larger context that involves considering what conditions are required in order to create or sustain a reasonably just society. Approached in this way, these issues come within the purview of a justice account of citizenship. Let me consider how they might be addressed in this context.

2 Integration and community cohesion

Some liberal thinkers, such as Rawls, have supposed that a just society—a society in which principles that are justifiable to all reasonable people govern its basic structure—would generate its own support. If we could create such a society, then individuals growing up under its institutions would come to endorse the principles that underwrite these institutions, sustaining them from one generation to the next.[14] But that position has been vigorously challenged by a number of critics who contend that the creation and sustainability of a reasonably just society in the face of diversity requires more than shared principles of justice and a just basic structure. We can identify two rather different perspectives here, one focused on the importance of community or social cohesion, the other on the importance of sharing a national identity, though it seems to me that only the first of these is genuinely integrationist. They are potentially mutually consistent but provide us with rather different approaches to the question of what bonds between citizens are needed to create and then sustain a reasonably just society.

According to the first perspective, it is *community cohesion* that is of crucial importance for creating and sustaining a reasonably just society, where community cohesion is measured, and sometimes even defined, in terms of the frequency and quality of contact between communities and their members. This integrationist perspective lies at the heart of the Cantle Report, published in Britain after the disturbances in Oldham, Burnley, and Bradford in northern England (and so called because it was the report of the 'Community Cohesion Review' chaired by Ted Cantle). That report claimed 'there is an urgent need to promote community cohesion, based upon a greater knowledge of, contact between, and respect for, the various cultures that now make Great Britain such a rich and diverse nation.'[15] Different ideas are combined together here but one plausible way of disentangling them is to think of community cohesion as fostered by greater contact between cultural groups because (when it is of the right kind at least) it tends to improve understanding between them.[16] The thought then is that better understanding will help prevent the growth of fear, and promote mutual respect and trust, which helps to make a society more just, stable and enduring.[17]

These ideas owe much to Gordon Allport's contact hypothesis in social psychology.[18] Allport argued that when four conditions are met, interactions between members of different groups tend to reduce prejudice. The contact involved must (a) be frequent enough to lead to personal acquaintance; (b) be cooperative and involve the pursuit of shared goals; (c) be supported by institutional authorities, law or custom; (d) take place amongst participants of equal status. We might say that when contact between members of different groups fulfils these conditions, it is *meaningful* in a way that mere economic transactions, in which the interaction does not go beyond the exchanging of money for goods and services, are not.

If the importance of meaningful contact (so defined) is predicated on the way in which that contact promotes mutual trust, we need to understand better why mutual trust is important, and indeed how it might help to create and sustain a just society. Let me begin by drawing a familiar distinction between trust and well-founded trust. A may trust B to behave in a particular manner, but her trust is badly-founded if B does not regard himself as having a reason to behave in that way. If A's trust of B is to be well-founded, A must be justified in believing that B will behave in the manner that A expects; and for that to be the case B must generally regard himself as having a relatively strong reason to do so. (If B regards himself as having such a reason, then we might also say that, from A's point of view, B is trustworthy.) In what follows I shall focus specifically on trusting others *to act fairly*. When fellow citizens who have not met before, and are unlikely to meet again in the future, trust each other to act fairly when they encounter each other in civil society, and this trust is well-founded, the benefits are obvious: they are better able to go about their daily lives, for they can be justified in expecting shopkeepers not to short-change them, builders to use the materials they say they will, and dentists to do what work is needed rather than what pays them the most.

Institutions can often be designed in such a way that those who occupy roles within them have strong reasons to behave fairly; for example, they can often be designed so that corruption is readily detectable and career progression, or retaining one's job, depends on not behaving corruptly.[19] But in general in civil society, even when there is extensive legal regulation, there is bound to be relatively wide scope for individuals to act unfairly without detection. Unless individuals regard the unfairness of a course of action as itself providing a significant reason not to perform it, trust will not be well-founded, and we have reason to expect levels of trust to decline across society. The problem of trust in society in effect has two dimensions: first, individuals need to be motivated to act in trustworthy ways, that is, to act fairly when there is little chance that they will be found out if they don't do so;[20] second, individuals need to learn to trust others when it is reasonable for them to do so, that is, they need to learn to be trusting. Both of these can present significant barriers, and there is evidence that they pose a larger problem in heterogeneous compared to homogeneous societies.[21] Integrationist approaches that emphasize the importance of 'meaningful contact' address the second dimension, in effect presupposing that individuals are, in general, motivated to act in trustworthy ways, at least when they know that others are as well: the idea is that when individuals from different groups are so motivated, and contact between them is of the right quality and frequency, then this promotes mutual understanding and respect, which in turn leads to higher levels of trusting behaviour.[22] (A secondary mechanism might also be postulated: the kind of meaningful contact which the community cohesion approach aims to promote may generate a sense amongst people that they are 'in it together', which may in turn raise levels of trusting behaviour.)

It is tempting to respond to the idea that meaningful contact can provide a solution to the problem of lack of trust by arguing that this problem is caused by discrimination and material inequality rather than by lack of integration. But those who defend the importance of meaningful contact for mutual trust may argue that discrimination and material inequality are *in part* a product of the stereotyping which occurs when groups lead largely separate lives.[23] And they need not deny that discrimination and material inequality are also independent causes of lack of trust:[24] when people feel that they have been unfairly treated in the allocation of jobs or in terms of their share of wealth and income, they may not be disposed to trust those they see as the beneficiaries. At best, the dispute here is over the relative importance of different causes of lack of trust and that is not an easy matter to settle empirically.

It is clear that integrationism, understood as an approach which emphasizes the importance of community contact, is *potentially* assimilationist in a wide-ranging way. For it is just a short step from here to the idea that meaningful contact of the right level and quality is hindered by separate faith schools and impeded by specific minority practices, such as the wearing of full-face veils by some Muslim women, lending support to policies which deny public funding for faith schools or discourage the wearing of these veils. But it is also clear, I think, that these policies, and their more extreme counterparts that seek to ban the wearing of full-face veils in public or to outlaw faith schools, could only be justified (if at all) by appeal to empirical hypotheses that are likely to be controversial in relation to the societies they address.[25] Those who emphasize the importance of meaningful contact must allow that different levels of it might be required in different societies—and at different times in the same society—to make them reasonably just, stable, and enduring. The level of meaningful contact required may depend, for example, upon the history of the relations between the different groups, including the extent of mistrust that has been generated between them as a result of discriminatory practices or other forms of unjust treatment, and the extent to which segregation is itself a cause of a range of injustices. In societies that have experienced deep conflicts, perhaps even civil war, mistrust may be so great that considerable 'high quality' community contact would be required to restore or create even minimum levels of trust. Securing the conditions for it would involve putting an end to forms of segregation that are the direct cause of various specific forms of injustice because they serve to deny minorities fair access to a range of important goods, such as jobs, public goods, consumer goods and services, and various forms of capital.[26] It might also justify putting in place a range of different schemes designed to bring different groups into greater contact with each other, for example, some form of compulsory national service. In contrast, in societies where relations are relatively healthy, it might be the case that sufficient trust can be created and sustained without such measures, so long as members of different groups come into meaningful contact with each other in at least one important sphere, such as neighbourhoods, schools, workplaces, or civil society associations—so that a state of affairs is avoided in which groups lead largely separate or parallel lives, encountering each other only in market transactions that involve nothing more than the buying and selling of goods and services.

If a society is unstable or unjust (or both) because levels of trust are low as a result of lack of integration, then from the perspective of the justice account this would provide clear support for the claim that all of its members are under a duty to integrate, understood as a duty to seek greater contact with other cultural groups on some occasions, in some spheres of activity—in other words, an imperfect duty, since it does not command specific forms of behaviour on specific occasions. It might also be thought to justify a range of perfect duties that had particular salience for immigrants, such as a duty to learn the official language of the state, since the fulfilment of such a duty would help to facilitate meaningful contact between different groups. In circumstances where there are low levels of trust, the importance of increasing those levels might also justify perfect duties which had greater significance for members of the majority cultural or ethnic group; for example, parents might be under a duty to send their child to a school where she will encounter children from other religions, cultures, or ethnic groups.

When a society is relatively just, and levels of trust are sufficient to sustain it, but these levels could be increased through deepening contact between different groups within spheres of activity, and by expanding it across different spheres, would this justify the idea that citizens were under an imperfect duty to integrate further or were under more specific perfect duties to do so? When levels of trust in a society are sufficiently high for it to be reasonably just, stable and enduring, it is not clear that a duty to integrate further could be justified, even if levels of trust could be increased through compliance with such a duty. It is justifiable to demand that citizens make different choices about where, for example, they send their children to school, when the viability of a just society is at stake, but not merely when such a society would function better as a result. The benefits higher levels of trust would bring have to be weighed against the costs potentially borne by those who, in order to comply with this duty, might need to make different decisions concerning where they lived, or which schools their children attended, in a way that they might legitimately regard as unnecessary if trust between groups is already sufficiently high for society to be reasonably just, stable, and enduring and there is no reason to think that this level of trust cannot be sustained.

3 Sharing a national identity

In policy discourses in Britain, the community cohesion approach has also been combined with a rather different one which maintains that a shared national identity is important in order for a reasonably just society to be achieved and sustained, where a national identity is constituted in part by a particular set of values.[27] Although in Britain policymakers have regarded this approach as a kind of integrationism—believing that a society is integrated when it is united around a set of shared values—in my view it is not helpful to do so. For this approach does not require the lives of members of different groups to become more entwined, for them to lead more of their lives together. Two people, or two groups, may share values but their lives not be integrated in the least—indeed, they might be geographically separated in such a way that their lives do not even come into contact with each other. Therefore, to label this second approach as integrationist masks the very real differences between it and one which argues for greater community contact on the ground that this will lead to greater understanding between communities, and promote mutual respect and trust between them. The only clear way of linking these two approaches would be to maintain that without a core set of shared values, a national identity which binds together different communities, it will be difficult when members of different communities do come into contact for them to understand each other or at least to find common ground and therefore to interact meaningfully. But how much sharing of values is required to facilitate mutual understanding or meaningful engagement? Even if sharing distinctive values makes it easier for people to converse with each other and develop a sustained relationship, why think that it is important for each citizen to share the *same* set of distinctive values? Citizens might find that when they encounter each other they generally have some distinctive values in common, and that this provides a sufficient basis for them to interact meaningfully, but that the distinctive values they share varies depending on the person.

Approaches that emphasize the importance of a shared national identity based upon shared values, and which suppose that a state is entitled to use various means to promote those values when they are not fully shared, are better regarded as assimilationist in character. They nevertheless have something in common with integrationist approaches, which can be seen by asking why we should think that sharing a national identity is important for a reasonably just diverse society to be viable. The most plausible answer to this question appeals to the way in which sharing a national identity might be thought to promote the mutual trust that is crucial for creating and sustaining a just society.[28] When people share a national identity, they have a sense of belonging together; indeed the latter is partially constitutive of the former. By a sense of belonging together, I mean a belief amongst them that there is some reason why they should associate together or cooperate with each other which goes beyond the fact that they have been thrown together for a variety of different reasons. (Sharing a distinctive set of values is not the only basis for a sense of belonging together. Historically speaking, a belief that one shares the same race or ethnicity, the same culture or history, or the same first language as others, has provided such a basis. But it might be thought that sharing values has the potential to be more inclusive since it does not exclude people on the basis of unchangeable facts about them.) Whatever its source, a sense of belonging together is likely to increase levels of trust of the relevant sort, for a person who sees herself as deeply bonded to her fellow citizens in general will be more likely to behave fairly towards them even in circumstances where she knows she will not come into contact with them in the future, and her fellow nationals in general will (again, partly because of their bond) expect her to behave in this way.[29] In other words, a shared national identity, partially constituted by a sense of belonging together, can address both dimensions of the problem of trust that I distinguished in the previous section, by promoting both trustworthy and trusting behaviour.

The idea that a shared national identity based on shared values promotes the mutual trust that is important for a reasonably just diverse society to be viable is bound to raise worries, however. Some of these worries can be presented in the form of a dilemma. Either the values that are supposed to constitute the shared national identity are 'thin' and widely shared but not distinctive to a particular political community, in which case it will be unclear how this position goes beyond the idea that when citizens are brought to converge upon a set of reasonable principles of justice, and their institutions embody these principles, then these institutions will generate their own support. These principles do not provide a basis for a *distinctive* national identity—indeed it is not clear that a set of reasonable principles of justice can provide the basis for an *identity* at all.[30] Or these values are 'thick' and controversial, in which case any attempt to impose them, or even to foster them by non-coercive means, would threaten to be oppressively assimilationist, and the idea that members of cultural minorities were under a duty to change their behaviour so that it conformed to these values, that is, a duty to assimilate, would seem to go beyond what can be reasonably demanded of them.

The second horn of this dilemma is not necessarily inescapable. As I argued in section 1, assimilationist policies may not be unjust, especially when they are pursued using non-coercive means. Nor can we rule out the possibility of forging a national identity that goes beyond a commitment to shared principles of justice through non-oppressive means, such as a process of collective deliberation that involves mutual accommodation. But it is the first horn of the dilemma which theorists and indeed policymakers risk becoming impaled upon in practice.[31] For example, British policy and strategy documents, together with a number of ministerial speeches, have identified a set of values as 'British' which are widely shared but not at all distinctive. One strategy document singled out 'respect for others and the rule of law, including tolerance and mutual obligations between citizens' as 'essential elements of Britishness'.[32] Tony Blair listed Britain's essential values as 'belief in democracy, the rule of law, tolerance, equal treatment for all, respect for this country and its shared heritage'.[33] (The last of these might seem to involve something distinctively British but only because it is an attitude towards Britain rather than a specific value.) Gordon Brown argued that a 'distinctive set of values' has emerged from 'the long tidal flows of British history', but his list of liberty, civic responsibility, fairness, and tolerance does not fulfil its promise.[34] David Cameron has identified freedom of speech, freedom of worship, democracy, the rule of law, equal rights regardless of race, sex, or sexuality as what defines Britain as a society.[35] When we cast our net wider and look at the pronouncements of other public figures who think it important for British citizens to share a national identity, the values which they pick out are equally unexceptional (at the level of principled commitment at least, even if it remains remarkably difficult for societies to live up to them).

One apparent way out of the problem I have raised might be to say that what is distinctive is not the values themselves, but the specific interpretation that has been given of them or the specific way they have been understood within the nation's history and traditions. The most obvious way of making this case, however, is by reference to the institutional and historical realization of these values, that is, the concrete institutional forms in which democracy, liberty, tolerance, fairness and civic responsibility have been nurtured, and by reference to the (sometimes historically inaccurate) stories that are told about how these institutions were developed so as to realize such values.[36] So in Britain, for example, we might point to parliamentary institutions as the distinctively British way of realizing democracy, or to the National Health Service as the distinctively British way in which fairness in the context of health care has been institutionalized. But then it might seem that what provides the basis for the sense of belonging together is not these shared institutions—that we share these institutions does not give us a distinctive reason *why* we should do so—but the fact that we each *identify* with them.

It seems to me, however, that there is a better way of developing this underlying idea, one which makes no reference to the importance of sharing a national identity in the strict sense or having a sense of belonging together, and which does not suppose that the shared identification involved must be rooted in sharing the same values.

In order to bring this alternative into view, let me distinguish between a sense of belonging together and a sense of belonging to a polity, as I have done elsewhere.[37] Citizens possess a sense of belonging together if and only if they believe that there is some reason why they should be part of the same polity, other than that they happen to live within its borders. In contrast, they possess a sense of belonging to their polity if and only if they identify with it and feel at home in it. When a person identifies with a polity, he regards himself as having a special relationship to it: he sees it as *his* in an important sense. In order to be able to identify with it, he must be able to perceive a significant proportion of its major institutions and practices as valuable in at least some respects, and see his concerns reflected in them. When a person feels at home in a polity he is able to find his way around important parts of it, and experiences participation in at least some of its major institutions and practices as natural. In order to be able to feel this way, he must (in general at least) not be excluded from these practices and institutions, be marginalized in relation to them, or think that they are deeply unjust in some other way.[38] Might not a sense of belonging to the polity on its own, when it is widely shared by citizens, and each knows that it is widely shared by the others, provide a basis for them to trust *each other*, and thereby play an effective role in sustaining those institutions and practices (and creating the will to make them more just, even if citizens have different views about what that would involve)?

When citizens identify with their major institutions and practices and feel at home in them, and they know that their fellow citizens also think and feel the same way, there is a basis for them to trust each other. For they will be inclined to regard themselves as 'in it together', each with a stake in the continuation of their institutions and practices and with making them more just, and as a result be more inclined to treat each other fairly even when they know they could get away with not doing so; and they will also expect others to behave in the same way—even if there is no deep reason (in terms of distinctive shared values, shared ethnicity, shared history, or shared first language) why they should be fellow citizens.[39]

In effect I am questioning whether a reasonably just and diverse society *requires* a shared national identity in order for it to be viable. Those who deny that it does, might nevertheless accept that, other things being equal, a reasonably just diverse society is likely to be *more* resilient, that is, better able to adapt to changing circumstances of various kinds, when citizens share a national identity. My claim, however, is that levels of trust may be increased in ways that are not dependent on sharing a national identity,[40] and that a reasonably just diverse society may be viable when its citizens possess a common sense of belonging to the polity even in the absence of a shared national identity. The most obvious advantage of the alternative I am proposing is that it does not require citizens to share values in any substantial sense. So long as citizens converge on a range of specific value judgements regarding the desirability, on balance, of their major institutions and practices and they feel at home in them, then this provides the basis for them to identify with these institutions and practices. Different citizens may identify with the same institutions and practices for different reasons, and their contrasting reasons may derive from different values or very different interpretations of the same values,[41] so in Britain, for example, some may value the National Health Service on grounds of fairness—because, say, it provides health care for all independently of a person's ability to pay—whereas others may value it solely because of the quality of care it provides, or because it met their needs when they were ill.

It would not make any sense to suppose that cultural or religious minorities were under *a duty* to come to identify with the institutions that govern their lives, or to change their attitude towards these institutions. The state might, however, adopt a policy of seeking to foster a widespread sense of belonging to the polity amongst its citizens and other long-term residents. Fostering such a sense of belonging in a multi-faith, multi-racial, and culturally diverse society is a serious challenge, especially when minorities have a history of being discriminated against in it (and key institutions and organizations, such as the police force, have been deeply implicated in this history), or when there are high levels of unemployment that disproportionately affect these minorities. But at the very least it requires measures to promote individual security, end the discrimination to which these groups have been subjected, and to improve the opportunities of those who are most disadvantaged. Even the idea that we need to promote community cohesion might have a role to play here, on the basis that meaningful contact between members of different groups may enable citizens of different faiths and cultures to feel at home in civil society. Some measures which have an integrationist character might be justified in terms of the direct contribution they make to promoting a sense of belonging to the polity. For example, a policy of requiring applicants for citizenship to demonstrate the ability to communicate in the language of the state, and pass tests which require knowledge of life in that state, might be justified in part on the grounds that citizens will be unable to feel at home in it unless they are have a basic mastery of the language and at least a rudimentary understanding of the workings of these institutions and practices. The importance of promoting a sense of belonging, assuming that it does play a key role in creating and sustaining just institutions, might be thought to outweigh any injustice involved in denying long-term residents an automatic entitlement to citizenship,[42] especially if those who lack the linguistic ability required to pass these tests are exempted from the requirement.

Of course, fostering a widespread sense of belonging to the polity is a demanding project and there may be limits to what public policy can do. Such a sense of belonging is affected in complex and often unforeseen ways by policy decisions. There may be something in the idea that too much perceived focus on the needs and interests of minority groups alienates members of the majority cultural group by making it appear that these minority groups are receiving preferential treatment.[43] Even if these policies are required as a matter of justice, care needs to be taken in how they are presented and implemented. A group's sense of belonging to the polity may also be affected by foreign policy decisions: the way in which British foreign policy has adversely affected Muslims beyond UK borders surely has a key role to play in explaining why so many young Muslims find it hard to identify with the British polity and feel at home in it.[44]

4 Integration, prejudice, and the equal membership account

So far I have considered how a justice account might underpin a policy of integration and ground the idea that both immigrants and native citizens, under some circumstances, have a duty to integrate. But what significance does an equal membership account place on integration? An argument for the importance of integration can be developed that runs parallel to the one considered in the context of the justice account. Mutual trust might plausibly be regarded as crucial for creating and then sustaining institutions and practices that embody social and political equality, and (as before) meaningful contact between different cultural groups might be thought to play a key role in promoting mutual trust. In some circumstances the connections between meaningful contact, mutual trust, and the creation and sustainability of social and political equality may justify the idea that there is a duty to integrate. But the equal membership account also provides distinctive reasons for worrying about lack of integration. When groups lead largely separate or parallel lives within the same society, this is often a product of prejudice of various kinds that represent a failure to treat others as equals.[45] Recall from Chapter 2 my discussion of a case where someone chooses not to live in a neighbourhood in which there is a high proportion of a particular ethnic minority, will not sit next to a person from that minority when he catches a bus, will not send his child to a school with a high proportion of that minority in it, and discourages his child from playing with children in the neighbourhood who belong to that group.

If this pattern of behaviour is reproduced across a society, it will mean that members of this minority will lead largely separate lives, inhabiting different neighbourhoods and being educated in different schools. When lack of integration has such causes, then the good of equal membership is undermined. (Of course, injustice will also be the likely consequence since minorities tend to suffer from stigmatization or other kinds of involuntary disadvantage as a result of these forms of behaviour.)

Could these considerations justify the idea that citizens have a duty to integrate? The fundamental problem that is being identified is not lack of integration, but a failure to treat members of a minority as equals. Integration, however, might be accorded secondary significance through Allport's contact hypothesis, that is, in terms of the idea that prejudice is best eradicated by bringing members of different racial, ethnic, or religious groups into meaningful contact with each other. This would appeal to some of the same mechanisms which lie at the heart of the community cohesion-based defence of the value and importance of integration, but it would do so in the service of social equality rather than by appealing to the way in which meaningful contact promotes the trust that is important for the proper functioning of a just society. It could underpin the idea that there is a general duty to integrate, although in practice there might not be much point in appealing to such a duty to persuade people to change their behaviour, for those who are prejudiced are unlikely to be motivated to comply with it. It could also support various public policy initiatives designed to bring different groups into meaningful contact with each other, and to dismantle any barriers which may provide people with non-prejudiced reasons not to mix, for example, ensuring that the catchment areas of schools are not drawn in such a way that they contain a very high proportion of pupils whose first language is different from that of the majority community.

Defenders of a justice account can also ground a duty to integrate in similar considerations, independently of the role that lack of integration might be thought to play in undermining the mutual trust that is important for creating and sustaining a just society. But if they do so, they will ground this duty by appealing to the way that prejudice generates various forms of injustice, such as discrimination or stigmatization, or to the effects of segregation on fair access to various goods, rather than directly (as the equal membership account does) in the more fundamental requirement that citizens should treat each others as equals, not only in the political process or when selecting for advantaged social positions but more generally in civil society and beyond. In practice, the extent to which these approaches diverge will depend on the extent to which the failure to treat others as equals, and hence the failure to achieve social equality, itself involves or creates injustice.

The equal membership account may also provide distinctive grounds for justifying the idea that citizens are under specific duties that relate to acquiring the abilities and competencies that are required for political participation and for full access to civil society. These duties might include a duty to learn the official language of the state if they do not yet have adequate mastery of it, and to acquire basic knowledge of the way in which major social, political and economic institutions function, for in the absence of these competences, a person will not be able to *enjoy* the good of equal membership.

5 Conclusion

The idea that immigrants have a duty to integrate has gained considerable ground recently in many states. The issues raised by those who trumpet the importance of community cohesion and sharing a national identity are best viewed from the perspective of justice accounts of citizenship, since these accounts shed the most light on them. The key question is what role (if any) community cohesion and a shared national identity play in creating and sustaining a reasonably just society, and whether that role might ground a duty to integrate. In addressing this question, we need to achieve some clarity concerning the concepts that are being deployed. Indeed I argued that sharing a national identity has very little to do with integration, properly understood, even if it can play a role in creating and sustaining a just society. I also maintained that we would do well to distinguish the idea of sharing a national identity from that of sharing a sense of belonging to the polity, and that the latter may be important in creating and sustaining a just society in the absence of a shared national identity. When these distinctions have been drawn, the question of whether there is a duty to integrate will to a large extent rest upon empirical facts about the degree of mistrust in a society, and the role that integration could play in fostering mutual respect and trust, and promoting justice more generally.

Notes

1. This chapter draws upon G. Stoker, A. Mason, A. McGrew, C. Armstrong, D. Owen, G. Smith, M. Banya, D. McGhee, and C. Saunders, *Prospects for Citizenship* (London: Bloomsbury Academic, 2011), Ch. 4, for which I was the lead author.
2. T. Blair, 'Our Nation's Future—Multiculturalism and Integration', a speech delivered at Downing Street, hosted by the Runnymede Trust, 8 December 2006.
3. Laborde, *Critical Republicanism*, pp. 190, 198–9.

4. J. Kenney, 'Good Citizenship: The Duty to Integrate', a speech delivered at Huron University College's Canadian Leaders Speakers' Series, University of Western Ontario, 18 March 2009. Available at: <http://www.cic.gc.ca/english/department/media/speeches/2009/2009-03-18.asp>, accessed 6 December 2011.

5. See Kymlicka, *Multicultural Citizenship*, pp.10–15, 95–8.

6. This is not to deny that the characteristics of a group may make a difference to what they are entitled to claim from the state, or what obligations they have to it. National minorities, for example, may have different rights and obligations than immigrant groups that are justified by their different circumstances rather than any choice either has made.

7. See T. Modood, *Multiculturalism: A Civic Idea* (Cambridge: Polity, 2007), pp. 46–51. For relevant discussion, see also B. Parekh, 'Britain and the Social Logic of Pluralism' in *Britain: A Plural Society. Report of a Seminar* (London: Commission for Racial Equality, 1990), pp. 63–8; B. Parekh, *A New Politics of Identity: Political Principles for an Interdependent World* (Basingstoke: Palgrave, 2008), p. 85. Integration, so understood, is what some others refer to as mutual accommodation: see, for example, S. Scheffler, 'Immigration and the Significance of Culture', *Philosophy and Public Affairs*, Vol. 35, 2007, pp. 115–16.

8. Modood, *Multiculturalism*, p. 48.

9. Some might say that assimilation essentially involves a minority changing its values, but that seems to me to be too restrictive. For example, members of an immigrant group may decide that in order to fit in better they should stop speaking the language of their ancestors and instead use the established language of the polity to which they now belong, both at home and in public, and we should surely regard that as involving a degree of assimilation even if it involves no change of values.

10. To suppose that there is a clear-cut relationship between a cultural or ethnic group and a particular set of practices is generally to fall into the trap of essentialism. For a nuanced attempt to retain the notion of culture but avoid the pernicious cultural stereotyping that often goes along with it, see A. Phillips, *Multiculturalism Without Culture* (Princeton, NJ: Princeton University Press, 2007).

11. Needless to say comparable demands can also justifiably be made to members of the majority cultural group. For members of this group may routinely violate individual rights or deny equality of opportunity, and even when their conduct is not sanctioned by the norms that govern the group's practices, the values of that group may make it intelligible. Racist or sexist attitudes, for example, may pervade the values and practices of the majority group. Even when these attitudes would not sanction violence against women or racial groups, they may nevertheless make that violence intelligible, just as honour killings become intelligible in the light of a sexual morality which sees women's sexual activity outside of marriage as deeply shaming to their family.

12. For relevant discussion, see Mason, *Community, Solidarity and Belonging*, pp. 123–6.

13. Although the distinction between coercive and non-coercive assimilation policies is normatively significant, we should not suppose that the latter are always just or permissible. The category of 'non-coercive assimilation policies' is very broad and

includes policies that attach considerable costs to failures to assimilate, in a way that may be unjust even though it does not amount to coercion.

14. See Rawls, *A Theory of Justice*, sections 69 and 76. In fact Rawls thinks that principles of justice are inadequate unless they can be realized in a stable way in the best of foreseeable circumstances. For relevant discussion, see D. Copp, 'Pluralism and Stability in Liberal Theory', *Journal of Political Philosophy*, Vol. 4, 1996, pp. 191–206; A. Mason, 'Just Constraints', *British Journal of Political Science*, Vol. 34, 2004, pp. 252, 259–60; Cohen, *Rescuing Justice and Equality*, pp. 327–30.

15. Home Office, *Community Cohesion: A Report of the Independent Review Team Chaired by Ted Cantle* (London: HMSO, 2001), p. 10.

16. We might ask how the concept of community cohesion relates to that of social cohesion, which also has wide currency. It seems to me that there is no substantial difference between these notions, though Cantle argues that they mark out different ideas in the sociological literature. In his view, social cohesion is more concerned with bonds that reach across class, whereas community cohesion focuses on bonds that reach across religion and culture. See T. Cantle, *Community Cohesion: A New Framework for Race and Diversity*, Revised and Updated Edition (Palgrave Macmillan: Basingstoke, 2008), pp. 50–61.

17. 'The fact that people from the same background or culture choose to live or work together is not in itself a sign of breakdown in cohesion. But it is important that we foster mutual understanding and respect between people from different backgrounds and cultures. Communities are better equipped to organize themselves to tackle their common problems if they are not divided by mutual suspicion and misunderstanding of diverse cultures and faiths' (Home Office, *Strength in Diversity: Towards a Community Cohesion Strategy* (London: HMSO, 2004), section 5.3). These ideas are presented more rigorously in Cantle, *Community Cohesion*, esp. pp. 50–67, in which he also emphasizes the elements of a broader definition of community cohesion according to which community cohesion requires not just meaningful contact between communities but also an end to discrimination.

18. See G. Allport, *The Nature of Prejudice* (Cambridge, MA: Addison-Wesley, 1954); Anderson, *The Imperative of Integration*, p. 123. Robert Putnam expresses scepticism about contact theories of this sort (see R. Putnam, 'E Pluribus Unum: Diversity and Community in the Twenty-first Century: The 2006 Johan Skytte Prize Lecture', *Scandinavian Political Studies*, Vol. 30, 2007, pp. 148–9), but the evidence he provides does not refute community cohesion hypotheses when they are carefully formulated, since so much will depend on the proviso that the contact between cultural groups has to be of the right kind or quality, for example that it must be meaningful. As Putnam implies, however, there is a danger of making the hypothesis impossible to falsify, for example, by dismissing apparent counter-evidence on the grounds that there is a lack of the required meaningful contact (see Putnam, 'E Pluribus Unum', note 14). Eric Uslaner avoids this pitfall, marshalling evidence for the claim that, in the US at least, the contact that whites enjoy by living in diverse neighbourhoods boosts their generalized trust, with additional increases occurring when they have friends from other backgrounds or belong to the same groups, whereas for African-Americans having friends from different backgrounds

increases generalized trust though merely living together in the same neighbourhoods does not. See E. Uslaner, 'Segregation, Mistrust and Minorities', *Ethnicities*, Vol. 10, 2010, pp. 415–34. A meta-analysis of various studies claims strong support for the contact hypothesis applied to a number of different group divisions and settings: see T. Pettigrew and L. Tropp, 'A Meta-Analytic Test of Intergroup Contact Theory', *Journal of Personality and Social Psychology*, Vol. 90, 2006, 751–83.

19. See R. Hardin, 'Trusting Persons, Trusting Institutions', in R. J. Zeckhauser (ed.), *The Strategy of Choice* (Cambridge MA: MIT Press, 1991), especially pp. 201–5.

20. This could of course be achieved by people internalizing the kind of duty I defended in Chapter 5, that is, a duty not to seek unfair advantage, but the issue here is the empirical one, of what conditions are likely to facilitate the internalization of such a duty in a culturally diverse society.

21. See K. Newton, 'The New Liberal Dilemma: Social Trust in Mixed Societies', a paper prepared for the ECPR Workshop on Social Capital, The State and Diversity, Helsinki, 7–12 May 2007; Putnam, *'E Pluribus Unum'*.

22. In Robert Putnam's terms, the idea is that cross-cultural contact creates bridging social capital: see R. Putnam, *Bowling Alone: The Collapse and Revival of American Community* (New York: Simon and Schuster, 2000), pp. 22–3. See also Cantle, *Community Cohesion*, pp. 200–1.

23. Elizabeth Anderson has also argued forcefully that the segregation of African Americans is the underlying cause of many of the injustices from which they suffer, including lack of fair access to jobs, public goods, consumer goods and services, and various forms of capital (see Anderson, *The Imperative of Integration*, especially Chs. 1–4). Although her claims are specifically about the plight of African Americans, they may apply to some extent to groups in other countries, giving integration and the meaningful contact it involves wider normative significance. The extent to which ethnic minorities in Britain are segregated is a matter of some dispute: for a challenge to the idea that they lead 'parallel lives', see L. Simpson, 'Statistics of Racial Segregation: Measures, Evidence and Policy', *Urban Studies*, Vol. 41, 2004, pp. 661–81.

24. Cantle, *Community Cohesion*, p. 58.

25. I say 'if at all' because there is a powerful argument for saying that banning the wearing of full-face veils in public, and outlawing even privately funded faith schools, involves a violation of individual rights. It is not clear that such an injustice could be outweighed by gains in social cohesion and mutual trust, except when a strong case can be made for holding that these gains are required in order for an otherwise just society to be viable.

26. See Anderson, *The Imperative of Integration*, especially Chs. 1–4 and note 23 above.

27. This section draws upon my 'Integration, Cohesion, and National Identity: Theoretical Reflections on Recent British Policy', *British Journal of Political Science*, Vol. 40, 2010, pp. 857–74.

28. This is not the only possible answer, however. Some have argued that widespread support for redistribution on grounds of social justice requires, or is facilitated by, a shared 'solidaristic' national identity because of the greater fellow feeling that this involves or creates. See, for example, D. Miller, *On Nationality* (Oxford: Oxford

University Press, 1995), pp. 93–6. It is not clear, however, that Miller's claim is borne out by the empirical evidence: for relevant discussion, see K. Banting et al., 'Do Multicultural Societies Erode the Welfare State? An Empirical Analysis', in K. Banting and W. Kymlicka (eds), *Multiculturalism and the Welfare State: Recognition and Redistribution in Contemporary Democracies* (Oxford: Oxford University Press, 2006); N. Holtug, 'Immigration and the Politics of Social Cohesion', *Ethnicities*, Vol. 10, 2010, especially pp. 438–40. An argument for the importance of a shared national identity that appeals to its role in promoting mutual trust, and then to the role that mutual trust plays in promoting just behaviour, has relevance even for those who deny that justice has demanding redistributive implications. But the mutual trust generated by a shared national identity might have an additional role in explaining support for the welfare state, on the grounds that people are more likely to support it politically if they expect others to fill in their tax returns honestly, not claim welfare benefits fraudulently, and avoid (when they can) putting themselves in a position where they have to rely on state-funded services—and they are more likely to behave in these ways themselves if they have confidence that others will do so as well: see D. Miller, 'Social Justice in Multicultural Societies', in P. van Parijs (ed.), *Cultural Diversity versus Economic Solidarity* (Brussels: De Boeck University Press, 2004), pp. 26–7.

29. It would be rash, however, to claim that a sense of belonging together is *always* likely to increase trust, whatever its source. If people have a sense of belonging together because of their shared inclination to cheat and deceive, then (in the absence of some special story) their sense of belonging together is unlikely to promote trust between them. If it is to promote trust, the source of their sense of belonging together must generally give them some reason to think that their fellows are not *untrustworthy*. See Holtug, 'Immigration and the Politics of Social Cohesion', p. 442.

30. See Miller, *On Nationality*, p. 175.

31. Miller thinks that a shared British national identity needs to be forged out of a distinctive shared public culture, but offers little help in outlining what form it might take: see Miller, *On Nationality*, especially pp. 172–80.

32. Home Office, *Improving Opportunity, Strengthening Society: The Government's Strategy to Increase Race Equality and Community Cohesion* (London: HMSO, 2005), Ch. 4, section 4.

33. See Blair, 'Our Nation's Future'.

34. See G. Brown, 'The Future of Britishness', a speech delivered to the Fabian Society 'The Future of Britishness' conference, London, 14 January 2006. Available at <http://fabians.org.uk/events/speeches/the-future-of-britishness>, accessed 16 March 2011. In his speech on 'Managed Migration and Earned Citizenship', delivered at the Camden Centre, London, 20 February 2008, Brown added 'internationalism' to his list, understood as a kind of outward lookingness.

35. See David Cameron's speech at the Munich Security Conference, delivered on 5 February 2011, available at: <http://www.number10.gov.uk/news/speeches-and-transcripts/2011/02/pms-speech-at-munich-security-conference-60293>, accessed 16 March 2011.

36. This would have resonances with Habermas's idea of constitutional patriotism: see J. Habermas, 'Appendix II: Citizenship and National Identity', in his *Between Facts and Norms: Contributions to a Discourse Theory of Law and Democracy*, translated by W. Rehg (Cambridge, MA: MIT Press, 1996), pp. 491–515. Rogers Smith gives 'ethically constitutive stories' a key role in explaining the emergence of what he calls 'peoples'—a wider category than nations: see R. Smith, *Stories of Peoplehood: The Politics and Morals of Political Membership* (Cambridge: Cambridge University Press, 2003), Ch. 2.

37. See Mason, *Community, Solidarity and Belonging*, p. 127. However, I have modified the account I give there of what it is to possess a sense of belonging to a polity, partly in response to John Horton's comment that identification with a polity does not require that one endorse each and every practice or institution that is part of it, or even most of them: see Horton, 'In Defence of Associative Political Obligations: Part Two', pp. 12–13.

38. Some have seen the distinction between possessing a sense of belonging together and possessing a sense of belonging to a polity as at least a partial basis for a distinction between ethnic nationalism and civic nationalism: see Barry, *Culture and Equality*, p. 80. This is not how I see the distinction, however. Even under civic nationalism, the idea is that people have a sense of belonging together, fostered by, for example, national myths or shared values. The distinction between a sense of belonging together and a sense of belonging to the polity might, however, form the basis of a distinction between nationalism and patriotism. And I don't have any objection to saying, for example, that those who share a sense of belonging to the British polity have a 'British identity', or that they constitute a people, provided that this is not taken to imply that they have a sense of belonging together in the technical sense I have identified. (Rogers Smith uses the term 'people' in a broad sense that encompasses more than nations in his *Stories of Peoplehood*, p. 12.)

39. We should also not underestimate the role that various other mechanisms may play in providing people with reasons to behave in a trustworthy fashion. Philip Pettit, for example, emphasizes the way in which a desire for the acceptance or approval of others can motivate people to behave fairly even when the probability of being found out is relatively low: see P. Pettit, *The Common Mind: An Essay on Psychology, Society, and Politics* (Oxford: Oxford University Press, 1993), pp. 330–3.

40. For relevant discussion, see D. Weinstock, 'Building Trust in Divided Societies', *Journal of Political Philosophy*, Vol. 7, 1999, especially pp. 300–5.

41. In this respect my proposal differs from the one which might be derived from Habermas's model of constitutional patriotism, for according to that model the identification with major institutions derives from agreement on fundamental universal principles. See Habermas, 'Appendix II: Citizenship and National Identity'.

42. For a defence of the idea that long-term residents have an automatic entitlement to citizenship, and that citizenship tests are therefore unjust, see J. Carens, 'The most liberal citizenship test is none at all', in R. Baubock and C. Joppke (eds), 'How Liberal Are Citizenship Tests', EU Working Papers, Eudo Citizenship, RSCAS 2010/41. Available at <http://eudo-citizenship.eu/docs/RSCAS_2010_41.

pdf>, accessed 16 March 2011. See also J. Carens, 'Why Naturalization Should Be Easy: A Response to Noah Pickus', in N. Pickus (ed.), *Immigration and Citizenship in the 21st Century* (Totowa, NJ: Rowman and Littlefield, 1998), 141–6; Carens, 'The Integration of Immigrants', pp. 39–40.

43. This idea is gestured towards in Charles Clarke's Foreword to *Improving Opportunity*: 'This strategy is not about putting all people from minority ethnic communities in one category and those from the majority in another. That fails to recognize the progress of many, and can fuel the politics of division.' See D. McGhee, *The End of Multiculturalism: Terrorism, Integration and Human Rights* (Maidenhead: Open University Press/McGraw-Hill, 2008), pp. 100ff and pp. 113ff, for further discussion.

44. See McGhee, *The End of Multiculturalism*, pp. 64ff; Modood, *Multiculturalism*, p. 150.

45. For some empirical evidence that lack of integation in various contexts is a product of prejudice, see Uslaner, 'Segregation, Mistrust, and Minorities', pp. 428–30.

8

A Duty to Act as a Global or Ecological Citizen?

Like all political concepts, the concept of citizenship has evolved in response to changing social, political, and economic circumstances. Indeed, we should not be surprised that notions of cosmopolitan and ecological citizenship have emerged in the light of concerns about global inequality and environmental degradation. But how far can we transform the concept of citizenship without subverting its underlying rationale or emptying it of content? In this chapter, I ask whether citizenship is a relationship that can be coherently conceived as extending across state borders in the absence of transnational political institutions, and whether it makes sense to suppose that a person might have duties of citizenship of some transnational kind that are owed to those who live beyond the borders of the state to which she belongs when she and they are not subject to any common political authority.[1]

I begin by examining the issue of whether it is intelligible to think that we owe obligations of ecological or environmental citizenship to those beyond the borders of the state we inhabit but who are vulnerable to the impact we have on the environment. I focus on a model of ecological citizenship that has been worked out in some depth by Andrew Dobson, which holds that people may be fellow ecological citizens, even though they live in different states, in virtue of being linked by obligations of justice as a result of either participating in, or experiencing the adverse effects of, a practice that is unsustainable from an environmental point of view.[2] According to Dobson, participants in such a practice are bound by obligations of justice to compensate those who are harmed by it and are under an obligation to reduce the size of their ecological footprints to sustainable levels. It might seem that Dobson's model is a version of the justice account applied specifically to environmental actions and concerns. But I argue that special obligations of the kind that his model invokes, which relate to past and present injustices, are insufficient on their own to give the idea of citizenship a secure foothold. Although it might appear to be a specialized version of the justice account of citizenship, Dobson's model is not really about citizenship at all.

My strategy is to employ the minimal core concept of citizenship that I described in the Introduction as a reference point for new uses of the term, namely, that citizenship is (in part) a relationship in which those involved enjoy rights within a common framework of protection, and incur special obligations to each other. In making my argument against the novel extension in usage which Dobson's ecological model advocates, I do not rule out the possibility of beneficial conceptual change, but I contend that we need to assess the costs and benefits associated with transforming our ways of thinking, and that the costs of his model are too high. In the third section of the chapter, I show how my argument might be extended to raise doubts about similar attempts to defend the reality of duties of global or cosmopolitan citizenship. Many of those who invoke the notion of global citizenship defend it by appeal to obligations of global justice or ethical obligations that have global reach. But the mere existence of demanding ethical obligations that extend across state borders, or even obligations of justice that do so, is insufficient to engage the concept of citizenship. My argument here is purely conceptual: it does not rest upon any scepticism towards the existence of duties of global justice; it does not question the emergence of a global civil society; it does not argue that the achievement of global citizenship is unnecessary in practice to secure the protection of human rights or to promote global justice; nor does it maintain that human beings lack the kind of connectedness or shared identity necessary for a global form of citizenship to be feasible.[3] I conclude with a discussion of James Tully's attempt to recover and develop a tradition of 'diverse citizenship' which, in my view, provides a more promising basis for claims that might be made about actually existing transnational citizenship, and for the idea that we are currently under an obligation to act as transnational citizens. Indeed these claims might be thought to involve a legitimate extension of the equal membership account.

1 Ecological obligations and the limits of citizenship

In the Introduction, I argued for a minimal core concept of citizenship that picks out elements that are central to our ordinary understanding of it. According to this core concept, citizenship is (in part) a relationship in which those involved enjoy rights or entitlements within a common framework of protection and provision and incur special obligations, duties or responsibilities to each other. Although this characterization is not intended to act as a brake on conceptual innovation, it poses a challenge for any new uses of the term which are inconsistent with it. It brings into question any attempt to extend the relationship of citizenship beyond the boundaries of the state that allows the possibility that two people may stand in this relationship even though they are not subject to any common framework for protecting their rights and securing their entitlements. The core concept does not rule out the possibility in principle that the relationship of citizenship might extend beyond the boundaries of the nation state. But when categorising a transnational relationship as one of citizenship involves abandoning elements of the core concept, then the costs and benefits of this conceptual innovation need to be assessed in terms of whether it improves or impairs our understanding of the issues, or enhances or diminishes our powers of discrimination.

According to the core concept I identified, fellow citizens enjoy a set of rights within a common framework of protection. We can imagine a community the members of which were not subject to any legal institutions but who nevertheless enjoyed rights and received their entitlements as a result of voluntary arrangements and informal pressure or sanctions, but large-scale communities of this kind will be hard to sustain. In general, at least, the 'common framework of protection' will involve some methods of enforcement. This need not involve a full-blown state in the modern sense, but it will normally require some network of legal and political institutions. So we can make sense of the idea that people might enjoy rights as transnational citizens, within a transnational framework of protection, but with the exception perhaps of European Citizenship, it would seem that we are nevertheless a considerable distance away from realizing it in practice. (It might be argued that an *international* citizenship, in which nation states are conceived as the citizens,[4] has to some extent been realized through institutions such as the United Nations, but this is different from individuals enjoying rights as transnational citizens.)

The lack of transnational legal and political institutions to protect individual rights might not be regarded as an insuperable barrier to the realization of global or transnational citizenship. Notions of transnational citizenship can be faithful to the idea that fellow citizens are bound together by special obligations even if they do not enjoy rights as transnational citizens, thereby preserving at least one element of the core concept. Andrew Dobson's model of ecological citizenship, for example, dispenses with the idea that fellow ecological citizens enjoy rights as transnational citizens but preserves the idea that obligations of citizenship are special obligations that may extend across state boundaries. He distinguishes between *environmental* citizenship, which is primarily concerned with the enjoyment of rights within a state, and *ecological* citizenship, which is concerned with virtues and responsibilities that demand as a matter of justice that one reduce the size of one's ecological footprint to a sustainable level and compensate those who suffer (or have suffered) as a result of one's participation in unsustainable practices.[5] Unlike environmental citizenship, the responsibilities of ecological citizenship extend beyond the borders of the nation state because individuals are bound together by obligations of justice as a result of participating in practices or 'material activities', the effects of which are felt beyond state boundaries. Although the obligation to ensure that one's ecological footprint is sustainable (and to compensate others for the harm they suffer when it is unsustainable) is a general obligation, the various obligations of ecological citizenship that it underpins are special obligations: those who engage in environmentally damaging practices owe special obligations to those that are harmed as a result, to reduce the size of their ecological footprints and to compensate for the harm caused. So, for example, reflecting upon the wider effects of pollution, Dobson argues that those who are principally responsible for climate change may owe obligations of ecological citizenship to those who suffer many of the burdens of global warming despite not being responsible for it, such as the inhabitants of undeveloped islands that are threatened by rising sea levels.[6]

In this way, Dobson develops a model of ecological citizenship that might seem to be properly regarded as a justice account. But there are serious costs involved in travelling along this path, even if we bracket the issue of whether it makes sense to describe a relationship as one of citizenship when the rights and entitlements of those involved in it are not secured by any common framework of protection and provision. Even though Dobson's model preserves the idea that obligations of citizenship are special obligations, it appears to involve a problematic extension of the concept of citizenship because it does not seem able to explain why the special obligations of citizenship that it identifies are obligations that fellow citizens *owe to each other*, which is also a feature of the core concept. According to Dobson's model, obligations of ecological citizenship are owed by one *subset* of fellow citizens to another subset, that is, they are owed by participants in environmentally unfriendly practices to those who suffer the adverse effects of those practices. In this respect they are very different from more commonplace obligations of citizenship, such as the obligation to participate politically or to contribute to one's political community, which are owed by each citizen capable of fulfilling them to every other.

In response it might be argued that Dobson's account is on a par with other justice accounts of citizenship in terms of the difficulties it faces in justifying the idea that the special obligations it identifies really are obligations that fellow citizens owe to each other. In Chapter 1, I pointed out that justice accounts which appeal to the idea that there is a duty of citizenship to support and to further just institutions have difficulty in explaining why this obligation is owed by and to fellow citizens rather than being a general obligation. Furthermore, in Chapter 2, I argued that the justice account tends to ground a set of special obligations that are owed by and to the residents within a territory rather than obligations that are owed by and to fellow citizens in particular, yet for convenience I have been willing to grant that it provides us with an account of the special obligations of citizenship; so why not also, for convenience, allow that Dobson's model provides us with an account of the special obligations of ecological citizenship?

But Dobson's model is really very different from justice accounts. If the duty to support and further just institutions could not be understood as a special obligation that fellow citizens owe to each other, rather than as a general duty which everyone is under, then there would indeed be good reason to deny that it is an obligation of citizenship. Drawing upon Waldron's work, however, I argued in Chapter 1 that the manner in which citizens are subject to the institutions of the state to which they belong, with part of the point of these institutions being to give due weight to their interests, provides a basis for maintaining that they are bound by an obligation to each other to support these institutions when they are reasonably just (and to work towards their reform when they are unjust) in a way that others who aren't subject to these institutions are not. By the same reasoning of course, that obligation extends to resident aliens as well, for they too are subject to these institutions in a different manner to non-resident non-citizens, even when the latter may influence the functioning of these institutions. But Dobson's obligations of ecological citizenship are different in kind because they are owed by members of one subset of fellow citizens to a different subset of them, that is, they are owed by participants in unsustainable practices to those who are adversely affected by these practices.

In this context, it is instructive to consider again two general ways in which justice accounts have attempted (with varying degrees of success) to explain why the obligations it grounds are owed by and to fellow citizens, in order to see whether either of them could be extended to make sense of the obligations of ecological citizenship which Dobson defends. What these two approaches rely upon is the idea of membership in a common scheme for the distribution of benefits and burdens. The first strategy appeals to the principle of fair play and applies to those who participate in the same cooperative scheme for mutual advantage. This principle justifies the special obligations that fellow citizens owe to each other by maintaining that the enjoyment of various benefits (such as law and order, and perhaps also welfare payments, health care, and pensions) places the recipients of these benefits under an obligation to those who have contributed to their creation and maintenance, to bear their fair share of the burdens of sustaining them, such as, for example, obeying the law, making a productive contribution of one's own, and paying one's taxes. In its standard form, this strategy appeals to the rights and entitlements that are enjoyed in virtue of membership of, or at least residence in, the state, and for that reason the special obligations that it justifies bind those who are citizens of, or live together in, the same state.[7] But this strategy could, in principle, justify special obligations that extend beyond the borders of the state and indeed bind together those who belong to different states, for it would have potential application to membership of any cooperative scheme for mutual advantage. However, it does not seem to offer a promising means of underpinning a Dobson-style notion of ecological citizenship, at least in circumstances where there is not yet any cooperative scheme of the required kind.[8] The existence of a scheme of global trade, governed by international institutions, may give rise to special obligations to obey whatever rules and conventions govern these markets, but it is hard to see how it could by itself justify special obligations of environmental justice, even though trade has environmental effects.

This is not to deny that those committed to environmental sustainability might be understood as involved in a cooperative venture, one that benefits them as well as free riders outside the scheme who continue to degrade the environment. Under the principle of fair play, those involved in this cooperative scheme would have special obligations to each other to bear the burdens of acting in environmentally sustainable ways, but those outside the scheme would not—though they might be under a general obligation to become part of that scheme. Even if this could provide us with a possible model of transnational ecological citizenship, it is not one that is well suited to Dobson's aims, for it would not allow us to count the obligation that requires wanton polluters to mend their ways as an obligation of ecological citizenship; obligations of ecological citizenship would be incurred only by those who were already committed to sustainable practices and hence part of the relevant scheme.

The second strategy that justice accounts of citizenship have used to explain why the obligations they identify are owed by and to fellow citizens maintains that these obligations derive, at least in part, from a universal obligation to others, as fellow human beings, to protect their rights and secure their entitlements. (The argument that Waldron employs, successfully in my view, to explain how a duty to support and promote just institutions can satisfy the particularity requirement, and bind fellow citizens in a way that it does not bind non-citizens, can be understood as part of a general strategy of this kind.) Special obligations are viewed as a way of distributing responsibilities amongst human beings: our general obligations of justice are most effectively fulfilled by assigning particular groups of people with special obligations to each other. In other words, these special obligations arise from membership in a scheme for protecting rights and entitlements. This does not seem particularly promising in the context of Dobson-style ideas of ecological citizenship, however, for his model does not seem to be concerned with distributing responsibilities to protect rights and to secure entitlements in an analogous way. It is true that, for Dobson, different material circumstances mean different people are vulnerable in different ways to environmental degradation, and that groups of people who cause that degradation may acquire special responsibilities to compensate those who suffer as a result. But his account does not involve dividing the world into groups, and assigning each group with special responsibility to protect the rights and secure the entitlements of its members, in the way that the analogy would require.

So, even though justice accounts may have difficulty in explaining why the special obligations they identify are obligations that fellow citizens in particular owe to each other, as opposed to obligations that residents of the same state owe to each other, they may nevertheless have some success in identifying a collective or group the members of which lie in a particular relationship to each other as members of a common scheme, whether it is a scheme to distribute fairly the benefits and burdens of mutually advantageous cooperation, or a scheme that is (perhaps in addition) designed to ensure that its members' rights are secured and indeed that their needs are met irrespective of their contribution to the social product. Dobson's account, in contrast, is unable to identify such a relationship, for the only relationship that binds together fellow ecological citizens is that of 'harmer' through participation in unsustainable practices and 'victim' as a result of suffering the lion's share of the adverse effects of these practices. It is the absence of such a relationship that, at least in part, makes it hard to reconcile the special obligations which Dobson conceives as special obligations of ecological citizenship (owed by one subset of fellow ecological citizens to another subset) with the very idea of citizenship.

2 Conceptual innovation or conceptual confusion?

Dobson might question my insistence that obligations of citizenship must be special obligations that fellow citizens owe to each other. He might regard abandoning this idea as a conceptual innovation rather than as a mark of conceptual confusion.[9] Indeed he is appropriately critical of another attempt to restrict the concept of citizenship that may seem related to mine, namely, one which holds that obligations of citizenship must be based on reciprocity. Reciprocity in this context is the idea that citizens incur obligations to one another in return for enjoying benefits of various kinds, perhaps because they are understood as having entered some sort of contractual agreement.[10] Like Dobson, I do not see any reason to think that this notion of reciprocity is indispensible to the very concept of citizenship, even though it has been central to particular normative theories of citizenship. But the idea that the obligations of citizenship are obligations that fellow citizens owe to each other does not imply reciprocity in this sense, nor does it imply that a citizen owes an obligation to her fellows *because* they have fulfilled their obligations to her. So rejecting the idea that reciprocity is integral to citizenship is not equivalent to (and nor does it entail) that we must reject the idea that obligations of citizenship are obligations that fellow citizens owe to each other.

Dobson might nevertheless argue that we should reject the idea that obligations of citizenship are owed by fellow citizens to each other even if it is independent of the notion of reciprocity. There are apparent counter-examples to this idea that seem analogous in certain respects to cases in which some are harmed as a result of others participating in unsustainable practices, and which might appear to give the notion of ecological citizenship a foothold. In the first example, a state has committed some wrong against one of its neighbours—perhaps it has bombed an area of it—and as a result some of the citizens of this neighbouring state request or demand assistance from the citizens of the state that has committed the wrong. Aren't they obliged to help, not simply on humanitarian grounds but also because their state acted in their name when it committed this wrong? If so, they would be obliged in virtue of their citizenship to assist and in that sense they have an obligation of citizenship to do so. In the second example, a state has committed a wrong against a group of its own citizens—a particular ethnic or religious group, let us say. Perhaps it has dispossessed them or confiscated their savings. Don't the other citizens of that state owe an obligation to the victimized group to compensate them in some way, an obligation that is in effect owed by one subset of citizens to another subset in virtue of their citizenship? In this light it might be argued that what makes an obligation one of citizenship is that it is owed in virtue of one's citizenship—it does not need to be owed to each of one's fellow citizens or even to one's fellow citizens at all. But the two examples I have described do not help Dobson's case. They rely on the idea that the state acts in the name of its citizens, so that when it commits injustices or other moral wrongs, those citizens may incur obligations to those who are wronged, irrespective of the citizenship of the victims. In the kind of cases with which Dobson is primarily concerned, it is not the actions of the state which cause the harm, and the 'harmers' and 'the harmed' are in effect constituted as fellow citizens in virtue of the obligations incurred by the former, so the analogy breaks down.

The fundamental challenge which Dobson's account faces is this: what theoretical illumination is gained by speaking of obligations that are owed to fellow ecological citizens, rather than speaking of special obligations of justice that are owed by some to others because of the ways in which the former have acted, and continue to act, unjustly towards the latter? Why does the fact that some cause (or have caused) injustice to others in such a way that they owe obligations of compensatory justice to them mean that they stand in a relationship of citizenship to each other? Are those who benefited from colonial exploitation thereby automatically in a relationship of citizenship with those who suffered from it?[11] There are many to whom we owe special obligations of compensatory justice because of what we did in the past, and indeed because of how we continue to act in the present, but there is no reason to think of them as fellow citizens, or to think of these obligations as obligations of citizenship. Intellectually speaking, we gain nothing by invoking the idea of citizenship, and we lose what is distinctive about that relationship. Once we allow that obligations of citizenship can be owed to someone simply by virtue of unjust past or present interactions, we lose sight of what it is that makes them obligations of citizenship as opposed to merely obligations of justice, compensatory or otherwise. We can acknowledge our environmental interconnectedness, and indeed maintain that we have an obligation of justice (rather than merely charity) to humanity, including to future generations, to use resources in a sustainable way and to compensate others when we harm them by violating this obligation, without invoking the idea of citizenship at all.[12]

To this it might be responded that even if there is an intellectual cost incurred by invoking the idea of citizenship in these contexts, this cost is more than outweighed by the political gains: by representing the obligations of global environmental justice as demands of ecological citizenship, we promote compliance with these obligations. People are motivated to change their behaviour by the thought that they are acting as ecological citizens—or being good ecological citizens—in a way that they would not be motivated by the mere thought that they are complying with principles of justice, or acting justly or virtuously. I doubt this is true, but it is an empirical claim, a claim of moral psychology, that cannot be refuted (or indeed defended) except by appeal to empirical evidence. If we are going to speculate about the practical effects of using different forms of expression, we might also wonder whether introducing the language of ecological citizenship could result in the substance of what is being claimed getting lost in the rhetoric, with the result that movements for environmental justice lose their focus.

3 Global citizenship

Some have tried to motivate the idea of global citizenship, and the idea that we have demanding duties to act as global citizens, simply by appealing to the existence of obligations of justice that we owe to fellow human beings, and to obligations—perhaps also of justice—to establish, strengthen, and participate in transnational institutions and wider communities of discourse that enable us to fulfil these universal obligations.[13] In this section, I shall suggest that these ideas of global or cosmopolitan citizenship face much the same difficulties as Dobson's model of ecological citizenship. But I shall end by acknowledging that there may be a legitimate extension of the notion of citizenship to transnational relationships which dispenses with the idea that people enjoy a common citizenship only when they are subject to a common framework that protects their rights and secures their entitlements.

Nigel Dower suggests that those who are sceptical about notions of global citizenship face a dilemma: 'either one's ethical theory is robustly global so that commitment to global citizenship follows naturally from it, or one's denial of global citizenship has to be the denial of serious global obligation'.[14] But this is a false dilemma. Scepticism about the idea that we are global citizens need not rest upon denying the existence of robust duties of justice owed to fellow human beings wherever they live; nor need it involve denying that we have duties to promote the realization of institutions that enable us to fulfil them more effectively. We may be sceptical about the idea that the inhabitants of the world are already global citizens because we think that this would require a set of institutions with global reach that are capable of protecting people's rights and securing their entitlements or because we believe that duties of citizenship must be special duties that fellow citizens owe to each other. The mere existence of demanding obligations to other human beings, even if these obligations are obligations of justice, is not enough to give the idea of global or cosmopolitan citizenship a foothold.

Luis Cabrera's conception of global citizenship, even though it is more nuanced, does not give the notion any better grounding. He argues that individuals act as global citizens when they:

a) reach across international borders, or internal boundaries of differentiated citizenship
b) in order to help secure those fundamental rights that would be better protected if there were a just system of global institutions in place, and
c) work to help put such a system in place.[15]

Cabrera does not claim that we *are* already global citizens—he merely claims that we act *as* global citizens when we behave in a way that meets these criteria. (In fact, he seems to think that we act as global citizens whenever a and b are met, or when c is met.) I have no particular quarrel in this context with Cabrera's view that we have 'a natural duty to act as though there were a just global institutional scheme in place',[16] but it is unclear what this has to do with global citizenship. His claim that, even though we are not global citizens, we act as global citizens when we strive to fulfil this duty, provides little help. Indeed, it is tempting to respond that in acting on this duty we act *as if we were* global citizens rather than act as global citizens,[17] since in general when we speak of a person acting as something he is not, this is what we mean. For example, when someone says of a child that she is looking after that she is not the boy's mother but is acting as a mother to him, she means that she is acting as if she were his mother, either formally or informally assuming the duties to him that she would have if that were so. In some circumstances we might treat motherhood as a description of a role rather than as a biological fact and suppose that a person has a duty to occupy that role, that is, to *become* a child's mother and incur the responsibilities of the role. But this cannot be extrapolated to the case of global citizenship, for as Cabrera himself concedes, people cannot become global citizens in the absence of the relevant global institutions, so they cannot have a duty to do so.

My account of the core concept of citizenship does not entail that the very idea of global citizenship is incoherent. The idea that, say, each and every human being is a citizen of the world is not unintelligible. But any proposed model of global citizenship needs to be assessed against the core concept. It must at the very least explain how global citizens are, or could be, bound together by special obligations in a way that gives the notion of global citizenship a point, or it must justify abandoning this element of the core concept. Now, there are ways of grounding obligations of global justice which would allow us to derive special obligations, and it might be thought that these could underwrite ideas of global citizenship. For example, the kind of interdependence that arises from the existence of a global economic or institutional order (comprised, say, of institutions such as the World Bank, the International Monetary Fund, the World Trade Organization, and the United Nations, as well as the rules governing global trade) might be able to justify special obligations that are derived from universal obligations of global justice to aid others (or refrain from harming them), in conjunction with empirical facts concerning the ways in which our acts (and omissions) can cause poverty and suffering beyond the borders of the state in which we live. But, just as our special obligations to compensate others for the effects of the environmentally unsustainable practices in which we participate does not give reason to invoke the idea of ecological citizenship, so too these special obligations to aid or refrain from harming those beyond our borders who are vulnerable to our actions, do not give reason to invoke the idea of global citizenship. Nothing would be gained in terms of our understanding by doing so, for nothing would be added to the thought that we are bound by general obligations of justice that extend beyond our borders, or special obligations that are (perhaps through the addition of empirical premises) derived from these general obligations.

Are there any other more promising routes to the idea of global or transnational citizenship? It might be supposed that a global economic order of the kind described, governed in part by international institutions and conventions, is sufficient for us to be regarded as willing participants in a cooperative scheme for mutual advantage of a kind that would engage the principle of fair play at the global level. Could this then justify the existence of special obligations between the world's inhabitants in a way that would enable us to give content to the notion of global citizenship? Even if we are prepared to regard this as a cooperative scheme of the relevant kind, there is reason to be sceptical about whether it could ground a notion of global citizenship, since the kind of special obligations it could justify would be limited to requiring that those who trade with others (or lend money) beyond the borders of their state accept their fair share of the burdens of doing so, such as obeying whatever laws and conventions govern international trade and investment.[18] Given the limited range of a cooperative scheme of this kind, it is hard to see why on its own it would warrant talk of a shared global citizenship. Even to describe it as 'global economic citizenship' would be stretching things too far, given that the economic sphere encompasses so much more than market exchanges.

James Tully follows a rather different path, one that leads to a notion of transnational rather than global citizenship. He draws upon a tradition of 'diverse civic citizenship', which he understands as an activity or practice that does not require any institutional setting and takes place in the context of relationships, either between equals exercising power together, or between the governed and their governors, and which is oriented towards securing the enjoyment of public or civic goods, whether through (creative) use of the options available to them, or by employing strategies of negotiation or confrontation in order to expand that range of options.[19] So individuals act as transnational citizens—or as Tully would prefer to say, as glocal citizens—when they act on their own, or together with others, as part of transnational networks to uphold civic goods such as caring for the environment, mutual aid, fair trade, and social equality.[20]

This 'civic' way of understanding citizenship has elements in common with what I have been calling the equal membership account and in my view constitutes a more promising way of making sense of the idea that people may act as, and indeed be, transnational citizens, even in a context where they are not subject to any common political authority. It involves extending the equal membership account beyond its normal range since it allows that the relationship of citizenship may exist even when there is no common framework for securing rights and entitlements (though fellow transnational citizens may be part of other citizenship relationships in which their rights and entitlements are secured). But it seems to me that here the extension is intelligible, and in some cases at least there is some point to it: when people enjoy equal standing in a group and act together to secure a range of important civic or public goods, they express their social and political equality, and to the extent that their endeavours are successful, they secure some of the conditions required to sustain it. When in transnational networks in particular, people act together as equals to promote a range of goods such as environmental sustainability, poverty relief, and fair trade, and these networks give participants some measure of equality of opportunity to participate in decision-making processes, then the equal membership account provides a warrant for conceiving of them as transnational citizens. Fellow transnational citizens in this sense may be bound together by special obligations that they owe to each other which are partially constitutive of, and justified by, the wider relationship in which they participate as equals. (To the extent that they are also part of a cooperative scheme for mutual advantage, they might in addition be regarded as bound by special obligations grounded in a principle of fair play, thus drawing upon an element of the justice account of citizenship.) In this way the tradition of diverse civic citizenship provides a foothold for the idea of transnational citizenship which is lacking in those accounts which merely appeal to the notion of a global ethic or obligations of global justice.

4 Concluding remarks

In this chapter, I have expressed a degree of scepticism towards notions of ecological and cosmopolitan citizenship that appeal to the way in which our lives are deeply interconnected and our flourishing dependent upon the acts and omissions of individual and collective agents that are located, wholly or in part, beyond the borders of the state to which we belong. Our vulnerability to harms caused by these actors is undeniable, but the obligations of justice to which that vulnerability gives rise do not by themselves enable us to give content to ideas of ecological or cosmopolitan citizenship. My argument does not express (or imply) any scepticism about the possibility or desirability of transforming the state system in order to generate new transnational forms of government. There are a number of arguments in favour of dispersing the sovereignty that is currently concentrated in the hands of nation-states in order to create a variety of transnational political institutions, the existence of which might give the idea of cosmopolitan citizenship clear empirical application. But these institutions are not yet a reality, and neither the possibility nor desirability of them on its own would generate obligations *of citizenship* to work towards bringing them about—though, of course, there may be moral obligations, perhaps even obligations of justice, to do so.

Notes

1. This chapter draws upon my 'Environmental Obligations and the Limits of Transnational Citizenship', *Political Studies*, Vol. 57, 2009, pp. 280–97.
2. A. Dobson, *Citizenship and the Environment* (Oxford: Oxford University Press, 2003).
3. David Miller, for example, argues that global citizenship is unnecessary for the protection of human rights, and maintains that the empirical conditions for active citizenship to be possible at the global level do not obtain: see D. Miller, 'Bounded Citizenship' in his *Citizenship and National Identity* (Oxford: Polity, 2000).
4. See A. Linklater, 'What Is a Good International Citizen?', in P. Keal (ed.), *Ethics and Foreign Policy* (St Leonards, NSW: Allen and Unwin, 1992).
5. See Dobson, *Citizenship and the Environment*, pp. 88–90. See J. Barry, 'Sustainability, Political Judgement and Citizenship: Connecting Green Politics and Democracy', in B. Doherty and M. de Geus (eds), *Democracy and Green Political Thought* (London: Routledge, 1996), p. 126, and D. Bell, 'Liberal Environmental Citizenship', *Environmental Politics*, Vol. 14, 2005, pp. 179–94, for accounts which emphasize environmental rights.
6. See Dobson, *Citizenship and the Environment*, p. 31.
7. Note, however, that this strategy for defending special obligations for fellow citizens is not only over-inclusive (the obligations it justifies bind not only fellow citizens but also resident aliens) but may also be under-inclusive. Arguably those who are *unwilling* recipients of the benefits are not covered by it, since it is not clear that they are bound by obligations derived from a principle of fair play. If so, regarding the obligations derived from a principle of fair play as obligations of *citizenship* involves two simplifications.
8. See B. Barry, 'Humanity and Justice in Global Perspective', in J. Pennock and J. Chapman (eds), *Nomos Vol. 24: Ethics, Economics and the Law* (New York: NYU Press, 1982), especially pp. 231–4.
9. Indeed Dobson regards some of the resistance to ideas of ecological citizenship as an illegitimate attempt to police linguistic boundaries: see A. Dobson, 'Citizenship' in A. Dobson and R. Eckersley (eds), *Political Theory and the Ecological Challenge* (Cambridge: Cambridge University Press, 2006), p. 227). Cf. Tully, *Public Philosophy in a New Key, Volume II*, pp. 245, 268–9; Bosniak, *The Citizen and the Alien*, p. 120.
10. See Dobson, *Citizenship and the Environment*, pp. 45, 47, 118, 125.
11. Even if we deny that they are (as I think we should), we might insist that a state owes obligations of justice to those it colonized in the past, and that these include obligations to ensure that the colonized are given special access to citizenship in it. That is another issue, however.
12. Indeed the literature on global justice is full of contributions that advance the idea that we have demanding duties of global justice but do not invoke the idea of global citizenship. See, for example, S. Caney, *Justice Beyond Borders: A Global Political Theory* (Oxford: Oxford University Press, 2005); Pogge, *World Poverty and Human Rights*; O. O'Neill, *Bounds of Justice* (Cambridge: Cambridge University Press, 2000), Part II, and her *Towards Justice and Virtue: A Constructive Account of Practical Reasoning* (Cambridge: Cambridge University Press, 1996), esp. Ch. 4; P. Singer,

'Famine, Affluence and Morality', *Philosophy and Public Affairs*, Vol. 1, 1972, pp. 229–44; I. Young, 'Responsibility and Global Justice: A Social Connection Model', in E. F. Paul, F. D. Miller, and J. Paul (eds), *Justice and Global Politics* (Cambridge: Cambridge University Press, 2006).

13. See N. Dower, 'Global Citizenship: Yes or No?' in N. Dower and J. Williams (eds), *Global Citizenship: A Critical Reader* (Edinburgh: Edinburgh University Press, 2002), p. 40; A. Linklater, 'Cosmopolitan Citizenship', in K. Hutchings and R. Dannreuther (eds), *Cosmopolitan Citizenship* (Basingstoke: Macmillan, 1999). K. Anthony Appiah seeks to motivate the notion of world citizenship simply by appealing to the possibility and existence of respectful dialogue across borders: 'to engage respectfully in dialogue with others around the world about the questions great and small that we must solve together, about the many projects in which we can learn from each other, is already to live as fellow citizens' (K. A. Appiah, 'Citizens of the World', in M. Gibney (ed.), *Globalizing Rights* (Oxford: Oxford University Press, 2003), p. 230).

14. N. Dower, 'The Idea of Global Citizenship—A Sympathetic Assessment', *Global Society*, Vol. 14, 2000, p. 564.

15. L. Cabrera, 'Global Citizenship as the Completion of Cosmopolitanism', *Journal of International Political Theory*, Vol. 4, 2008, p. 94; Cf. L. Cabrera, *The Practice of Global Citizenship* (Cambridge: Cambridge University Press, 2010), p. 73, where 'a just system of global institutions' is replaced by 'a morally defensible system of global institutions'.

16. Cabrera, 'Global Citizenship as the Completion of Cosmopolitanism', p. 97.

17. See G. Stoker, A. Mason, A. McGrew, C. Armstrong, D. Owen, G. Smith, M. Banya, D. McGhee, and C. Saunders, *Prospects for Citizenship* (London: Bloomsbury Academic, 2011), Ch. 8, p. 171. Chris Armstrong was the lead author of this chapter.

18. See Barry, 'Humanity and Justice in Global Perspective', especially pp. 231–4.

19. Influenced by Wittgenstein, Tully rejects the idea that citizenship in general, or indeed any particular tradition of thinking about citizenship, can be captured in terms of some rule that governs the proper use of that term, so he might resist my general characterization of 'diverse civic citizenship' (see Tully, *Public Philosophy in a New Key, Vol. II*, pp. 244, 270–1, 279). But even if this characterization leaves out, or marginalizes, some strands of that tradition, it picks out a central way in which citizenship is understood within it.

20. See Tully, *Public Philosophy in a New Key, Vol. II*, pp. 292–3.

Conclusion

Citizenship makes a wide range of demands on us. In Part II, I explored a number of duties it might be thought to impose, but without aiming to compile a full list. My selection was informed by three criteria: first, the importance of the alleged duty; second, whether the two different conceptions of citizenship that I distinguished in Part I provide illuminating and interestingly different perspectives on how the duty might be justified; third, a particular focus on 'everyday citizenship', that is, the low-level decisions that we make in the course of our everyday lives, which, on reflection, duties of citizenship might be thought to govern, even though these decisions have generally been regarded as lying beyond their reach. As a result of applying and balancing these criteria, some duties which have played a significant, even major, role within the literature, such as a duty to serve one's political community in various ways (including, perhaps, a duty to serve in the military when needed) have received only relatively brief attention. Although I have indicated how a qualified version of this duty might be defended from within both the justice account and the equal membership account, it is not part of what I am calling everyday citizenship; nor are the different perspectives provided by the two accounts sufficiently distinctive or interesting in its case to merit devoting a whole chapter to its study.

My exploration began in the territory of ideal theory. In the first two chapters that comprise Part I, I treated citizenship as a moral notion that expresses an ideal: I focused on justice accounts that proceed by asking what duties citizens are under when they possess all the rights and entitlements that justice requires and equal membership accounts that proceed by asking what duties citizens are under when they possess the rights and entitlements that secure a range of conditions that are necessary for them to have equal standing, that is, various conditions that are required for the good of equal membership to be realized.[1] In Part II, I sometimes stayed at the level of ideal theory but in most of the chapters I also moved from ideal theory to our non-ideal circumstances, that is, from considering the duties that citizens would incur in a perfectly just society to those they would incur in a society that is unjust in various respects. (In some cases these duties are formulated in such a way that they straddle both ideal and non-ideal circumstances, for example the duty to support and further just institutions encompasses both a duty to comply with institutions that are already reasonably just and a duty to promote the reform of unjust institutions, at least in so far as that does not impose excessive costs upon us.)

There is much disagreement, however, about the purpose and value of ideal theory.[2] I hope to have made some contribution to these debates by illustrating how reasoning within ideal theory can be combined with reflection upon our non-ideal circumstances, and by showing that in at least some cases it is helpful to *begin* with ideal theory. But ideal theorizing about justice has been criticized from a number of directions, and my approach might be thought vulnerable to at least some of the charges that have been brought against it. Some maintain that ideal theory is pointless because it cannot provide adequate practical guidance since the gap between ideal theory and our non-ideal circumstances is too great.[3] In support of this argument it has been pointed out that ideal theory makes simplifying assumptions that are in fact false;[4] that it is constructed in the absence of any real understanding of what is possible in our historical circumstances;[5] that it pays insufficient attention to the way in which our actual institutions operate and of what motivates us;[6] and that it fails to analyse the power relations that govern societies.[7] Others argue that ideal theory is unnecessary for guiding reform because, for example, we can make comparative judgements about what institutions and policies would be *more* just without knowing what would be required for *perfect* justice.[8] Perhaps we can even make non-comparative judgements in some cases without a determinate ideal theory, for example, it might be thought that we can know that a state of affairs in which some live in affluence whilst others are starving is unjust without needing to know whether the correct principles of distributive justice are grounded in considerations of sufficiency, priority, or strict equality.

In the context of theorizing about the demands of citizenship, it might be thought that the dangers of ideal theory are especially acute. There are a number of ways in which actual societies can be non-ideal from the point of view of normative theories of citizenship. First, citizens may lack some or all of the rights and entitlements they ought to possess. Second, citizens may fail to live up to their duties or may lack the virtues required to be good citizens. Third, outsiders, including long-term residents, may be deprived of fair access to citizenship. In each type of case, non-ideal features may affect the duties of (other) citizens, and in this way cast doubt on the value of an ideal theory approach. If some or all of the residents of a state lack the rights and entitlements they ought to possess, then we may conclude that there is a real sense in which they are not full citizens whatever their legal status. Even if we think they possess enough of these rights and entitlements properly to be called citizens in the moral sense, the fact that they lack some of them may provide sufficient grounds for denying that they possess various duties to which they would otherwise be subject. If some do not fulfil their duties as citizens (either because they are weak-willed or because they would deny that they are under these duties), then this may affect the duties their fellow citizens are under. And if someone is deprived of fair access to citizenship, those who are citizens may be under a duty to treat her as if she were a citizen.

I do not want to deny that ideal theory may sometimes be unable to provide practical guidance because the gap between it and our non-ideal circumstances is too great or even unbridgeable.[9] Nor do I want to deny that fully defensible judgements about what is more or less just, or more or less desirable from the point of view of the good of equal membership, can often be made in the absence of any worked out ideal theory of justice or equal membership. I think that Rawls may nevertheless be right when he says that ideal theory provides the only basis for a *systematic grasp* of the issues that preoccupy us in our non-ideal circumstances.[10] This might be regarded as question-begging on the grounds that a systematic grasp of this kind is impossible, for example, it might be argued that no such grasp is available because there is no theory—no set of principles—which we can use to specify what would count as a perfectly just society. In response, I would maintain that whether such a grasp is available can only be determined by trying to provide it, and that improving our understanding of perfect justice, or indeed of the good of equal membership in its fullest and richest form, may be valuable even when it does not give us practical guidance.[11]

In the case of the demands of citizenship, it also seems to me that starting from ideal theory has certain advantages even if we are not seeking a systematic grasp of the issues. If we want to know what citizenship requires of us in non-ideal societies, that is, societies in which at least some do not enjoy rights and entitlements which they are due or in which at least some do not fully enjoy the good of equal membership, then a good place to begin is by asking what duties they and others would have in a perfectly just society or in a society that was ideal from the point of view of the good of equal membership. We can then examine how the lack of rights and entitlements, or inequalities of status, affect those duties. It is true that if we are seeking practical guidance, then ideal theory can only be a beginning.[12] That is why the arguments in this book have not remained at the level of ideal theory. In most of the chapters in Part II, I have also explored the issue of how the demands of citizenship are affected by living in unjust societies or societies in which the good of equal membership is only partially realized.

Consider some ways in which a lack of rights or entitlements may affect the duties of citizens: first, there are cases where citizens living in non-ideal societies are under duties that they would not be under in ideal circumstances; second, there are cases where the lack of rights or entitlements affects whether a duty that citizens would be under in ideal circumstances applies at all, or only to some of them, or affects the content of that duty; third, there are cases where non-ideal circumstances make a duty that would apply in ideal circumstances more demanding.

As a possible illustration of the first type of case, consider the argument in Chapter 7 that a duty to integrate might be justifiable in a culturally diverse society when levels of trust are sufficiently low that reasonably just institutions cannot be secured, but not when these levels are high enough to sustain such institutions—even if higher levels could be achieved by greater integration. As an illustration of the second type of case, consider the argument in Chapter 6 that the content of the duty to respect others, which is partially constitutive of the duty to treat them as equals, may depend upon the nature of the society in question, for example, whether it has a history of injustice which has damaged the relationships between different groups.

Contrast these cases with the third type of case where a duty that exists in an ideal society becomes more demanding in a non-ideal one. The duty not to seek or gain unfair advantages, discussed in Chapter 5, is more demanding in an unjust society, for when institutions are unjust, there is more scope for gaining such advantages. (As I pointed out, however, the content of this duty may also be different in an unjust society, for what counts as an unfair advantage may depend upon what injustices it contains: in an unjust society in which most children are deprived of the opportunity of an adequate education because state-funded education is so poor, even to secure an adequate education for one's child by sending her to a private school may be to gain an unfair advantage.) Furthermore, in Chapter 4, I claimed that the duty to share domestic burdens may become more demanding when women are disadvantaged by being discriminated against in the wider society: in such a society, male family members may have an obligation to take on a greater share of domestic burdens in order partially to redress the inequalities of access to jobs that are experienced by female members of their family.

So, one benefit of beginning from ideal theory is that it brings the issue of what demands citizenship places upon us into sharper relief. We can ask: given that we live in non-ideal societies, how does this affect the duties we would otherwise be under? This is not to deny that different ways of working may have other benefits. An approach, such as James Tully's, that might be thought to owe more to Wittgenstein's work, and which starts from the lived experience of citizenship and the traditions which inform it, brings other things into focus, for example, the cultural or historical specificity of some of the issues addressed by normative theories of citizenship, and the way in which various unjust norms can be seen as presuppositions of particular practices of citizenship.[13] But we should not in any case exaggerate the differences between these approaches. An approach which starts from our actual practices of citizenship will need to abstract from them to at least some degree when reflecting upon the duties and responsibilities of citizenship, for otherwise it will not be able to reach any understanding of the normative presuppositions of those practices or gain a critical perspective on them, whilst one which starts from ideal theory must move from it to reflection upon our actual practices if it is to have any relevance for our non-ideal circumstances. (Indeed Tully not only recovers the normative presuppositions of our actual practices, he also subjects them to critique on the basis of norms that he thinks give content to ideals of non-domination and non-exploitation.) Although Wittgenstein-inspired approaches, such as Tully's, that start from the historical complexity of our actual practices are sometimes accused of an indefensible moral relativism, there is no more reason to think that they *must* be flawed in this way than there is to think that approaches which start from ideal theory *must* misunderstand our non-ideal circumstances or be irrelevant to them. These approaches, I believe, represent different ways of mapping the same terrain, with different strengths and weaknesses depending in part upon the contours of that terrain and the purposes served by the exercise.

Notes

1. Ideal theory is sometimes characterized as theory which aims to describe a perfectly just society (perhaps employing various simplifying assumptions and responding to feasibility constraints grounded in facts about human nature). But there is good reason to suppose that there may be ideal theories of values other than justice, for example, an ideal theory of democracy that aimed to describe a perfectly democratic society. I am here supposing that there can also be an ideal theory of what I call equal membership, one that aims to describe a society in which the good of equal membership is fully realized.
2. See especially C. Farrelly, 'Justice in Ideal Theory: A Refutation', *Political Studies*, Vol. 55, 2007, pp. 844–64; A. Sen, 'What Do We Want from a Theory of Justice?', *Journal of Philosophy*, Vol. 103, 2006, pp. 215–38; I. Robeyns, 'Ideal Theory in Theory and Practice', *Social Theory and Practice*, Vol. 34, 2008, pp. 341–62; L. Valentini, 'On the Apparent Paradox of Ideal Theory' *Journal of Political Philosophy*, Vol. 17, 2009, pp. 332–55; A. J. Simmons, 'Ideal and Nonideal Theory', *Philosophy and Public Affairs*, Vol. 38, 2010, pp. 5–36; Z. Stemplowska and A. Swift, 'Ideal and Nonideal Theory', in D. Estlund (ed.) *Oxford Handbook of Political Philosophy* (Oxford: Oxford University Press, forthcoming).

3. See Farrelly, 'Justice in Ideal Theory'.

4. These are what Onora O'Neill calls idealizations, in contrast with abstractions: Abstraction 'is a matter of bracketing, but not of *denying*, predicates that are true of the matter under discussion' (O'Neill, *Towards Justice and Virtue*, p. 40), whereas idealization involves making claims that are strictly speaking false as a way of simplifying an argument or theory.

5. See J. Dunn, *Interpreting Political Responsibility* (Cambridge: Cambridge University Press, 1990), Ch. 12, pp. 193–215.

6. See R. Geuss, *Philosophy and Real Politics* (Princeton, NJ: Princeton University Press, 2008), p. 9.

7. See S. Wolin, 'The Liberal/Democratic Divide: On Rawls's Political Liberalism', *Political Theory*, Vol. 24, 1996, p. 101.

8. See Sen, 'What Do We Want from a Theory of Justice?', esp. pp. 216, 221–2, 237; A. Sen, *The Idea of Justice* (London: Penguin Books, 2009), pp. 12–18. For a response, see Simmons, 'Ideal and Nonideal Theory', pp. 34–6.

9. See Valentini, 'On the Apparent Paradox of Ideal Theory'.

10. Rawls, *A Theory of Justice*, p. 9/8.

11. If moral particularism is true, then it follows that there is no reason to think that there must be a set of principles of justice which determine what a perfectly just society would look like, but it does not follow that there cannot be a set of principles of this sort. See Mason, 'Justice, Holism, and Principles'.

12. There is of course the additional question of whether we must always be seeking practical guidance when we theorize about justice or other ideals. G. A. Cohen endorses what Adam Swift calls an epistemological rather than a practical conception of the role of political philosophy: 'the question for political philosophy is not what we should do but what we should think, even when what we should think makes no practical difference' (Cohen, *Rescuing Justice and Equality*, p. 268; A. Swift, 'The Value of Philosophy in Nonideal Circumstances', *Social Theory and Practice*, Vol. 34, 2008, pp. 366–8. See also Mason, 'Just Constraints'.)

13. See Tully, *Public Philosophy in a New Key, Vol. II*, especially Ch. 9; see also A. Norval, *Aversive Democracy: Inheritance and Originality in the Democratic Tradition* (Cambridge: Cambridge University Press, 2007).

Bibliography

Abizadeh, A., 'Cooperation, Pervasive Impact, and Coercion: On the Scope (not Site) of Distributive Justice', *Philosophy and Public Affairs*, Vol. 35, 2007, pp. 318–58

—— 'Democratic Theory and Border Coercion: No Right to Unilaterally Control Your Borders', *Political Theory*, Vol. 36, 2008, pp. 37–65

—— 'Democratic Legitimacy and State Coercion: A Reply to David Miller', *Political Theory*, Vol. 38, 2010, pp. 121–30

Allport, G., *The Nature of Prejudice* (Cambridge, MA: Addison-Wesley, 1954)

Anderson, E., 'What is the Point of Equality?', Ethics, Vol. 109, 1999, pp. 287–337

—— *The Imperative of Integration* (Princeton, NJ: Princeton University Press, 2010)

Appiah, K. A., 'Citizens of the World', in M. Gibney (ed.), *Globalizing Rights* (Oxford: Oxford University Press, 2003), pp. 189–232

Archard, D., 'Political Disagreement, Legitimacy, and Civility', *Philosophical Explorations*, Vol. 4, 2001, pp. 207–22

Armstrong, C., 'Coercion, Reciprocity, and Equality Beyond the State', *Journal of Social Philosophy*, Vol. 40, 2009, pp. 297–316

Banting, K., Johnston, R., Kymlicka, W., and Soroka, S., 'Do Multicultural Societies Erode the Welfare State? An Empirical Analysis', in K. Banting and W. Kymlicka (eds), *Multiculturalism and the Welfare State: Recognition and Redistribution in Contemporary Democracies* (Oxford: Oxford University Press, 2006), pp. 49–91

Barry, B., 'Humanity and Justice in Global Perspective', in J. Pennock and J. Chapman (eds), *Nomos Vol. 24: Ethics, Economics and the Law* (New York: NYU Press, 1982), pp. 219–52

—— *Culture and Equality: An Egalitarian Critique of Multiculturalism* (Cambridge: Polity, 2001)

Barry, J., 'Sustainability, Political Judgement and Citizenship: Connecting Green Politics and Democracy', in B. Doherty and M. de Geus (eds), *Democracy and Green Political Thought* (London: Routledge, 1996), pp. 115–31

Baubock, R., 'The Rights and Duties of External Citizenship', *Citizenship Studies*, Vol. 13, 2009, pp. 475–99

—— 'Temporary Migration, Partial Citizenship, and Hypermigration', *Critical Review of International Social and Political Philosophy*, Vol. 14, 2011, pp. 665–93

Beckman, L., 'Citizenship and Voting Rights: Should Resident Aliens Vote?', *Citizenship Studies*, Vol. 10, 2006, pp. 153–65

—— *The Frontiers of Democracy: The Right to Vote and its Limits* (Basingstoke: Palgrave Macmillan, 2009)

Beckman, L., 'Is Citizenship Special? Democracy in the Age of Migration and Human Mobility', a paper presented at the conference on 'The Dynamics of Citizenship in the Post-Political World', University of Stockholm, 26–28 May 2010

Bell, D., 'Liberal Environmental Citizenship', *Environmental Politics*, Vol. 14, 2005, pp. 179–94

Bellamy, R., *Liberalism and Pluralism: Towards a Politics of Compromise* (London: Routledge, 1999)

—— *Political Constitutionalism: A Republican Defence of the Constitutionality of Democracy* (Cambridge: Cambridge University Press, 2007)

Blake, M., 'Distributive Justice, Coercion, and Autonomy', *Philosophy and Public Affairs*, Vol. 30, 2001, pp. 257–96

Blum, L., 'Race, National Ideals, and Civic Virtue', *Social Theory and Practice*, 2007, Vol. 33, pp. 533–56

Bohman J. and Richardson, H., 'Liberalism, Deliberative Democracy, and "Reasons that All Can Accept"', *Journal of Political Philosophy*, Vol. 17, 2009, pp. 253–74

Bosniak, L., *The Citizen and the Alien: Dilemmas of Contemporary Membership* (Princeton, NJ: Princeton University Press, 2006)

Bou-Habib, P., 'Compulsory Insurance Without Paternalism', *Utilitas*, Vol. 18, 2006, pp. 243–63

Braybooke, D., *Meeting Needs* (Princeton, NJ: Princeton University Press, 1987)

Brighouse, H. and Swift, A., 'Legitimate Parental Partiality', *Philosophy and Public Affairs*, Vol. 37, 2009, pp. 43–80

Brown, G., 'The Future of Britishness'. Available at <http://fabians.org.uk/events/speeches/the-future-of-britishness>, accessed 16 March 2011

Bubeck, D., *Care, Gender and Justice* (Oxford: Oxford University Press, 1995)

—— 'A Feminist Approach to Citizenship', EUI Working Paper, 1995, EUF No. 95/1

Burtt, S., 'Is Inclusion a Civic Virtue? Adoption, Disability and the Liberal State', *Social Theory and Practice*, Vol. 33, 2007, pp. 557–78

Cabrera, L., 'Global Citizenship as the Completion of Cosmopolitanism', *Journal of International Political Theory*, Vol. 4, 2008, pp. 84–104

—— *The Practice of Global Citizenship* (Cambridge: Cambridge University Press, 2010)

Callan, E., *Creating Citizens: Political Education and Liberal Democracy* (Oxford: Oxford University Press, 1997)

Caney, S., *Justice Beyond Borders: A Global Political Theory* (Oxford: Oxford University Press, 2005)

Cantle, T., *Community Cohesion: A New Framework for Race and Diversity*, Revised and Updated Edition (Palgrave Macmillan: Basingstoke, 2008)

Carens, J., 'Why Naturalization Should Be Easy: A Response to Noah Pickus', in N. Pickus (ed.), *Immigration and Citizenship in the 21st Century* (Totowa, NJ: Rowman and Littlefield, 1998), pp. 141–6

—— 'The Integration of Immigrants', *Journal of Moral Philosophy*, Vol. 2, 2005, pp. 29–46

—— 'The most liberal citizenship test is none at all', in R. Baubock and C. Joppke (eds), 'How Liberal Are Citizenship Tests', EU Working Papers, Eudo Citizenship, RSCAS 2010/41. Available at <http://eudo-citizenship.eu/docs/RSCAS_2010_41.pdf>, accessed 16 March 2011

Carter, I., 'Equal Opportunity and Equal Freedom', a paper presented to the workshop on Equality of Opportunity at the ECPR Joint Sessions, Granada, 14–19 April 2005

—— 'How are Power and Freedom Related?', in C. Laborde and J. Maynor (eds), *Republicanism and Political Theory* (Oxford: Blackwell, 2008), pp. 58–82

Casal, P., and Williams, A., 'Rights, Equality and Procreation', *Analyse und Kritik*, Vol. 17, 1995, pp. 93–116

—— —— 'Equality of Resources and Procreative Justice' in J. Burley (ed.), *Dworkin and his Critics* (Oxford: Blackwell, 2004), pp. 150–69

Chambers, C., 'All Must Have Prizes: The Liberal Case for Interference in Cultural Practices', in P. Kelly (ed.), *Multiculturalism Reconsidered* (Cambridge: Polity, 2002), pp. 151–72

—— *Sex, Culture, and Justice: The Limits of Choice* (University Park, PA: Pennsylvania State University Press, 2008)

Chodorow, N., *The Reproduction of Mothering: Psychoanalysis and the Sociology of Gender.* (Berkeley and Los Angeles, CA: University of California Press, 1978)

Christiano, T., 'The Significance of Public Deliberation', in J. Bohman and W. Rehg (eds), *Deliberative Democracy: Essays on Reason and Politics* (Cambridge, MA: MIT Press, 1997), pp. 243–77

Clayton, M., *Justice and Legitimacy in Upbringing* (Oxford: Oxford University Press, 2006)

—— and Stevens, D., 'School Choice and the Burdens of Justice', *Theory and Research in Education*, Vol. 2, 2004, pp. 111–26

Cohen, G. A., 'On the Currency of Egalitarian Justice', *Ethics*, Vol. 99, 1989, pp. 906–44

—— 'Casting the First Stone: Who Can, and Who Can't, Condemn the Terrorists?', in A. O'Hear (ed.), *Political Philosophy* (Cambridge: Cambridge University Press, 2006), pp. 113–36

—— *Rescuing Justice and Equality* (Cambridge, MA: Harvard University Press, 2008)

—— 'Fairness and Legitimacy in Justice, and: Does Option Luck Ever Preserve Justice?', in G. A. Cohen, *On the Currency of Egalitarian Justice, and Other Essays in Political Philosophy* (Princeton, NJ: Princeton University Press, 2011), pp. 124–43

Connolly, W., *The Terms of Political Discourse*, second edition (Oxford: Martin Robertson, 1983)

Conover, P, Crewe, I., and Searing, D., 'The Nature of Citizenship in the United States and Great Britain: Empirical Comments on Theoretical Themes', *Journal of Politics*, Vol. 53, 1991, pp. 800–32

Copp, D., 'Pluralism and Stability in Liberal Theory', *Journal of Political Philosophy*, Vol. 4, 1996, pp. 191–206

Crisp, R., *Reasons and the Good* (Oxford: Oxford University Press, 2006)

Dagger, R., *Civic Virtues: Rights, Citizenship, and Republican Liberalism* (Oxford: Oxford University Press, 1997)

Dancy, J., *Ethics Without Principles* (Oxford: Oxford University Press, 2004)

Delphy, C., and Leonard, D., *Familiar Exploitation: A New Analysis of Marriage in Contemporary Western Societies* (Cambridge: Polity, 1992)

Dobson, A., *Citizenship and the Environment* (Oxford: Oxford University Press, 2003)

—— 'Citizenship' in A. Dobson and R. Eckersley (eds), *Political Theory and the Ecological Challenge* (Cambridge: Cambridge University Press, 2006), pp. 216–31

Dower, N., 'The Idea of Global Citizenship—A Sympathetic Assessment', *Global Society*, Vol. 14, 2000, pp. 553–67

—— 'Global Citizenship: Yes or No?' in N. Dower and J. Williams (eds), *Global Citizenship: A Critical Reader* (Edinburgh: Edinburgh University Press, 2002), pp. 39–40

Dunn, J., *Interpreting Political Responsibility* (Cambridge: Cambridge University Press, 1990)

Dworkin, A., *Pornography: Men Possessing Women* (New York: G. P. Putnam's Sons, 1979)

Dworkin, R., *Sovereign Virtue: The Theory and Practice of Equality* (Cambridge, MA: Harvard University Press, 2000)

Elster, J., 'The Market and the Forum: Three Varieties of Political Theory', in J. Bohman and W. Rehg (eds), *Deliberative Democracy: Essays on Reason and Politics* (Cambridge, MA: MIT Press, 1997), pp. 3–34

Estlund, D., 'Liberalism, Equality, and Fraternity in Cohen's Critique of Rawls', *The Journal of Political Philosophy*, Vol. 6, 1998, pp. 99–112

Etzioni, A., *The Spirit of Community: Rights, Responsibilities, and the Communitarian Agenda* (New York: Crown Publishers, 1993)

Fabre, C., *Whose Body is it Anyway? Justice and the Integrity of the Person* (Oxford: Oxford University Press, 2006)

Farrelly, C., 'Justice in Ideal Theory: A Refutation', *Political Studies*, Vol. 55, 2007, pp. 844–64

Fine, S., *Immigration and the Right to Exclude* (Oxford: Oxford University Press, forthcoming)

Fleurbaey, M., *Fairness, Responsibility, and Welfare* (Oxford: Oxford University Press, 2008)

Forst, R., *The Right to Justification* (New York: Columbia University Press, forthcoming)

Fourie, C., 'Justice and the Duties of Social Equality', PhD thesis, University College London, 2007

Fraser, N., 'After the Family Wage: Gender Equity and the Welfare State', *Political Theory*, Vol. 22, 1994, pp. 591–618

Galston, W., *Liberal Purposes: Goods, Virtues, and Diversity in the Liberal State* (Cambridge: Cambridge University Press, 1991)

—— 'Diversity, Toleration, and Deliberative Democracy: Religious Minorities and Public Schooling', in S. Macedo (ed.), *Deliberative Politics: Essays on Disagreement and Democracy* (New York: Oxford University Press, 1999), pp. 39–48

Gaus, G., *Justificatory Liberalism: An Essay on Epistemology and Political Theory* (Oxford: Oxford University Press, 1996)

—— 'The Place of Religious Belief in Public Reason Liberalism', in M. Dimova-Cookson and P. Stirk (eds), *Multiculturalism and Moral Conflict* (London: Routledge, 2010), pp. 19–37

George, R. P., 'On the External Benefits of Children', in D. T. Myers, K. Kipnis, and C. F. Murphy (eds), *Kindred Matters: Rethinking the Philosophy of the Family* (Ithaca, NY: Cornell University Press, 1993), pp. 209–17

Geuss, R., *Philosophy and Real Politics* (Princeton, NJ: Princeton University Press, 2008)

Gilligan, C., *In a Different Voice: Psychological Theory and Women's Development* (Cambridge, MA: Harvard University Press, 1982)

Goodin, R., 'What Is So Special about Our Fellow Countrymen?', *Ethics*, Vol. 98, 1988, pp. 663–86

—— 'Enfranchising All Affected Interests, and its Alternatives', *Philosophy and Public Affairs*, 2007, Vol. 35, pp. 40–68

Habermas, J., 'Appendix II: Citizenship and National Identity', in his *Between Facts and Norms: Contributions to a Discourse Theory of Law and Democracy*, translated by W. Rehg (Cambridge, MA: MIT Press, 1996)

Hamilton, L., *The Political Philosophy of Needs* (Cambridge: Cambridge University Press, 2003)

Hardin, R., 'Trusting Persons, Trusting Institutions', in R. J. Zeckhauser (ed.), The *Strategy of Choice* (Cambridge MA: MIT Press, 1991), pp. 185–209

Held, V., *The Ethics of Care: Personal, Political, and Global* (New York: Oxford University Press, 2005)

Holtug, N., 'Immigration and the Politics of Social Cohesion', *Ethnicities*, Vol. 10, 2010, pp. 435–51

—— *Persons, Interests, and Justice* (Oxford: Oxford University Press, 2010)

Home Office, *Community Cohesion: A Report of the Independent Review Team Chaired by Ted Cantle* (London: HMSO, 2001)

—— *Strength in Diversity: Towards a Community Cohesion Strategy* (London: HMSO, 2004)

—— *Improving Opportunity, Strengthening Society: The Government's Strategy to Increase Race Equality and Community Cohesion* (London: HMSO, 2005)

Honohan, I., *Civic Republicanism* (London: Routledge, 2002)

Horton, J., 'In Defence of Associative Political Obligations: Part One', *Political Studies*, Vol. 54, 2006, pp. 427–43

—— 'In Defence of Associative Political Obligations: Part Two', *Political Studies*, Vol. 55, 2007, pp. 1–19

—— *Political Obligation*, second edition (Basingstoke: MacMillan, 2010)

Jeske, D., 'Associative Obligations, Voluntarism and Equality', *Pacific Philosophical Quarterly*, Vol. 77, 1996, pp. 289–309

—— 'Special Obligations', *Stanford Encyclopedia of Philosophy*, at <http://plato.stanford.edu/entries/special-obligations/>, accessed 30 July 2010

Julius, A. J., 'Basic Structure and the Value of Equality', *Philosophy and Public Affairs*, Vol. 31, 2003, pp. 321–55

Kant, I., *Critique of Pure Reason*, translated by N. Kemp Smith (London: Macmillan, 1929)

Kenney, J., 'Good Citizenship: The Duty to Integrate', at: <http://www.cic.gc.ca/english/department/media/speeches/2009/2009-03-18.asp>, accessed 6 December 2011

Kernohan, A., *Liberalism, Equality, and Cultural Oppression* (Cambridge: Cambridge University Press, 1998)

Kittay, E. F., *Love's Labor: Essays on Women, Equality, and Dependency* (London: Routledge, 1999)

Klosko, G., *The Principle of Fairness and Political Obligation* (Lanham, MD: Rowman and Littlefield, 1992)

Kramer, M, 'Liberty and Domination', in C. Laborde and J. Maynor (eds), *Republicanism and Political Theory* (Oxford: Blackwell, 2008), pp. 31–57

Kymlicka, W., *Multicultural Citizenship: A Liberal Theory of Minority Rights* (Oxford: Oxford University Press, 1995)

—— *Politics in the Vernacular: Nationalism, Multiculturalism, and Citizenship* (Oxford: Oxford University Press, 2001)

—— and Norman, W., 'Return of the Citizen: A Survey of Recent Work on Citizenship Theory', *Ethics*, Vol. 104, 1994, pp. 352–81

Laborde, C., *Critical Republicanism: The Hijab Controversy and Political Philosophy* (Oxford: Oxford University Press, 2008)

Laden, A., *Reasonably Radical: Deliberative Liberalism and the Politics of Identity* (Ithaca: Cornell University Press, 2001)

Linklater, A., 'What Is a Good International Citizen?', in P. Keal (ed.), *Ethics and Foreign Policy* (St Leonards, NSW: Allen and Unwin, 1992), pp. 21–43

—— 'Cosmopolitan Citizenship', in K. Hutchings and R. Dannreuther (eds), *Cosmopolitan Citizenship* (Basingstoke: Macmillan, 1999), pp. 35–59

Lippert-Rasmussen, K., 'Egalitarianism, Option Luck, and Responsibility', *Ethics*, Vol. 111, 2001, pp. 548–79

Lister, R., *Citizenship: Feminist Perspectives*, second edition (Basingstoke: Palgrave Macmillian, 2003)

Lovett, F., *A General Theory of Domination and Justice* (Oxford: Oxford University Press, 2010)

Macedo, S., *Liberal Virtues: Citizenship, Virtue, and Community in Liberal Constitutionalism* (Oxford: Oxford University Press, 1990)

Mackinnon, C., *Feminism Unmodified: Discourses on Life and Law* (Cambridge, MA: Harvard University Press, 1987)

Mason, A., 'Gilligan's Conception of Moral Maturity', *Journal for the Theory of Social Behavior*, Vol. 20, 1990, pp. 167–79

—— *Community, Solidarity and Belonging: Levels of Community and Their Normative Significance* (Cambridge: Cambridge University Press, 2000)

—— 'Equality, Personal Responsibility, and Gender Socialisation', *Proceedings of the Aristotelian Society*, Vol. 100, 2000, pp. 227–46

—— 'Just Constraints', *British Journal of Political Science*, Vol. 34, 2004, pp. 251–68

—— ' *Levelling the Playing Field: The Idea of Equal Opportunity and its Place in Egalitarian Thought* (Oxford: Oxford University Press, 2006)

—— 'Public Justifiability, Deliberation, and Civic Virtue', *Social Theory and Practice*, Vol. 33, 2007, pp. 679–700

—— 'Environmental Obligations and the Limits of Transnational Citizenship', *Political Studies*, Vol. 57, 2009, pp. 280–97

—— 'Justice, Holism, and Principles' *Res Publica*, Vol. 15, 2009, pp. 179–94

—— 'Integration, Cohesion, and National Identity: Theoretical Reflections on Recent British Policy', *British Journal of Political Science*, Vol. 40, 2010, pp. 857–74

—— 'Citizenship and Justice', *Politics, Philosophy, and Economics*, Vol. 10, 2011, pp. 263–81

—— 'Putting Story-Reading to Bed: A Reply to Segall', *Critical Review of International Social and Political Philosophy*, Vol. 14, 2011, pp. 81–8

Mason, A., 'Citizens, Resident Aliens and the Good of Equal Membership', in L. Beckman and E. Urman (eds), *The Territories of Citizenship* (Basingstoke: Palgrave Macmillan, forthcoming)

May, S., 'Moral Compromise, Political Reconciliation, and Civic Friendship', *Critical Review of International Social and Political Philosophy*, Vol. 14, 2011, pp. 581–602

Maynor, J., *Republicanism in the Modern World* (Cambridge: Polity, 2003)

McGhee, D., *The End of Multiculturalism: Terrorism, Integration and Human Rights* (Maidenhead: Open University Press/McGraw-Hill, 2008)

McKeever, S., and Ridge, M., *Principled Ethics: Generalism as a Regulative Ideal* (Oxford: Oxford University Press, 2006)

Mead, L., *Beyond Entitlement: The Social Obligations of Citizenship* (New York: Free Press, 1986)

Miller, D., 'Constraints on Freedom', *Ethics*, Vol. 94, 1983, pp. 66–86

—— *On Nationality* (Oxford: Oxford University Press, 1995)

—— 'Equality and Justice', in A. Mason (ed.), *Ideals of Equality* (Oxford: Blackwell, 1998), pp. 21–36

—— 'Bounded Citizenship' in his *Citizenship and National Identity* (Oxford: Polity, 2000), pp. 81–96

—— 'Social Justice in Multicultural Societies', in P. van Parijs (ed.), *Cultural Diversity versus Economic Solidarity* (Brussels: De Boeck University Press, 2004), pp. 13–31

—— 'Reasonable Partiality Towards Compatriots', *Ethical Theory and Moral Practice*, Vol. 8, 2005, pp. 63–81

—— 'Democracy's Domain', *Philosophy and Public Affairs*, Vol. 37, 2009, pp. 201–28

—— 'Why Immigration Controls Are Not Coercive: A Reply to Arash Abizadeh', *Political Theory*, Vol. 38, 2010, pp. 111–20

Modood, T., *Multiculturalism: A Civic Idea* (Cambridge: Polity, 2007)

Moore, G. E., *Principia Ethica*, revised edition (Cambridge: Cambridge University Press, 1993), p. 79

Moore A., and Crisp, R., 'Welfarism in Moral Theory', *Australasian Journal of Philosophy*, Vol. 74, 1996, pp. 598–613

Murphy, L., 'Institutions and the Demands of Justice', *Philosophy and Public Affairs*, Vol. 27, 1998, pp. 251–91

Nagel, T., *Equality and Partiality* (New York: Oxford University Press, 1991)

—— 'The Problem of Global Justice,' *Philosophy and Public Affairs*, Vol. 33, 2005, pp. 113–47

Newton, K., 'The New Liberal Dilemma: Social Trust in Mixed Societies', a paper prepared for the ECPR Workshop on Social Capital, The State and Diversity, Helsinki, 7–12 May 2007

Norval, A., *Aversive Democracy: Inheritance and Originality in the Democratic Tradition* (Cambridge: Cambridge University Press, 2007)

Nozick, R., *Anarchy, State and Utopia*, (Oxford: Blackwell, 1974)

O' Flynn, I., *Deliberative Democracy and Divided Societies* (Basingstoke: Palgrave Macmillan, 2006)

Okin, S., *Justice, Gender and the Family* (New York: Basic Books, 1989)

—— 'Is Multiculturalism Bad for Women?', in J. Cohen, M. Howard, and M. Nussbaum (eds), *Is Multiculturalism Bad for Women?* (Princeton, NJ: Princeton University Press, 1999)

—— '"Mistresses of Their Own Destiny": Group Rights, Gender, and Realistic Rights of Exit', *Ethics*, Vol. 112, 2002, pp. 205–30

O'Neill, O., *Towards Justice and Virtue: A Constructive Account of Practical Reasoning* (Cambridge: Cambridge University Press, 1996)

—— *Bounds of Justice* (Cambridge: Cambridge University Press, 2000)

Osiel, M., *Mass Atrocity, Collective Memory, and the Law* (New Brunswick: Transaction Publishers, 1997)

Otsuka, M., 'Prerogatives to Depart from Equality', in A. O'Hear (ed.), *Political Philosophy* (Cambridge: Cambridge University Press, 2006), pp. 95–111

Owen, D., 'Transnational Citizenship and the Democratic State: Modes of Membership and Voting Rights', *Critical Review of International Social and Political Philosophy*, Vol. 14, 2011, pp. 641–63

Parekh, B., 'Britain and the Social Logic of Pluralism' in B. Parekh (ed.), *Britain: A Plural Society. Report of a Seminar* (London: Commission for Racial Equality, 1990), pp. 58–76

—— *A New Politics of Identity: Political Principles for an Interdependent World* (Basingstoke: Palgrave, 2008)

Parfit, D., 'Equality and Priority', in A. Mason (ed.), *Ideals of Equality* (Oxford: Blackwell, 1998), pp. 1–20

—— 'Equality or Priority?', in M. Clayton and A. Williams (eds), *The Ideal of Equality* (Basingstoke, UK: Macmillan, 2000), pp. 81–125

Pettigrew, T., and Tropp, L., 'A Meta-Analytic Test of Intergroup Contact Theory', *Journal of Personality and Social Psychology*, Vol. 90, 2006, pp. 751–83

Pettit, P., *The Common Mind: An Essay on Psychology, Society, and Politics* (Oxford: Oxford University Press, 1993)

—— *Republicanism: A Theory of Freedom and Government* (Oxford: Oxford University Press, 1997)

—— 'Republican Freedom: Three Axioms, Four Theorems', in C. Laborde and J. Maynor (eds), *Republicanism and Political Theory* (Oxford: Blackwell, 2008)

Phillips, A., 'Citizenship and Feminist Theory', in G. Andrews (ed.), *Citizenship* (London: Lawrence and Wishart, 1991), pp. 76–88

—— *Multiculturalism Without Culture* (Princeton, NJ: Princeton University Press, 2007)

Plant, R., *Modern Political Thought* (Oxford: Blackwell, 1991)

Pocock, J., 'The Ideal of Citizenship since Classical Times', in R. Beiner (ed.), *Theorizing Citizenship* (Albany, NY: State University of New York Press, 1995), pp. 29–52

Pogge, T., *Realizing Rawls* (Ithaca, NY: Cornell University Press, 1989)

—— 'On the Site of Distributive Justice: Reflections on Cohen and Murphy', *Philosophy and Public Affairs*, Vol. 29, 2000, pp. 137–69

—— *World Poverty and Human Rights* (Cambridge: Polity, 2002)

Putnam, R., *Bowling Alone: The Collapse and Revival of American Community* (New York: Simon and Schuster, 2000)

—— 'E Pluribus Unum: Diversity and Community in the Twenty-first Century: The 2006 Johan Skytte Prize Lecture', *Scandinavian Political Studies*, Vol. 30, 2007, pp. 137–74

Quine, W., 'Two Dogmas of Empiricism', in his *From a Logical Point of View*, second edition (Cambridge, MA: Harvard University Press, 1961)

Quong, J., 'The Scope of Public Reason', *Political Studies*, Vol. 52, 2004, pp. 233–50

—— *Liberalism Without Perfection* (Oxford: Oxford University Press, 2011)

Rakowski, E., *Equal Justice* (Oxford: Oxford University Press, 1991)

Rawls, J., *Political Liberalism*, paperback edition (New York: Columbia University Press, 1996)

—— *A Theory of Justice* (Cambridge, MA: Harvard University Press, 1971; revised edition 1999)

—— 'The Idea of Public Reason Revisited', in S. Freeman (ed.), *J. Rawls: Collected Papers* (Cambridge, MA: Harvard University Press, 1999), pp. 573–615

—— *Justice as Fairness: A Restatement* (Cambridge, MA: Harvard University Press, 2001)

Raz, J., *The Morality of Freedom* (Oxford: Oxford University Press, 1986)

Risse, M., 'What to Say About the State', *Social Theory and Practice*, Vol. 32, 2006, pp. 671–98

Robeyns, I., 'Ideal Theory in Theory and Practice', *Social Theory and Practice*, Vol. 34, 2008, pp. 341–62

Rubio-Marin, R., *Immigration as a Democratic Challenge: Citizenship and Inclusion in Germany and the United States* (Cambridge, Cambridge University Press, 2000)

Sangiovanni, A., 'Global Justice, Reciprocity, and the State', *Philosophy and Public Affairs*, Vol. 35, 2007, pp. 3–39

Scanlon, T. M., *What We Owe to Each Other* (Cambridge, MA: Harvard University Press, 1998)

Scheffler, S., 'Families, Nations, and Strangers', in his *Boundaries and Allegiances: Problems of Justice and Responsibility in Liberal Thought* (Oxford: Oxford University Press, 2001), pp. 48–65

—— 'Immigration and the Significance of Culture', *Philosophy and Public Affairs*, Vol. 35, 2007, pp. 93–125

—— 'Is the Basic Structure Basic?' in C. Sypnowich (ed.), *The Egalitarian Conscience: Essays in Honour of G. A. Cohen* (Oxford: Oxford University Press, 2006), pp. 102–29

Segall, S., 'In Solidarity with the Imprudent: A Defence of Luck Egalitarianism', *Social Theory and Practice*, Vol. 33, 2007, pp. 177–98

—— *Health, Luck, and Justice* (Princeton, NJ: Princeton University Press, 2010)

—— 'If You're a Luck-Egalitarian, How Come You Read Bedtime Stories to Your Children?', *Critical Review of International Social and Political Philosophy*, Vol. 14, 2011, pp. 23–40

Seglow, J., 'Associative Duties and Global Justice', *Journal of Moral Philosophy*, Vol. 7, 2010, pp. 54–73

Selbourne, D., *The Principle of Duty* (London: Sinclair-Stevenson, 1994)

Sen, A., 'What Do We Want from a Theory of Justice?', *Journal of Philosophy*, Vol. 103, 2006, pp. 215–38

—— *The Idea of Justice* (London: Penguin Books, 2009)

Shiffrin, S., 'Incentives, Motives, and Talents', *Philosophy and Public Affairs*, Vol. 38, 2010, pp. 111–42

Simmons, A. J., *Moral Principles and Political Obligations* (Princeton, NJ: Princeton University Press, 1979)

—— *Justification and Legitimacy: Essays on Rights and Obligations* (Cambridge: Cambridge University Press, 2001)

—— 'The Duty to Obey and Our Natural Moral Duties', in C. H. Wellman and A. J. Simmons, *Is There a Duty to Obey the Law?* (Cambridge: Cambridge University Press, 2005)

—— 'Ideal and Nonideal Theory', *Philosophy and Public Affairs*, Vol. 38, 2010, pp. 5–36

Simpson, L., 'Statistics of Racial Segregation: Measures, Evidence and Policy', *Urban Studies*, Vol. 41, 2004, pp. 661–81

Singer, P., 'Famine, Affluence and Morality', *Philosophy and Public Affairs*, Vol. 1, 1972, pp. 229–44

Skinner, Q., *Liberty Before Liberalism* (Cambridge: Cambridge University Press, 1997)

—— 'Freedom as the Absence of Arbitrary Power', in C. Laborde and J. Maynor (eds), *Republicanism and Political Theory* (Oxford: Blackwell, 2008), pp. 83–101

Smith, R., *Stories of Peoplehood: The Politics and Morals of Political Membership* (Cambridge: Cambridge University Press, 2003)

Spinner, J., *The Boundaries of Citizenship* (Baltimore: Johns Hopkins University Press, 1994)

Statman, D., 'Who Needs Imperfect Duties?', *American Philosophical Quarterly*, Vol. 33, 1996, pp. 211–24

Steiner, H., *An Essay on Rights* (Oxford: Blackwell, 1994)

—— 'Silver Spoons and Golden Genes: Talent Differentials and Distributive Justice', in D. Archard and C. M. McLeod (eds), *The Moral and Political Status of Children* (Oxford: Oxford University Press, 2002), pp. 183–95

Stemplowska, Z. and Swift, A., 'Ideal and Nonideal Theory', in D. Estlund (ed.), *Oxford Handbook of Political Philosophy* (Oxford: Oxford University Press, forthcoming)

Stoker, G., Mason, A., McGrew, A., Armstrong, C., Owen, D., Smith, G., Banya, M., McGhee, D., and Saunders, C., *Prospects for Citizenship* (London: Bloomsbury Academic, 2011)

Sunstein, C., 'The Law of Group Polarization', *Journal of Political Philosophy*, Vol. 10, 2002, pp. 175–95

Swift, A., *How Not to Be a Hypocrite: School Choice for the Morally Perplexed Parent* (London: Routledge, 2003)

—— 'The Value of Philosophy in Nonideal Circumstances', *Social Theory and Practice*, Vol. 34, 2008, pp. 363–87

Taylor, C., 'Irreducibly Social Goods', in his *Philosophical Arguments* (Cambridge, MA: Harvard University Press, 1995), pp. 127–45

Tomasi, J., *Liberalism Beyond Justice: Citizens, Society, and the Boundaries of Political Theory* (Princeton, NJ: Princeton University Press, 2001)

Tully, J., *Public Philosophy in a New Key, Vol. II: Imperialism and Civic Freedom* (Cambridge: Cambridge University Press, 2008)

Uslaner, E., 'Segregation, Mistrust and Minorities', *Ethnicities*, Vol. 10, 2010, pp. 415–34

Valentini, L., 'On the Apparent Paradox of Ideal Theory', *Journal of Political Philosophy*, Vol. 17, 2009, pp. 332–55

Vallentyne, P., 'Brute Luck, Option Luck, and Equality of Initial Opportunities', *Ethics*, Vol. 112, 2002, pp. 529–57

Voigt, K., 'The Harshness Objection: Is Luck Egalitarianism Too Harsh on the Victims of Option Luck', *Ethical Theory and Moral Practice*, Vol. 10, 2007, pp. 389–407

Waldron, J., 'Special Ties and Natural Duties', *Philosophy and Public Affairs*, Vol. 22, 1993, pp. 3–30

Weinstock, D., 'Building Trust in Divided Societies', *Journal of Political Philosophy*, Vol. 7, 1999, pp. 287–307

Wellman, C., 'Friends, Compatriots, and Special Political Obligations', *Political Theory*, Vol. 29, 2001, pp. 217–36

White, S., *The Civic Minimum: On the Rights and Obligations of Economic Citizenship* (Oxford: Oxford University Press, 2003)

Williams, A., 'Incentives, Inequality, and Publicity', *Philosophy and Public Affairs*, Vol. 27, 1998, pp. 225–47

—— 'Justice, Incentives and Constructivism', *Ratio*, Vol. 21, 2008, pp. 476–93

Wittgenstein, L., *Philosophical Investigations*, third edition, trans. G. E. M. Anscombe (Oxford: Blackwell, 1967)

Wolff, J., 'Fairness, Respect, and the Egalitarian Ethos', *Philosophy and Public Affairs*, Vol. 27, 1998, pp. 97–122

Wolin, S., 'The Liberal/Democratic Divide: On Rawls's Political Liberalism', *Political Theory*, Vol. 24, 1996, pp. 97–119

Young, I. M., 'Polity and Group Difference: A Critique of the Ideal of Universal Citizenship', *Ethics*, Vol. 99, 1989, pp. 250–74

—— 'Activist Challenges to Deliberative Democracy', in J. S. Fishkin and P. Laslett (eds), *Debating Deliberative Democracy* (Oxford: Blackwell, 2003), pp. 102–20

—— 'Responsibility and Global Justice: A Social Connection Model', in E. F. Paul, F. D. Miller, and J. Paul (eds), *Justice and Global Politics* (Cambridge: Cambridge University Press, 2006), pp. 102–30

Index

Abizadeh, A. 57, 72, 74
accumulation of wealth principle, *see* principle, accumulation of wealth
advantage, non-comparative 147 n. 1
all-affected interests principle, *see* principle, all-affected interests
Allport, G. 174, 184
all-subjected principle, *see* principle, all-subjected
analytic
  versus synthetic statements 15, 21 n. 13
Anderson, E. 81 nn. 13, 17, and 21, 103 nn. 15 and 17, 187 n. 18, 188 nn. 23 and 26
Appiah, K. A. 206 n. 13
Archard, D. 155
Armstrong, C. 47 n. 4, 206 n. 17
assimilation 170–80
  coercive versus non-coercive policies 173, 179, 186 n. 13
  versus integration 171–3
associative duties, *see* duties, associative
atomism, *see* holism
authority
  legal 73–5
  political 12, 192, 203
autonomy
  personal 83 n. 39, 84 n. 53, 87, 116, 130 n. 9

Banting, K. 189 n. 28
Barry, B. 117, 120 n. 21, 130 n. 21, 190 n. 38, 205 n. 8, 206 n. 18
Barry, J. 205 n. 5
basic skills principle, *see* principle, basic skills
basic structure 27, 29–30, 55, 57–60, 78, 105, 108–9, 118, 140, 143–4, 170, 174
Baubock, R. 66, 77, 83 n. 31, 84 nn. 53–5
Beckman, L. 75, 83 nn. 32, 39, 45, and 48–51, 104 n. 25
bedtime stories 138, 140–1
Bell, D. 205 n. 5
Bellamy, R. 54 nn. 61 and 65, 167 n. 24
belonging
  sense of belonging to the polity 149, 161–2, 170, 181–3

sense of belonging together 179–81
Blair, T. 169, 180
Blake, M. 47 n. 4
Blum, L. 81 n. 12, 168 n. 33
Bohman, J. 164 n. 2, 166 nn. 17–18
Bosniak, L. 21 n. 12, 205 n. 9
Bou-Habib, P. 104 n. 18
Braybooke, D. 102 n. 4
Brighouse, H. 107, 148 n. 15
Brown, G. 180
Bubeck, D. 49 n. 24, 129 n. 6
Burtt, S. 166 n. 19

Cabrera, L. 201–2
Callan, E. 50 n. 29
Cameron, D. 180
Caney, S. 205 n. 12
Cantle, T. 174, 187 nn. 16–17, 188 nn. 22 and 24
care
  ethics of, 107–8
  of children, *see* children, caring for
Carens, J. 81 n. 16, 84 n. 54, 190 n. 42
Carter, I. 54 nn. 63–4, 103 n. 17
Casal, P. 131 n. 35
Chambers, C. 130 n. 19, 130 n. 20
childcare, *see* children, caring for
children
  benefiting one's own 133–5, 137–43
  caring for 8–9, 105, 107–28
  educating 134–5, 137–43
Chodorow, N. 132 n. 39
Christiano, T. 166 n. 13, 167 n. 27
circumstances, *see* social circumstances
citizenship
  civic 4, 203–4
  civil 4
  common good account 25, 31–4, 36, 42, 53 n. 58
  core concept 1, 12–16, 25, 193–5, 202
  diverse, *see* citizenship, civic
  ecological 6, 12–13, 92–202
  environmental 192, 194

225

Printed and bound by CPI Group (UK) Ltd, Croydon, CR0 4YY